마이갓 5 Step 모의고사 공부법

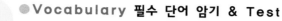

1 ● **Vocabulary** 필수 단어 암기 & Test
① 단원별 필수 단어 암기 ② 영어 → 한글 Test ③ 한글 → 영어 Test

2 ● **Text** 지문과 해설
① 전체 지문 해석 ② 페이지별 필기 공간 확보 ③ N회독을 통한 지문 습득

3 ● **Practice 1** 빈칸 시험 (w/ 문법 힌트)
① 해석 없는 반복 빈칸 시험 ② 문법 힌트를 통한 어법 숙지
③ 주요 문법과 암기 내용 최종 확인

4 ● **Practice 2** 빈칸 시험 (w/ 해석)
① 주요 내용/어법/어휘 빈칸 ② 한글을 통한 내용 숙지
③ 반복 시험을 통한 빈칸 암기

5 ● **Quiz** 객관식 예상문제를 콕콕!
① 수능형 객관식 변형문제 ② 100% 자체 제작 변형문제 ③ 빈출 내신 문제 유형 연습

영어 내신의 끝
마이갓 모의고사 고1, 2

1 등급을 위한 5단계 노하우
2 모의고사 연도 및 시행월 별 완전정복
3 내신변형 완전정복

영어 내신의 끝
마이갓 교과서 고1, 2

1 등급을 위한 10단계 노하우
2 교과서 레슨별 완전정복
3 영어 영역 마스터를 위한 지름길

마이갓 교재
보듬책방 온라인 스토어 (https://smartstore.naver.com/bdbooks)

마이갓 10 Step 영어 내신 공부법

Vocabulary

필수 단어 암기 & Test
① 단원별 필수 단어 암기
② 영어 → 한글 Test
③ 한글 → 영어 Test

Grammar

단원별 중요 문법과 연습 문제
① 기초 문법 설명
② 교과서 적용 예시 소개
③ 기초/ Advanced Test

Text

지문과 해설
① 전체 지문 해석
② 페이지별 필기 공간 확보
③ N회독을 통한 지문 습득

Practice 3

빈칸 시험 (w/ 해석)
① 주요 내용/어법/어휘 빈칸
② 한글을 통한 내용 숙지
③ 반복 시험을 통한 빈칸 암기

Practice 2

빈칸 시험 (w/ 해석)
① 주요 내용/어법/어휘 빈칸
② 한글을 통한 내용 숙지
③ 반복 시험을 통한 빈칸 암기

Practice 1

어휘 & 어법 선택 시험
① 시험에 나오는 어법 어휘 공략
② 중요 어법/어휘 선택형 시험
③ 반복 시험을 통한 포인트 숙지

Quiz

객관식 예상문제를 콕콕!
① 수능형 객관식 변형문제
② 100% 자체 제작 변형문제
③ 빈출 내신 문제 유형 연습

Final Test

주관식 서술형 예상문제
① 어순/영작/어법 등
　 주관식 서술형 문제 대비!
② 100% 자체 제작 변형문제

전체 영작 연습

직접 영작 해보기
① 주어진 단어를 활용한
　 전체 서술형 영작 훈련
② 쓰기를 통한 내용 암기

학교 기출 문제

지문과 해설
① 단원별 실제 학교 기출
　 문제 모음
② 객관식부터 서술형까지
　 완벽 커버!

24년 고1
3월 모의고사

마
이
갓

연습과 실전 모두 잡는 내신대비 완벽
| workbook |

보듬영어

2024 고1

3월

WORK BOOK

2024년 고1 3월 모의고사 내신대비용 WorkBook & 변형문제

보듬영어

CONTENTS

2024 고1 3월 WORK BOOK

보듬영어

Voca

❶ voca	❷ text	❸ [/]	❹ _____	❺ quiz 1	❻ quiz 2	❼ quiz 3	❽ quiz 4	❾ quiz 5

18	science	과학		21	consider	고려하다	
	recently	최근에			sight	시각	
	impressed	감명을 받은			philosopher	철학자	
	environment	환경			doubt	의심하다	
	discussion	토론			perception	인식	
	lecture	강의			balance	균형	
	suit	맞추다			link	연결	
	grateful	감사한			categorize	분류하다	
19	sandcastle	모래성			detect	감지하다	
	enormous	거대한			prey	먹잇감	
	destroy	부수다			divide	나누다	
	stream	흐르다			specific	특정한	
	ocean	바다			bucket	양동이	
	respond	반응하다		22	historical	역사적인	
	enthusiasm	열정			far-reaching	광범위한	
20	magic	마법, 마술			influence	영향력	
	challenge	어려움, 도전			noble	고귀한	
	statement	진술			possess	가지다, 소유하다	
	positive	긍정적인			aspect	측면	
	struggle	어려움을 겪다			improve	개선하다	
	witness	목격하다			diligence	근면	
	confidence	자신감			feedback	피드백	
	surprise	놀라게 하다			constantly	끊임없이	
	shift	변화			accomplish	성취하다	
	powerful	강력한			potential	잠재력	

Voca

❶ voca　　❷ text　　❸ [/]　　❹ _____　　❺ quiz 1　　❻ quiz 2　　❼ quiz 3　　❽ quiz 4　　❾ quiz 5

	potential	잠재력	27	delightful	즐거운
	community	공동체		experience	경험하다
	regardless of	~와 관계없이		various	다양한
23	crop rotation	윤작		host	(파티 등을) 주최하다
	field	밭		in advance	미리
	rotate	순환하다	28	upcycled	업사이클된
	original	원래의		environment	환경
	enrich	비옥하게 하다		passionate	열정적인
	soil	토양		fashion	패션, 의류
24	concentrate	집중하다		contest	대회
	assess	평가하다		announce	발표하다
	spoil	망쳐 놓다		local	지역의
	impact	영향(력)	29	overstate	과장해서 말하다
	overwork	과하게 작업하다		fulfillment	성취감
	benefit	득을 보다		empowerment	권한
25	extent	정도		energizing	활기찬
	climate	기후		satisfying	만족감을 주는
	extremely	극도로		employment	직업, 고용
	generation	세대		source	원천
26	secondary school	중등학교		conduct	수행하다
	chemistry	화학		numerous	수많은
	physics	물리학		psychology	심리
	mathematics	수학		workplace	업무 현장, 직장
	throughout	내내		quality	질
	military	군대의		output	성과

Voca

❶ voca　　❷ text　　❸ [/]　　❹ ____　　❺ quiz 1　　❻ quiz 2　　❼ quiz 3　　❽ quiz 4　　❾ quiz 5

	generally	일반적으로		capable	~할 수 있는
	income	수입		seed	씨앗
	overall	전반적으로		larva	유충
30	rate	빠르기		occupy	점유하다
	determine	결정하다		survive	생존하다
	ability	능력		reproduce	번식하다
	adapted	맞추어진, 적응된	32	respectable	존경할 만한
	ideally	이상적으로		make it a point	반드시 ~하도록 하다
	suited	적합한		discourage	못하게 하다
	motorist	운전자		speak up	자유롭게 의견을 내다
	limited	제한된		maintain	유지하다
	appreciate	감상하다, 제대로 인식하다		get aired	공공연히 알려지다
	on the other hand	반면에		if anything	오히려
	allow for	가능하게 하다, 허락하다		conversation	대담, 대화
	polar	극과 극의		corporate	기업
	opposite	반대의 것		nonprofit	비영리인
	ordinarily	보통		publish	발행하다, 출판하다
	typical	전형적인		feature	(기사로) 다루다
31	climatic	기후의		management	경영
	requirement	요건		techniques	기법
	endure	견디다		regularly	어김없이, 규칙적으로
	satisfy	충족시키다		claim	주장하다
	force	강요하다		remark	말하다
	creature	생명체	33	striking	두드러진
	immobile	움직이지 않는		characteristics	특징

❶ voca	❷ text	❸ [/]	❹ _____	❺ quiz 1	❻ quiz 2	❼ quiz 3	❽ quiz 4	❾ quiz 5

	eyelid	눈꺼풀	35	psychologist	심리학자
	mammal	포유류		severe	심각한
	apparently	분명히		mental	정신적
	process	처리하다		compose	작곡하다
	shorten	짧아지다		improve	개선하다
	weaken	약해지다		session	활동, 기간
	register	등록하다		review	검토하다
	function	기능		treatment	치료
	definition	정의		finding	결과
	essential	필수적인		choir	합창단
	derive	얻다		wellbeing	행복
	perceptual	지각의		significantly	상당히
34	research	연구		enhance	강화하다
	expert	전문가	36	realize	깨닫다
	difficulty	어려움		impossibility	불가능
	newcomer	초보		competitive	경쟁적인
	genuine	실제		structure	구조
	remarkably	놀랍게		period	기간
	accurate	정확한		racket	라켓
	judge	판단하다		appropriate	적절한
	insensitive	무감각한		progressive	점진적인
	acquire	습득하다		relate to	~와 관련되다
	underestimate	과소평가하다		arena	경기장
	session	기간, 시간		equipment	장비
	assumption	추정, 가정		common sense	(일반인들의) 공통된 견해, 상식

Voca

❶ voca　　❷ text　　❸ [/]　　❹ ＿＿＿　　❺ quiz 1　　❻ quiz 2　　❼ quiz 3　　❽ quiz 4　　❾ quiz 5

	adaptation	조정		perceive	지각하다
37	available	구할 수 있는		intensity	강도
	empire	제국		mechanism	기제
	deliver	전달하다	39	determine	결정하다
	near	다가가다		display	보이다
	repeat	반복하다		therefore	그런 까닭에
	relay	이어가다		session	활동
	condition	사정, 상황		rescue	구조하다
	station	배치하다		domestic	가정의
	royal	왕의, 왕실의		illness	질병
	hut	오두막		confusion	동요, 혼란
	apart	떨어진		explore	탐구하다
	direction	방향		specific	특정한, 구체적인
	hurry out	서둘러 나오다		constant	끊임없는
38	demonstrate	보여 주다		process	과정
	explanation	설명	40	conscious	의식적
	map	(지도에) 구획하다		subconscious	잠재의식(적)
	register	등록하다		recognition	인식
	tip	끝		frequently	자주, 빈번히
	sourness	신맛		judgment	판단(력)
	bitterness	쓴맛		cloud	(기억력, 판단력 등을) 흐리게 하다
	misinterpretation	오해		bias	편견
	mistranslation	오역		negativity	부정성
	conduct	수행하다		originate	비롯되다
	specialty	특화된 분야		fear	두려움

❶ voca	❷ text	❸ [/]	❹ _____	❺ quiz 1	❻ quiz 2	❼ quiz 3	❽ quiz 4	❾ quiz 5
41-42	norm	규범						
	define	규정하다						
	interpretation	해석						
	stranger	낯선 사람						
	marked	눈에 띄는						
	responsible	책임이 있는						
	worthy	받을 만한						
	criticism	비난						
	central	중심적인						
	translatable	번역할 수 있는						
	cost	대가, 비용						
	considerable	상당한						
	ridiculous	우스꽝스러운						
	unexpected	예상치 못한						
	minor	사소한						
43-45	Native American	미국 원주민						
	spiritual	영적인						
	holy	성스러운						
	spin	짜다(과거형 spun)						
	cycle	순환						

❶ voca	❷ text	❸ [/]	❹ ____	❺ quiz 1	❻ quiz 2	❼ quiz 3	❽ quiz 4	❾ quiz 5

18	science		21	consider		
	recently			sight		
	impressed			philosopher		
	environment			doubt		
	discussion			perception		
	lecture			balance		
	suit			link		
	grateful			categorize		
19	sandcastle			detect		
	enormous			prey		
	destroy			divide		
	stream			specific		
	ocean			bucket		
	respond		22	historical		
	enthusiasm			far-reaching		
20	magic			influence		
	challenge			noble		
	statement			possess		
	positive			aspect		
	struggle			improve		
	witness			diligence		
	confidence			feedback		
	surprise			constantly		
	shift			accomplish		
	powerful			potential		

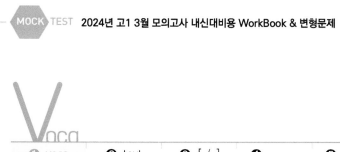

❶ voca	❷ text	❸ [/]	❹ _____	❺ quiz 1	❻ quiz 2	❼ quiz 3	❽ quiz 4	❾ quiz 5
	potential							
	community							
	regardless of							
23	crop rotation							
	field							
	rotate							
	original							
	enrich							
	soil							
24	concentrate							
	assess							
	spoil							
	impact							
	overwork							
	benefit							
25	extent							
	climate							
	extremely							
	generation							
26	secondary school							
	chemistry							
	physics							
	mathematics							
	throughout							
	military							

27	delightful							
	experience							
	various							
	host							
	in advance							
28	upcycled							
	environment							
	passionate							
	fashion							
	contest							
	announce							
	local							
29	overstate							
	fulfillment							
	empowerment							
	energizing							
	satisfying							
	employment							
	source							
	conduct							
	numerous							
	psychology							
	workplace							
	quality							
	output							

Voca

	❶ voca	❷ text	❸ [/]	❹ ____	❺ quiz 1	❻ quiz 2	❼ quiz 3	❽ quiz 4	❾ quiz 5
	generally								
	income								
	overall								
30	rate								
	determine								
	ability								
	adapted								
	ideally								
	suited								
	motorist								
	limited								
	appreciate								
	on the other hand								
	allow for								
	polar								
	opposite								
	ordinarily								
	typical								
31	climatic								
	requirement								
	endure								
	satisfy								
	force								
	creature								
	immobile								

	❶ voca	❷ text	❸ [/]	❹ ____	❺ quiz 1	❻ quiz 2	❼ quiz 3	❽ quiz 4	❾ quiz 5
	capable								
	seed								
	larva								
	occupy								
	survive								
	reproduce								
32	respectable								
	make it a point								
	discourage								
	speak up								
	maintain								
	get aired								
	if anything								
	conversation								
	corporate								
	nonprofit								
	publish								
	feature								
	management								
	techniques								
	regularly								
	claim								
	remark								
33	striking								
	characteristics								

Voca Test

❶ voca	❷ text	❸ [/]	❹ _____	❺ quiz 1	❻ quiz 2	❼ quiz 3	❽ quiz 4	❾ quiz 5

	eyelid			35	psychologist			
	mammal				severe			
	apparently				mental			
	process				compose			
	shorten				improve			
	weaken				session			
	register				review			
	function				treatment			
	definition				finding			
	essential				choir			
	derive				wellbeing			
	perceptual				significantly			
34	research				enhance			
	expert			36	realize			
	difficulty				impossibility			
	newcomer				competitive			
	genuine				structure			
	remarkably				period			
	accurate				racket			
	judge				appropriate			
	insensitive				progressive			
	acquire				relate to			
	underestimate				arena			
	session				equipment			
	assumption				common sense			

Voca Test

영 한

❶ voca	❷ text	❸ [/]	❹ _____	❺ quiz 1	❻ quiz 2	❼ quiz 3	❽ quiz 4	❾ quiz 5
	adaptation							
37	available							
	empire							
	deliver							
	near							
	repeat							
	relay							
	condition							
	station							
	royal							
	hut							
	apart							
	direction							
	hurry out							
38	demonstrate							
	explanation							
	map							
	register							
	tip							
	sourness							
	bitterness							
	misinterpretation							
	mistranslation							
	conduct							
	specialty							
	perceive							
	intensity							
	mechanism							
39	determine							
	display							
	therefore							
	session							
	rescue							
	domestic							
	illness							
	confusion							
	explore							
	specific							
	constant							
	process							
40	conscious							
	subconscious							
	recognition							
	frequently							
	judgment							
	cloud							
	bias							
	negativity							
	originate							
	fear							

Voca Test

영 ▶ 한

❶ voca	❷ text	❸ [/]	❹ ____	❺ quiz 1	❻ quiz 2	❼ quiz 3	❽ quiz 4	❾ quiz 5
41-42	norm							
	define							
	interpretation							
	stranger							
	marked							
	responsible							
	worthy							
	criticism							
	central							
	translatable							
	cost							
	considerable							
	ridiculous							
	unexpected							
	minor							
43-45	Native American							
	spiritual							
	holy							
	spin							
	cycle							

Voca Test

영 ○ 한

❶ voca	❷ text	❸ [/]	❹ _____	❺ quiz 1	❻ quiz 2	❼ quiz 3	❽ quiz 4	❾ quiz 5
18		과학						
		최근에						
		감명을 받은						
		환경						
		토론						
		강의						
		맞추다						
		감사한						
19		모래성						
		거대한						
		부수다						
		흐르다						
		바다						
		반응하다						
		열정						
20		마법, 마술						
		어려움, 도전						
		진술						
		긍정적인						
		어려움을 겪다						
		목격하다						
		자신감						
		놀라게 하다						
		변화						
		강력한						

❶ voca	❷ text	❸ [/]	❹ _____	❺ quiz 1	❻ quiz 2	❼ quiz 3	❽ quiz 4	❾ quiz 5
21		고려하다						
		시각						
		철학자						
		의심하다						
		인식						
		균형						
		연결						
		분류하다						
		감지하다						
		먹잇감						
		나누다						
		특정한						
		양동이						
22		역사적인						
		광범위한						
		영향력						
		고귀한						
		가지다, 소유하다						
		측면						
		개선하다						
		근면						
		피드백						
		끊임없이						
		성취하다						
		잠재력						

Voca Tes

영 > 한

❶ voca	❷ text	❸ [/]	❹ _____	❺ quiz 1	❻ quiz 2	❼ quiz 3	❽ quiz 4	❾ quiz 5

		잠재력	27	즐거운
		공동체		경험하다
		~와 관계없이		다양한
23		윤작		(파티 등을) 주최하다
		밭		미리
		순환하다	28	업사이클된
		원래의		환경
		비옥하게 하다		열정적인
		토양		패션, 의류
24		집중하다		대회
		평가하다		발표하다
		망쳐 놓다		지역의
		영향(력)	29	과장해서 말하다
		과하게 작업하다		성취감
		득을 보다		권한
25		정도		활기찬
		기후		만족감을 주는
		극도로		직업, 고용
		세대		원천
26		중등학교		수행하다
		화학		수많은
		물리학		심리
		수학		업무 현장, 직장
		내내		질
		군대의		성과

Voca Test

영 ⟩ 한

❶ voca	❷ text	❸ [/]	❹ ____	❺ quiz 1	❻ quiz 2	❼ quiz 3	❽ quiz 4	❾ quiz 5
		일반적으로				~할 수 있는		
		수입				씨앗		
		전반적으로				유충		
30		빠르기				점유하다		
		결정하다				생존하다		
		능력				번식하다		
		맞추어진, 적응된	32			존경할 만한		
		이상적으로				반드시 ~하도록 하다		
		적합한				못하게 하다		
		운전자				자유롭게 의견을 내다		
		제한된				유지하다		
		감상하다, 제대로 인식하다				공공연히 알려지다		
		반면에				오히려		
		가능하게 하다, 허락하다				대담, 대화		
		극과 극의				기업		
		반대의 것				비영리인		
		보통				발행하다, 출판하다		
		전형적인				(기사로) 다루다		
31		기후의				경영		
		요건				기법		
		견디다				어김없이, 규칙적으로		
		충족시키다				주장하다		
		강요하다				말하다		
		생명체	33			두드러진		
		움직이지 않는				특징		

Voca Test

❶ voca	❷ text	❸ [/]	❹ ___	❺ quiz 1	❻ quiz 2	❼ quiz 3	❽ quiz 4	❾ quiz 5
		눈꺼풀	35			심리학자		
		포유류				심각한		
		분명히				정신적		
		처리하다				작곡하다		
		짧아지다				개선하다		
		약해지다				활동, 기간		
		등록하다				검토하다		
		기능				치료		
		정의				결과		
		필수적인				합창단		
		얻다				행복		
		지각의				상당히		
34		연구				강화하다		
		전문가	36			깨닫다		
		어려움				불가능		
		초보				경쟁적인		
		실제				구조		
		놀랍게				기간		
		정확한				라켓		
		판단하다				적절한		
		무감각한				점진적인		
		습득하다				~와 관련되다		
		과소평가하다				경기장		
		기간, 시간				장비		
		추정, 가정				(일반인들의) 공통된 견해, 상식		

❶ voca	❷ text	❸ [/]	❹ _____	❺ quiz 1	❻ quiz 2	❼ quiz 3	❽ quiz 4	❾ quiz 5
		조정				지각하다		
37		구할 수 있는				강도		
		제국				기제		
		전달하다	39			결정하다		
		다가가다				보이다		
		반복하다				그런 까닭에		
		이어가다				활동		
		사정, 상황				구조하다		
		배치하다				가정의		
		왕의, 왕실의				질병		
		오두막				동요, 혼란		
		떨어진				탐구하다		
		방향				특정한, 구체적인		
		서둘러 나오다				끊임없는		
38		보여 주다				과정		
		설명	40			의식적		
		(지도에) 구획하다				잠재의식(적)		
		등록하다				인식		
		끝				자주, 빈번히		
		신맛				판단(력)		
		쓴맛				(기억력, 판단력 등을) 흐리게 하다		
		오해				편견		
		오역				부정성		
		수행하다				비롯되다		
		특화된 분야				두려움		

Voca Test

	❶ voca	❷ text	❸ [/]	❹ ____	❺ quiz 1	❻ quiz 2	❼ quiz 3	❽ quiz 4	❾ quiz 5
41-42			규범						
			규정하다						
			해석						
			낯선 사람						
			눈에 띄는						
			책임이 있는						
			받을 만한						
			비난						
			중심적인						
			번역할 수 있는						
			대가, 비용						
			상당한						
			우스꽝스러운						
			예상치 못한						
			사소한						
43-45			미국 원주민						
			영적인						
			성스러운						
			짜다(과거형 spun)						
			순환						

2024 고1 3월 모의고사

❶ voca　❷ text　❸ [/]　❹ ____　❺ quiz 1　❻ quiz 2　❼ quiz 3　❽ quiz 4　❾ quiz 5

18 목적

❶ Dear Ms. Jane Watson,

친애하는 Jane Watson 씨,

❷ I am John Austin, a science teacher at Crestville High School.

저는 Crestville 고등학교의 과학 교사 John Austin입니다.

❸ Recently I was impressed by the latest book you wrote about the environment.

최근에, 저는 환경에 관해 당신이 쓴 최신 도서에 감명받았습니다.

❹ Also my students read your book and had a class discussion about it.

또한 저의 학생들은 당신의 책을 읽었고 그것에 대해 토론 수업을 하였습니다.

❺ They are big fans of your book, so I'd like to ask you to visit our school and give a special lecture.

그들은 당신의 책을 아주 좋아하고, 그래서 저는 당신이 우리 학교에 방문하여 특별 강연을 해 주시기를 요청드리고 싶습니다.

❻ We can set the date and time to suit your schedule.

우리는 당신의 일정에 맞춰 날짜와 시간을 정하겠습니다.

❼ Having you at our school would be a fantastic experience for the students.

당신이 우리 학교에 와주신다면 학생들에게 멋진 경험이 될 것 같습니다.

❽ We would be very grateful if you could come.

우리는 당신이 와 주신다면 정말 감사하겠습니다.

❾ Best regards, John Austin

안부를 전하며, John Austin

19 심경

❶ Marilyn and her three-year-old daughter, Sarah, took a trip to the beach, where Sarah built her first sandcastle.

Marilyn과 세 살 된 딸 Sarah는 해변으로 여행을 떠났고, 그곳에서 Sarah는 처음으로 모래성을 쌓았다.

❷ Moments later, an enormous wave destroyed Sarah's castle.

잠시 후, 거대한 파도가 Sarah의 성을 무너뜨렸다.

❸ In response to the loss of her sandcastle, tears streamed down Sarah's cheeks and her heart was broken.

모래성을 잃은 것에 반응하여 눈물이 Sarah의 뺨을 타고 흘러내렸고, 그녀의 마음은 무너졌다.

❹ She ran to Marilyn, saying she would never build a sandcastle again.

그녀는 다시는 모래성을 쌓지 않겠다고 말하며 Marilyn에게 달려갔다.

❺ Marilyn said, "Part of the joy of building a sandcastle is that, in the end, we give it as a gift to the ocean."

Marilyn은 "모래성을 쌓는 즐거움 중 일부는 결국에는 우리가 그것을 바다에게 선물로 주는 것이란다." 라고 말했다.

❻ Sarah loved this idea and responded with enthusiasm to the idea of building another castle — this time, even closer to the water so the ocean would get its gift sooner!

Sarah는 이 생각이 마음에 들었고 또 다른 모래성을 만들 생각에 이번에는 바다와 훨씬 더 가까운 곳에서 바다가 그 선물을 더 빨리 받을 수 있도록 하겠다며 열정적으로 반응했다.

20 요지

❶ Magic is what we all wish for to happen in our life.

마법은 우리 모두 자신의 삶에서 일어나기를 바라는 바이다.

❷ Do you love the movie Cinderella like me?

여러분도 나처럼 신데렐라 영화를 사랑하는가?

❸ Well, in real life, you can also create magic. Here's the trick.

그러면, 실제 삶에서, 여러분도 마법을 만들 수 있다. 여기 그 요령이 있다.

❹ Write down all the real-time challenges that you face and deal with.

여러분이 직면하고 처리하는 모든 실시간의 어려움을 적어라.

❺ Just change the challenge statement into positive statements.

그 어려움에 관한 진술을 긍정적인 진술로 바꾸어라.

❻ Let me give you an example here.

여기서 여러분에게 한 예시를 제시하겠다.

❼ If you struggle with getting up early in the morning, then write a positive statement such as "I get up early in the morning at 5:00 am every day."

만약 여러분이 아침 일찍 일어나는 것에 어려움을 겪는다면, 그러면 '나는 매일 일찍 아침 5시에 일어난다.'와 같은 긍정적인 진술을 써라.

❽ Once you write these statements, get ready to witness magic and confidence.

일단 여러분이 이러한 진술을 적는다면, 마법과 자신감을 목격할 준비를 하라.

❾ You will be surprised that just by writing these statements, there is a shift in the way you think and act.

여러분은 단지 이러한 진술을 적음으로써 여러분이 생각하고 행동하는 방식에 변화가 있다는 것에 놀랄 것이다.

❿ Suddenly you feel more powerful and positive.

어느 순간 여러분은 더 강력하고 긍정적이라고 느끼게 된다.

21 주장

❶ Consider the seemingly simple question How many senses are there?
'얼마나 많은 감각이 존재하는가?'라는 겉으로 보기에 단순한 질문을 고려해 봐라.

❷ Around 2,370 years ago, Aristotle wrote that there are five, in both humans and animals — sight, hearing, smell, taste, and touch.
약 2,370년 전 Aristotle은 인간과 동물 둘 다에게 시각, 청각, 후각, 미각, 그리고 촉각의 다섯(감각)이 있다고 썼다.

❸ However, according to the philosopher Fiona Macpherson, there are reasons to doubt it.
그러나, 철학자 Fiona Macpherson에 따르면, 그것을 의심할 이유가 존재한다.

❹ For a start, Aristotle missed a few in humans: the perception of your own body which is different from touch and the sense of balance which has links to both touch and vision.
우선, Aristotle은 인간에게서 몇 가지를 빠뜨렸는데, 그것은 촉각과는 다른 여러분 자신의 신체에 대한 인식과, 촉각과 시각 모두에 관련되어 있는 균형 감각이었다.

❺ Other animals have senses that are even harder to categorize.
다른 동물들은 훨씬 더 범주화하기 어려운 감각을 가지고 있다.

❻ Many vertebrates have a different sense system for detecting odors.
많은 척추동물은 냄새를 탐지하기 위한 다른 감각 체계를 가지고 있다.

❼ Some snakes can detect the body heat of their prey.
어떤 뱀은 그들의 먹잇감의 체열을 감지할 수 있다.

❽ These examples tell us that "senses cannot be clearly divided into a limited number of specific kinds," Macpherson wrote in The Senses.
Macpherson이 'The Senses'에서 쓰기를, 이러한 사례는 우리에게 '감각은 제한된 수의 특정 종류로 명확하게 나누어지지 않을 수 있다.'라는 것을 알려 준다.

❾ Instead of trying to push animal senses into Aristotelian buckets, we should study them for what they are.
동물의 감각을 Aristotle의 양동이로 밀어 넣는 대신, 우리는 그것들을 존재하는 그대로 연구해야 한다.

22 의미

❶ When we think of leaders, we may think of people such as Abraham Lincoln or Martin Luther King, Jr.

우리가 리더에 대해 생각할 때, 우리는 Abraham Lincoln 혹은 Martin Luther King, Jr. 와 같은 사람들에 대해 생각할지 모른다.

❷ If you consider the historical importance and far-reaching influence of these individuals, leadership might seem like a noble and high goal.

만약 여러분이 이러한 인물들의 역사적 중요성과 광범위한 영향력을 고려한다면, 리더십은 고귀하고 높은 목표처럼 보일지도 모른다.

❸ But like all of us, these people started out as students, workers, and citizens who possessed ideas about how some aspect of daily life could be improved on a larger scale.

그러나 우리 모두와 마찬가지로, 이러한 인물들은 일상생활의 어느 측면이 더 큰 규모로 어떻게 개선될 수 있는지에 대한 생각을 가졌던 학생, 근로자, 그리고 시민으로 시작했다.

❹ Through diligence and experience, they improved upon their ideas by sharing them with others, seeking their opinions and feedback and constantly looking for the best way to accomplish goals for a group.

근면함과 경험을 통해, 그들은 자신의 생각을 다른 사람들과 공유하고, 그들의 의견과 반응을 구하며, 끊임없이 집단의 목표를 성취할 수 있는 가장 좋은 방법을 찾음으로써 자신의 생각을 발전시켰다.

❺ Thus we all have the potential to be leaders at school, in our communities, and at work, regardless of age or experience.

그러므로 우리는 모두, 나이나 경험에 관계없이, 학교, 공동체, 그리고 일터에서 리더가 될 수 있는 잠재력을 가지고 있다.

23 주제

❶ Crop rotation is the process in which farmers change the crops they grow in their fields in a special order.

윤작은 농부가 자신의 밭에서 재배하는 작물을 특별한 순서로 바꾸는 과정이다.

❷ For example, if a farmer has three fields, he or she may grow carrots in the first field, green beans in the second, and tomatoes in the third.

예를 들면, 만약 한 농부가 세 개의 밭을 가지고 있다면, 그들은 첫 번째 밭에는 당근을, 두 번째 밭에는 녹색 콩을, 세 번째 밭에는 토마토를 재배할 수 있다.

❸ The next year, green beans will be in the first field, tomatoes in the second field, and carrots will be in the third.

그 다음 해에 첫 번째 밭에는 녹색 콩을, 두 번째 밭에는 토마토를, 세 번째 밭에는 당근을 재배할 것이다.

❹ In year three, the crops will rotate again.

3년 차에 작물은 다시 순환할 것이다.

❺ By the fourth year, the crops will go back to their original order.

4년째에 이르면 작물은 원래의 순서로 되돌아 갈 것이다.

❻ Each crop enriches the soil for the next crop.
각각의 작물은 다음 작물을 위한 토양을 비옥하게 한다.

❼ This type of farming is sustainable because the soil stays healthy.
이 유형의 농업은 토양이 건강하게 유지되기 때문에 지속 가능하다.

24 제목

❶ Working around the whole painting, rather than concentrating on one area at a time, will mean you can stop at any point and the painting can be considered "finished."

한 번에 한 영역에만 집중하기보다 전체 그림에 대해서 작업하는 것은 여러분이 어떤 지점에서도 멈출 수 있고 그림이 '완성'된 것으로 간주될 수 있다는 것을 의미할 것이다.

❷ Artists often find it difficult to know when to stop painting, and it can be tempting to keep on adding more to your work.

화가인 여러분은 종종 언제 그림을 멈춰야 할지 알기 어렵다는 것을 발견하고, 자신의 그림에 계속해서 더 추가하고 싶은 유혹을 느낄 수도 있다.

❸ It is important to take a few steps back from the painting from time to time to assess your progress.

때때로 자신의 진행 상황을 평가하기 위해 그림에서 몇 걸음 뒤로 물러나는 것이 중요하다.

❹ Putting too much into a painting can spoil its impact and leave it looking overworked.

한 그림에 너무 많은 것을 넣으면 그것의 영향력을 망칠 수 있고 그것이 과하게 작업된 것처럼 보이게 둘 수 있다.

❺ If you find yourself struggling to decide whether you have finished, take a break and come back to it later with fresh eyes.

만약 여러분이 끝냈는지를 결정하는 데 자신이 어려움을 겪고 있음을 알게 된다면, 잠시 휴식을 취하고 나중에 새로운 눈으로 그것(그림)으로 다시 돌아와라.

❼ Then you can decide whether any areas of your painting would benefit from further refinement.

그러면 여러분은 더 정교하게 꾸며서 자신의 그림 어느 부분이 득을 볼지를 결정할 수 있다.

26 일치

❶ Jaroslav Heyrovsky was born in Prague on December 20, 1890, as the fifth child of Leopold Heyrovsky.

Jaroslav Heyrovsky는 1890년 12월 20일 Prague에서 Leopold Heyrovsky의 다섯째 자녀로 태어났다.

❷ In 1901 Jaroslav went to a secondary school called the Akademicke Gymnasium.

1901년 Jaroslav는 Akademicke Gymnasium이라고 불리는 중등학교에 다녔다.

❸ Rather than Latin and Greek, he showed a strong interest in the natural sciences.

그는 라틴어와 그리스어보다는 자연 과학에 강한 흥미를 보였다.

❹ At Czech University in Prague he studied chemistry, physics, and mathematics.

그는 라틴어와 그리스어보다는 자연 과학에 강한 흥미를 보였다.

❺ From 1910 to 1914 he continued his studies at University College, London.

1910년부터 1914년까지 그는 런던의 University College에서 학업을 이어 나갔다.

❻ Throughout the First World War, Jaroslav served in a military hospital.
제1차 세계 대전 내내 Jaroslav는 군 병원에 복무했다.

❼ In 1926, Jaroslav became the first Professor of Physical Chemistry at Charles University in Prague.
1926년에 Jaroslav는 Prague에 있는 Charles University 최초의 물리화학 교수가 되었다.

❽ He won the Nobel Prize in chemistry in 1959.
그는 1959년에 노벨 화학상을 수상했다.

29 어법

❶ It would be hard to overstate how important meaningful work is to human beings — work that provides a sense of fulfillment and empowerment.

인간에게 의미 있는 일, 즉 성취감과 권한을 제공하는 일이 얼마나 중요한지를 과장해서 말한다는 것은 어려울 것이다.

❷ Those who have found deeper meaning in their careers find their days much more energizing and satisfying, and count their employment as one of their greatest sources of joy and pride.

자신의 직업에서 더 깊은 의미를 찾은 사람은 자신의 하루하루가 훨씬 더 활기차고 만족감을 준다는 것을 발견하고, 자신의 직업을 기쁨과 자부심의 가장 큰 원천 중 하나로 꼽는다.

❸ Sonya Lyubomirsky, professor of psychology at the University of California, has conducted numerous workplace studies showing that when people are more fulfilled on the job, they not only produce higher quality work and a greater output, but also generally earn higher incomes.

University of California의 심리학 교수인 Sonya Lyubomirsky는 사람이 직업에 더 많은 성취감을 느낄 때 그들은 더 질 높은 업무와 더 큰 성과를 만들어 낼 뿐만 아니라 일반적으로 더 높은 수입을 거둔다는 것을 보여 주는 수 많은 업무 현장 연구를 수행했다.

❹ Those most satisfied with their work are also much more likely to be happier with their lives overall.

자신의 일에 가장 만족하는 사람은 또한 전반적으로 자신의 삶에 더 행복해할 가능성이 훨씬 더 크다.

❺ For her book Happiness at Work, researcher Jessica Pryce-Jones conducted a study of 3,000 workers in seventy-nine countries, finding that those who took greater satisfaction from their work were 150 percent more likely to have a happier life overall.

자신의 저서 'Happiness at Work'를 위해 연구자 Jessica PryceJones는 79개 국가의 3,000명의 근로자에 대한 연구를 수행했고, 자신의 일로부터 더 큰 만족감을 갖는 사람이 전반적으로 더 행복한 삶을 살 가능성이 150퍼센트 더 크다는 것을 알아냈다.

30 어휘

❶ The rate of speed at which one is traveling will greatly determine the ability to process detail in the environment.

사람이 이동하는 속도의 빠르기는 환경 속 세세한 것을 처리하는 능력을 크게 결정할 것이다.

❷ In evolutionary terms, human senses are adapted to the speed at which humans move through space under their own power while walking.

진화론적 관점에서, 인간의 감각은 그 자신의 힘으로 걸으며 공간을 이동하는 속도에 적응되어 있다.

❸ Our ability to distinguish detail in the environment is therefore ideally suited to movement at speeds of perhaps five miles per hour and under.

환경 속에서 세세한 것을 구별하는 우리의 능력은 그래서 대략 시속 5마일 또는 그 속도 이하의 이동에 이상적으로 맞추어져 있다.

❹ The fastest users of the street, motorists, therefore have a much more limited ability to process details along the street — a motorist simply has little time or ability to appreciate design details.

그러므로 도로의 가장 빠른 사용자인 운전자는 도로를 따라서 (이동하며) 세세한 것을 처리하는 훨씬 더 제한된 능력을 가지고 있고, 그래서 운전자는 단지 디자인의 세세한 것을 감상할 수 있는 적은 시간이나 능력이 있다.

❺ On the other hand, pedestrian travel, being much slower, allows for the appreciation of environmental detail.

반면에 보행자 이동은 훨씬 더 느려서, 환경의 세세한 것을 감상할 수 있도록 허용해 준다.

❻ Joggers and bicyclists fall somewhere in between these polar opposites; while they travel faster than pedestrians, their rate of speed is ordinarily much slower than that of the typical motorist.

조깅하는 사람과 자전거를 타는 사람은 이러한 극과 극 사이의 어딘가에 해당한다. 그들은 보행자보다 더 빨리 이동하지만, 속도의 빠르기는 보통 전형적인 운전자의 그것보다 훨씬 더 느리다.

31 빈칸

❶ Every species has certain climatic requirements — what degree of heat or cold it can endure, for example.

모든 종은, 예를 들자면 어느 정도의 더위나 추위를 견딜 수 있는지와 같은, 특정한 기후 요건을 가지고 있다.

❷ When the climate changes, the places that satisfy those requirements change, too.

기후가 변할 때, 그러한 요건을 충족시키는 장소도 역시 변한다.

❸ Species are forced to follow.

종은 따르도록 강요받는다.

❹ All creatures are capable of some degree of movement.

모든 생명체는 어느 정도의 이동이 가능하다.

❺ Even creatures of dispersal at some stage of their life — as a seed, in the case of the tree, or as a larva, in the case of the barnacle.

심지어 나무나 따개비처럼 움직이지 않는 것처럼 보이는 생명체도, 나무의 경우는 씨앗으로, 따개비의 경우는 유충으로, 그들 일생의 어느 단계에서 분산할 수 있다.

❻ A creature must get from the place it is born — often occupied by its parent — to a place where it can survive, grow, and reproduce.

생명체는 종종 자신의 부모에 의해서 점유된, 그래서 자신이 태어난 장소로부터 생존하고 성장하며 번식할 수 있는 장소로 이동해야 한다.

❼ From fossils, scientists know that even creatures like trees moved with surprising speed during past periods of climate change.

화석으로부터, 과학자들은 심지어 나무와 같은 생명체는 기후 변화의 과거 시기 동안 놀라운 속도로 이동했다는 것을 알고 있다.

32 빈칸

❶ No respectable boss would say, "I make it a point to discourage my staff from speaking up, and I maintain a culture that prevents disagreeing viewpoints from ever getting aired."

존경할 만한 상사라면 누구라도 '나는 반드시 내 직원이 자유롭게 의견을 내지 못하도록 하고, 동의하지 않는 관점이 언제든 공공연히 알려지는 것을 가로막는 문화를 유지한다.'라고 말하지는 않을 것이다.

❷ If anything, most bosses even say that they are pro-dissent.

오히려, 대부분의 상사는 심지어 자신은 반대에 찬성한다고 말 한다.

❸ This idea can be found throughout the series of conversations with corporate, university, and nonprofit leaders, published weekly in the business sections of newspapers.

이러한 생각은 매주 발행되는 신문의 경제란에 기업, 대학, 그리고 비영리 (단체의) 리더와의 일련의 대담을 통해서 발견될 수 있다.

❹ In the interviews, the featured leaders are asked about their management techniques, and regularly claim to continually encourage internal protest from more junior staffers.

인터뷰에서, (기사에) 다루어진 리더는 자신의 경영 기법에 대해 질문을 받고, 내부적인 저항이 더 많은 부하 직원에게서 (나오기를) 계속해서 장려하고 있다고 어김없이 주장한다.

❺ As Bot Pittman remarked in one of these conversations: "I want us to listen to these dissenters because they may intend to tell you why we can't do something, but if you listen hard, what they're really telling you is what you must do to get something done."

Bot Pittman은 이러한 대담 중 하나에서 "저는 우리가 이러한 반대자에게 귀 기울이기를 원합니다. 왜냐하면 그들은 여러분에게 우리가 무엇인가를 할 수 없는 이유를 말하려고 의도할 수 있겠지만, 그러나 만약에 여러분이 열심히 귀 기울이면, 그들이 정말로 여러분에게 말하고 있는 것은 어떤 일이 이루어지도록 하기 위해서 여러분이 무엇을 해야만 하는가이기 때문입니다." 라고 말했다.

33 빈칸

❶ One of the most striking characteristics of a sleeping animal or person is that they do not respond normally to environmental stimuli.

잠을 자고 있는 동물이나 사람의 가장 두드러진 특징 중 하나는 그들이 환경의 자극에 정상적으로 반응하지 않는다는 것이다.

❷ If you open the eyelids of a sleeping mammal the eyes will not see normally — they are functionally blind.

만약 당신이 잠을 자고 있는 포유류의 눈꺼풀을 열면, 그 눈은 정상적으로 볼 수 없을 것인데, 즉 그 눈은 기능적으로는 실명 상태이다.

❸ Some visual information apparently gets in, but it is not normally processed as it is shortened or weakened; same with the other sensing systems.

어떤 시각적 정보는 명백히 눈으로 들어오지만, 그것은 짧아지거나 약화되어서 정상적으로 처리되지 않는데, 이는 다른 감각 체계도 마찬가지다.

❹ Perceptual disengagement probably serves the function of protecting sleep, so some authors do not count it as part of the definition of sleep itself.

지각 이탈은 추측하건대 수면을 보호하는 기능을 제공해서 어떤 저자는 그것을 수면 자체의 정의의 일부로 여기지 않는다.

❺ But as sleep would be impossible without it, it seems essential to its definition.

그러나 수면이 그것 없이는 불가능하기 때문에 그것(지각 이탈)은 그것(수면)의 정의에 필수적인 것으로 보여진다.

❻ Nevertheless, many animals (including humans) use the intermediate state of drowsiness to derive some benefits of sleep without total perceptual disengagement.

그럼에도 (인간을 포함한) 많은 동물은 완전한 지각 이탈 없이 수면의 일부 이득을 끌어내기 위해서 졸음이라는 중간 상태를 이용한다.

34 빈칸

❶ A number of research studies have shown how experts in a field often experience difficulties when introducing newcomers to that field.

많은 조사 연구는 한 분야의 전문가가 그 분야로 초보자를 입문시킬 때 어떻게 어려움을 종종 겪는지를 보여 주었다.

❷ For example, in a genuine training situation, Dr Pamela Hinds found that people expert in using mobile phones were remarkably less accurate than novice phone users in judging how long it takes people to learn to use the phones.

예를 들어, 실제 교육 상황에서 Pamela Hinds 박사는 휴대 전화기를 사용하는 데 능숙한 사람들이 휴대 전화기 사용법을 배우는 것에 얼마나 오랜 시간이 걸리는지를 판단하는 데 있어서, 초보 휴대 전화기 사용자보다 놀랍도록 덜 정확하다는 것을 알아냈다.

❸ Experts can become insensitive to how hard a task is for the beginner, an effect referred to as the 'curse of knowledge'.

전문가는 한 과업이 초보자에게 얼마나 어려운지에 대해 무감각해질 수 있는데, 즉 '지식의 저주'로 칭해지는 효과이다.

❹ Dr. Hinds was able to show that as people acquired the skill, they then began to underestimate the level of difficulty of that skill.

Hinds 박사는 사람이 기술을 습득했을 때 그 이후에 그 기술의 어려움의 정도를 과소평가 하기 시작했다는 것을 보여 줄 수 있었다.

❺ Her participants even underestimated how long it had taken themselves to acquire that skill in an earlier session.

그녀의 참가자는 심지어 자신들이 이전 기간에 그 기술을 습득 하는 데 얼마나 오래 걸렸는지를 과소평가했다.

❻ Knowing that experts forget how hard it was for them to learn, we can understand the need to look at the learning process through students' eyes, rather than making assumptions about how students 'should be' learning.

전문가가 자신이 학습하는 것이 얼마나 어려웠는지를 잊어 버린다는 것을 안다면, 우리는 학생이 어떻게 학습을 '해야 하는지'에 대한 (근거 없는) 추정을 하기보다 학생들의 눈을 통해 학습 과정을 바라봐야 할 필요성을 이해할 수 있을 것이다.

35 무관

❶ A group of psychologists studied individuals with severe mental illness who experienced weekly group music therapy, including singing familiar songs and composing original songs.

한 심리학자 그룹이 친숙한 노래 부르기와 독창적인 작곡하기를 포함한 집단 음악 치료를 매주 경험한 심각한 정신 질환이 있는 사람들을 연구했다.

❷ The results showed that the group music therapy improved the quality of participants' life, with those participating in a greater number of sessions experiencing the greatest benefits.

그 연구 결과는 참여자가 (치료) 활동에 참여한 횟수가 많을수록 가장 큰 효과를 경험했기에, 집단 음악 치료가 참여자의 삶의 질을 개선하였음을 보여 주었다.

❸ Focusing on singing, another group of psychologists reviewed articles on the efficacy of group singing as a mental health treatment for individuals living with a mental health condition in a community setting.

노래 부르기에 초점을 두고, 또 다른 그룹의 심리학자는 집단 생활의 환경에서 정신적인 건강 문제를 가지고 살고 있는 이들에게 미치는 집단 가창의 효능에 대한 논문을 검토했다.

❹ The findings showed that, when people with mental health conditions participated in a choir, their mental health and wellbeing significantly improved.

발견된 결과는, 정신적인 건강 문제를 가진 사람이 합창단에 참여했을 때, 정신 건강과 행복이 상당히 개선되었음을 보여 주었다.

❺ Group singing provided enjoyment, improved emotional states, developed a sense of belonging and enhanced self-confidence.

집단 가창은 즐거움을 제공했고 감정 상태를 개선하였으며 소속감을 키웠고 자신감을 강화하였다.

36 순서

❶ In many sports, people realized the difficulties and even impossibilities of young children participating fully in many adult sport environments.

많은 스포츠에서 사람들은 어린아이들이 여러 성인 스포츠 환경에 완전히 참여하기란 어렵고 심지어 불가능하다는 것을 깨달았다.

❷ They found the road to success for young children is unlikely if they play on adult fields, courts or arenas with equipment that is too large, too heavy or too fast for them to handle while trying to compete in adult-style competition.

어린아이들이 너무 크거나 너무 무겁고 또는 너무 빨라서 그들(어린아이들)이 다룰 수 없는 장비를 가지고 성인 스타일의 시합에서 경쟁하려고 하면서 성인용 운동장, 코트 또는 경기장에서 운동한다면 그들(어린아이들)이 성공으로 가는 길이 있을 것 같지 않다는 것을 그들은 발견했다.

❸ Common sense has prevailed: different sports have made adaptations for children.

이러한 공통된 견해가 널리 퍼졌기에 여러 스포츠는 어린아이들을 위한 조정을 했다.

❹ As examples, baseball has T ball, football has flag football and junior soccer uses a smaller and lighter ball and (sometimes) a smaller field.

예를 들자면, 야구에는 티볼이 있고, 풋볼에는 플래그 풋볼이 있고, 유소년 축구는 더 작고 더 가벼운 공과 (가끔은) 더 작은 경기장을 사용한다.

❺ All have junior competitive structures where children play for shorter time periods and often in smaller teams.

모두가 어린아이들이 더 짧아진 경기 시간 동안 그리고 종종 더 작은 팀으로 경기하는 유소년 시합의 구조를 가진다.

❻ In a similar way, tennis has adapted the court areas, balls and rackets to make them more appropriate for children under 10.

비슷한 방식으로, 테니스는 코트 면적, 공, 라켓을 10세 미만의 어린아이에게 더 적합하도록 만들기 위해 조정했다.

❼ The adaptations are progressive and relate to the age of the child.

이러한 조정은 점진적이고 어린아이의 연령과 관련이 있다.

❽ He won the Nobel Prize in chemistry in 1959.

그는 1959년에 노벨 화학상을 수상했다.

37 순서

❶ With no horses available, the Inca empire excelled at delivering messages on foot.

구할 수 있는 말이 없어서, Inca 제국은 걸어서 메시지를 전달하는 데 탁월했다.

❷ The messengers were stationed on the royal roads to deliver the Inca king's orders and reports coming from his lands.

전령들은 Inca 왕의 명령과 그의 영토에서 오는 보고를 전달하기 위해 왕의 길에 배치되었다.

❸ Called Chasquis, they lived in groups of four to six in huts, placed from one to two miles apart along the roads.

Chasquis라고 불리는, 그들은 네 명에서 여섯 명의 집단을 이루어 길을 따라 1마일에서 2마일 간격으로 떨어져 배치된 오두막에서 생활했다.

❹ They were all young men and especially good runners who watched the road in both directions.

그들은 모두 젊은 남자였고, 양방향으로 길을 주시하는 특히 잘 달리는 이들이었다.

❺ If they caught sight of another messenger coming, they hurried out to meet them.

그들은 다른 전령이 오는 것을 발견하면 그들을 맞이하기 위해 서둘러 나갔다.

❻ The Inca built the huts on high ground, in sight of one another.

Inca 사람들은 서로를 볼 수 있는 높은 지대에 오두막을 지었다.

❼ When a messenger neared the next hut, he began to call out and repeated the message three or four times to the one who was running out to meet him.

전령은 다음 오두막에 다가갈 때, 자신을 만나러 달려 나오고 있는 전령에게 소리치기 시작했고 메시지를 서너 번 반복했다.

❽ The Inca empire could relay messages 1,000 miles (1,610 km) in three or four days under good conditions.

Inca 제국은 사정이 좋으면 사나흘 만에 1,000마일(1,610km) 정도 메시지를 이어 갈 수 있었다.

38 삽입

❶ The tongue was mapped into separate areas where certain tastes were registered: sweetness at the tip, sourness on the sides, and bitterness at the back of the mouth.

혀는 특정 맛이 등록되는 개별적인 영역으로 구획되었는데, 즉, 끝에는 단맛, 측면에는 신맛, 그리고 입의 뒤쪽에는 쓴맛이 있었다.

❷ Research in the 1980s and 1990s, however, demonstrated that the "tongue map" explanation of how we taste was, in fact, totally wrong.

그러나 1980년대와 1990년대의 연구는 우리가 맛을 느끼는 방식에 대한 '혀 지도' 설명이 사실은 완전히 틀렸다는 것을 보여 주었다.

❸ As it turns out, the map was a misinterpretation and mistranslation of research conducted in Germany at the turn of the twentieth century.

밝혀진 바와 같이, 그 지도는 20세기 초입 독일에서 수행된 연구를 오해하고 오역한 것이었다.

❹ Today, leading taste researchers believe that taste buds are not grouped according to specialty.

오늘날, 선도적인 미각 연구자는 미뢰가 맛을 느끼는 특화된 분야에 따라 분류되지 않는다고 믿는다.

❺ Sweetness, saltiness, bitterness, and sourness can be tasted everywhere in the mouth, although they may be perceived at a little different intensities at different sites.

비록 그것들이 여러 위치에서 조금씩 다른 강도로 지각될지도 모르겠지만, 단맛, 짠맛, 쓴맛 그리고 신맛은 입안 어디에서나 느낄 수 있다.

❻ Moreover, the mechanism at work is not place, but time.

게다가, 작동 중인 기제는 위치가 아니라 시간이다.

❼ It's not that you taste sweetness at the tip of your tongue, but rather that you register that perception first.

여러분은 혀끝에서 단맛을 느낀다기보다 오히려 그 지각(단맛)을 '가장 먼저' 등록하는 것이다.

39 삽입

❶ No two animals are alike.

어떤 두 동물도 똑같지 않다.

❷ Animals from the same litter will display some of the same features, but will not be exactly the same as each other; therefore, they may not respond in entirely the same way during a healing session.

한 배에서 태어난 동물은 똑같은 몇몇 특성을 보여 줄 수 있겠지만, 서로 정확히 같지는 않을 것이다. 그런 까닭에, 그들은 치료 활동 중에 완전히 똑같은 방식으로 반응하지 않을지도 모른다.

❸ Environmental factors can also determine how the animal will respond during the treatment.

또한 환경적 요인은 치료 중에 동물이 어떻게 반응할지를 결정할 수 있다.

❹ For instance, a cat in a rescue center will respond very differently than a cat within a domestic home environment.

예를 들어, 구조 센터에 있는 고양이는 가정집 환경 내에 있는 고양이와는 매우 다르게 반응할 것이다.

❺ In addition, animals that experience healing for physical illness will react differently than those accepting healing for emotional confusion.

게다가, 신체적 질병의 치료를 받는 동물은 감정적 동요의 치료를 받는 동물과는 다르게 반응할 것이다.

❻ With this in mind, every healing session needs to be explored differently, and each healing treatment should be adjusted to suit the specific needs of the animal.

이를 염두에 두어, 모든 치료 활동은 다르게 탐구되어야 하고, 각각의 치료법은 동물의 특정한 필요에 맞도록 조정되어야 한다.

❼ You will learn as you go; healing is a constant learning process.

여러분은 치료가 끊임없는 학습의 과정인 것을 직접 겪으면서 배우게 될 것이다.

40 요약

❶ The mind has parts that are known as the conscious mind and the subconscious mind.

마음은 의식적 마음과 잠재의식적 마음이라고 알려진 부분을 갖고 있다.

❷ The subconscious mind is very fast to act and doesn't deal with emotions.

잠재의식적 마음은 매우 빠르게 작동하며 감정을 다루지 않는다.

❸ It deals with memories of your responses to life, your memories and recognition.

그것은 여러분의 삶에 대한 반응의 기억, 기억 및 인식을 다룬다.

❹ However, the conscious mind is the one that you have more control over.

그러나 의식적 마음은 여러분이 더 많은 통제력을 갖고 있는 부분이다.

❺ You think.

여러분은 생각한다.

❻ You can choose whether to carry on a thought or to add emotion to it and this is the part of your mind that lets you down frequently because — fueled by emotions — you make the wrong decisions time and time again.

여러분은 생각을 계속할지 또는 그 생각에 감정을 더할지를 선택할 수 있다. 그리고 이것은 감정에 북받쳐 잘못된 결정을 반복해서 내리게 만들기 때문에 여러분을 빈번하게 낙담시키는 마음의 부분이기도 하다.

❼ When your judgment is clouded by emotions, this puts in biases and all kinds of other negativities that hold you back.

감정에 의해 여러분의 판단력이 흐려질 때 이것은 편견과 그 밖의 여러분을 억제하는 모든 종류의 부정성을 자리 잡게 만든다.

❽ Scared of spiders? Scared of the dark?

거미를 무서워하는가? 어둠을 무서워하는가?

❾ There are reasons for all of these fears, but they originate in the conscious mind.

이러한 두려움 전부 이유가 있지만 그것들은 의식적 마음에서 비롯된다.

❿ They only become real fears when the subconscious mind records your reactions.

그것들은 오직 잠재의식적 마음이 여러분의 반응을 기록할 때 실제 두려움이 된다.

41~42 제목, 어휘

❶ Norms are everywhere, defining what is "normal" and guiding our interpretations of social life at every turn.

규범은 무엇이 '정상적'인지를 규정하고 모든 순간 사회적 생활에 대한 우리의 해석을 안내해 주며 어디에나 존재한다.

❷ As a simple example, there is a norm in Anglo society to say Thank you to strangers who have just done something to help, such as open a door for you, point out that you've just dropped something, or give you directions.

간단한 예로, 문을 열어 주거나, 여러분이 물건을 방금 떨어뜨렸다는 것을 짚어 주거나, 길을 알려주는 것과 같이 도움을 줄 수 있는 무언가를 이제 막 해준 낯선 사람에게 '감사합니다'라고 말하는 규범이 Anglo 사회에 있다.

❸ There is no law that forces you to say Thank you.

여러분이 '감사합니다'라고 말하도록 강요하는 법은 없다.

❹ But if people don't say Thank you in these cases it is marked.

하지만 이런 상황에서 사람들이 '감사합니다'라고 말하지 않으면 그것은 눈에 띄게 된다.

❺ People expect that you will say it.

사람들은 여러분이 그렇게 말하기를 기대한다.

❻ You become responsible.

여러분은 책임을 지게 되는 것이다.

❼ Failing to say it will be both surprising and worthy of criticism.

그렇게 말하지 못하는 것은 (주변을) 놀라게 하기도 하고 비판을 받을 만하다.

❽ Not knowing the norms of another community is the central problem of cross-cultural communication.

다른 집단의 규범을 모른다는 것은 문화 간 의사소통에서 중심적인 문제이다.

❾ To continue the Thank you example, even though another culture may have an expression that appears translatable (many don't), there may be different norms for its usage, for example, such that you should say Thank you only when the cost someone has caused is considerable.

'감사합니다'의 예를 이어 보자면, 비록 또 다른 문화권이 번역할 수 있는 것처럼 보이는 어떤 표현(다수는 그렇지 못하지만)을 가지고 있다 할지라도, 그것의 사용법에 대해, 예를 들어, 누군가가 초래한 대가가 상당할 때만 '감사합니다'라고 말해야 한다는 것처럼 다른 규범이 있을 수 있다.

❿ In such a case it would sound ridiculous (i.e., unexpected, surprising, and worthy of criticism) if you were to thank someone for something so minor as holding a door open for you.

그 같은 상황에서 만약 여러분이 혹시라도, 여러분을 위해 문을 잡아주는 것과 같이 아주 사소한 일에 대해 누군가에게 감사해한다면, 그것은 우스꽝스럽게(즉, 예상치 못하게, 놀랍게, 비판을 받을 만하게) 들릴 수 있을 것이다.

43~45 순서, 지칭, 세부 내용

❶ Long ago, when the world was young, an old Native American spiritual leader Odawa had a dream on a high mountain.

오래전, 세상이 생겨난지 오래지 않을 무렵, 아메리카 원주민의 늙은 영적 지도자인 Odawa는 높은 산에서 꿈을 꾸었다.

❷ In his dream, Iktomi, the great spirit and searcher of wisdom, appeared to him in the form of a spider.

자신의 꿈속에서 위대한 신령이자 지혜의 구도자인 Iktomi가 거미의 형태로 그에게 나타났다.

❸ Iktomi spoke to him in a holy language.

Iktomi는 성스러운 언어로 그에게 말했다.

❹ Iktomi told Odawa about the cycles of life.

Iktomi는 Odawa에게 삶의 순환에 관해서 말했다.

❺ He said, "We all begin our lives as babies, move on to childhood, and then to adulthood.

그는 "우리는 모두 아기로 삶을 출발하고, 유년기를 거쳐 그다음 성년기에 이르게 된다.

❻ Finally, we come to old age, where we must be taken care of as babies again."

결국 우리는 노년기에 도달하고, 거기서 우리는 다시 아기처럼 보살핌을 받아야 한다."라고 말했다.

❼ Iktomi also told him that there are good and bad forces in each stage of life.

또한 Iktomi는 삶의 각 단계에는 좋고 나쁜 힘이 있다고 그에게 말했다.

❽ "If we listen to the good forces, they will guide us in the right direction.

"우리가 좋은 힘에 귀를 기울이면 그들은 우리를 올바른 방향으로 인도할 것이다.

❾ But if we listen to the bad forces, they will lead us the wrong way and may harm us," Iktomi said.

하지만 만약 나쁜 힘에 귀를 기울이면 그들은 우리를 잘못된 길로 이끌고 우리를 해칠 수도 있다."라고 Iktomi는 말했다.

❿ When Iktomi finished speaking, he spun a web and gave it to Odawa.

Iktomi가 말을 끝냈을 때, 그는 거미집을 짜서 Odawa에게 주었다.

❶ He said to Odawa, "The web is a perfect circle with a hole in the center.
그가 Odawa에게 말하기를, "그 거미집은 가운데 구멍이 뚫린 완벽한 원이다.

❷ Use the web to help your people reach their goals.
너의 마을 사람들이 자신들의 목표에 도달할 수 있도록 거미집을 사용해라.

❸ Make good use of their ideas, dreams, and visions.
그들의 생각, 꿈, 비전을 잘 활용해라.

❹ If you believe in the great spirit, the web will catch your good ideas and the bad ones will go through the hole."
만약 네가 위대한 신령을 믿는다면 그 거미집이 네 좋은 생각을 붙잡아 줄 것이고 나쁜 생각은 구멍을 통해 빠져 나갈 것이다."

❺ Right after Odawa woke up, he went back to his village.
Odawa는 잠에서 깨자마자 자기 마을로 되돌아갔다.

❻ Odawa shared Iktomi's lesson with his people.
Odawa는 Iktomi의 교훈을 그의 마을 사람들과 나누었다.

❼ Today, many Native Americans have dream catchers hanging above their beds.
오늘날 많은 미국 원주민은 침대 위에 드림 캐처를 건다.

❽ Dream catchers are believed to filter out bad dreams.
드림캐처는 나쁜 꿈을 걸러 준다고 믿어 진다.

❾ The good dreams are captured in the web of life and carried with the people.
좋은 꿈은 인생이라는 거미집에 걸리고 사람들 과 동반하게 된다.

❿ The bad dreams pass through the hole in the web and are no longer a part of their lives.
나쁜 꿈은 거미집의 구멍 사이로 빠져나가고 더 이상 그들의 삶의 한 부분이 되지 못한다.

2024 고1 3월 모의고사   ❶ 회차 :   점 / 200점

❶ voca   ❷ text   ❸ [/]   ❹ _____   ❺ quiz 1   ❻ quiz 2   ❼ quiz 3   ❽ quiz 4   ❾ quiz 5

18. Dear Ms. Jane Watson,

I am John Austin, a science teacher at Crestville High School. Recently I [**impressed / was impressed**]¹⁾ by the latest book you wrote about the environment. Also my students read your book and had a class discussion [**about / X**]²⁾ it. They are big fans of your book, so I'd like to [**ask / asking**]³⁾ you to visit our school and give a special lecture. We can set the date and time to suit your schedule. [**Have / Having**]⁴⁾ you at our school would be a fantastic experience for the students. We would be very grateful if you could come. / Best regards, John Austin

친애하는 Jane Watson 씨,
저는 Crestville 고등학교의 과학 교사 John Austin입니다. 최근에, 저는 환경에 관해 당신이 쓴 최신 도서에 감명받았습니다. 또한 저의 학생들은 당신의 책을 읽었고 그것에 대해 토론 수업을 하였습니다. 그들은 당신의 책을 아주 좋아하고, 그래서 저는 당신이 우리 학교에 방문하여 특별 강연을 해주시기를 요청드리고 싶습니다. 우리는 당신의 일정에 맞춰 날짜와 시간을 정하겠습니다. 당신이 우리 학교에 와주신다면 학생들에게 멋진 경험이 될 것 같습니다. 우리는 당신이 와주신다면 정말 감사하겠습니다. / 안부를 전하며, John Austin

19. Marilyn and her three-year-old daughter, Sarah, took a trip to the beach, [**where / which**]⁵⁾ Sarah built her first sandcastle. Moments later, an enormous wave [**destroyed / was destroyed**]⁶⁾ Sarah's castle. In response to the loss of her sandcastle, tears streamed down Sarah's cheeks and her heart [**broken / was broken**]⁷⁾. She ran to Marilyn, saying she [**should / would**]⁸⁾ never build a sandcastle again. Marilyn said, "Part of the joy of building a sandcastle is that, in the end, we give [**it / them**]⁹⁾ as a gift to the ocean." Sarah loved this idea and responded with enthusiasm to the idea of building [**another / other**]¹⁰⁾ castle — this time, even closer to the water so the ocean would get [**its / their**]¹¹⁾ gift sooner!

Marilyn과 세 살 된 딸 Sarah는 해변으로 여행을 떠났고, 그곳에서 Sarah는 처음으로 모래성을 쌓았다. 잠시 후, 거대한 파도가 Sarah의 성을 무너뜨렸다. 모래성을 잃은 것에 반응하여 눈물이 Sarah의 뺨을 타고 흘러내렸고, 그녀의 마음은 무너졌다. 그녀는 다시는 모래성을 쌓지 않겠다고 말하며 Marilyn에게 달려갔다. Marilyn은 "모래성을 쌓는 즐거움 중 일부는 결국에는 우리가 그것을 바다에게 선물로 주는 것이란다." 라고 말했다. Sarah는 이 생각이 마음에 들었고 또 다른 모래성을 만들 생각에 이번에는 바다와 훨씬 더 가까운 곳에서 바다가 그 선물을 더 빨리 받을 수 있도록 하겠다며 열정적으로 반응했다.

20. Magic is [**that / what**]¹²⁾ we all wish for to happen in our life. Do you love the movie Cinderella like me? Well, in real life, you can also create magic. Here's the trick. Write down all the real-time challenges [**that / when**]¹³⁾ you face and deal with. Just change the challenge statement into positive statements. Let me give you an example here. If you struggle [**of / with**]¹⁴⁾ getting up early in the morning, then write a positive statement such as "I get up early in the morning at 5:00 am every day." [**Once / Otherwise**]¹⁵⁾ you write these statements, get ready to witness magic and [**confidence / confident**]¹⁶⁾. You will be surprised that just by writing these statements, there is a shift in the way you think and act. Suddenly you feel [**less / more**]¹⁷⁾ powerful and positive.

마법은 우리 모두 자신의 삶에서 일어나기를 바라는 바이다. 여러분도 나처럼 신데렐라 영화를 사랑하는가? 그러면, 실제 삶에서, 여러분도 마법을 만들 수 있다. 여기 그 요령이 있다. 여러분이 직면하고 처리하는 모든 실시간의 어려움을 적어라. 그 어려움에 관한 진술을 긍정적인 진술로 바꾸어라. 여기서 여러분에게한 예시를 제시하겠다. 만약 여러분이 아침 일찍 일어나는 것에 어려움을 겪는다면, 그러면 '나는 매일 일찍 아침 5시에 일어난다.'와 같은 긍정적인 진술을 써라. 일단 여러분이 이러한 진술을 적는다면, 마법과 자신감을 목격할 준비를 하라. 여러분은 단지 이러한 진술을 적음으로써 여러분이 생각하고 행동하는 방식에 변화가 있다는 것에 놀랄 것이다. 어느 순간 여러분은 더 강력하고 긍정적이라고 느끼게 된다.

21. Consider the seemingly simple question How many senses are there? Around 2,370 years ago, Aristotle wrote [**that / what**]18) there are five, in both humans [**and / or**]19) animals — sight, hearing, smell, taste, and touch. However, according to the philosopher Fiona Macpherson, there are reasons to [**believe / doubt**]20) it. For a start, Aristotle missed a [**few / little**]21) in humans: the perception of your own body which is different [**at / from**]22) touch and the sense of balance [**where / which**]23) has links to both touch and vision. [**Other / The other**]24) animals have senses that are even [**hard / harder**]25) to categorize. Many vertebrates have a different sense system for detecting odors. Some snakes can [**be detected / detect**]26) the body heat of their [**predator / prey**]27). These examples tell us that "senses cannot be clearly divided into a [**limited / limitless**]28) number of specific kinds," Macpherson wrote in The Senses. Instead of trying [**pushing / to push**]29) animal senses into Aristotelian buckets, we should study them for [**what / which**]30) they are.

'얼마나 많은 감각이 존재하는가?'라는 겉으로 보기에 단순한 질문을 고려해 봐라. 약 2,370년 전 Aristotle은 인간과 동물 둘다에게 시각, 청각, 후각, 미각, 그리고 촉각의 다섯(감각)이 있다고 썼다. 그러나, 철학자 Fiona Macpherson에 따르면, 그 것을 의심할 이유가 존재한다. 우선, Aristotle은 인간에게서 몇 가지를 빠뜨렸는데, 그것은 촉각과는 다른 여러분 자신의 신체에 대한 인식과, 촉각과 시각 모두에 관련되어 있는 균형 감각이었다. 다른 동물들은 훨씬 더 범주화하기 어려운 감각을 가지고 있다. 많은 척추동물은 냄새를 탐지하기 위한 다른 감각 체계를 가지고 있다. 어떤 뱀은 그들의 먹잇감의 체열을 감지할 수 있다. Macpherson이 'The Senses'에서 쓰기를, 이러한 사례는 우리에게 '감각은 제한된 수의 특정한 종류로 명확하게 나누어지지 않을 수 있다.'라는 것을 알려 준다. 동물의 감각을 Aristotle의 양동이로 밀어 넣는 대신, 우리는 그것들을 존재하는 그대로 연구해야 한다.

22. When we think of leaders, we may [**think / think of**]31) people such as Abraham Lincoln or Martin Luther King, Jr. If you consider the historical importance and [**far-reached / far-reaching**]32) influence of these individuals, leadership might seem like a noble and high goal. But like all of us, these people started out as students, workers, and citizens [**who / whose**]33) possessed ideas about how some aspect of daily life could be [**improved / involved**]34) on a larger scale. Through diligence and experience, they improved upon their ideas by sharing them with others, [**seeked / seeking**]35) their opinions and feedback and constantly looking for the best way to accomplish goals for a group. Thus we all [**has / have**]36) the potential to be leaders at school, in our communities, and [**at / in**]37) work, regardless of age or experience.

우리가 리더에 대해 생각할 때, 우리는 Abraham Lincoln 혹은 Martin Luther King, Jr. 와 같은 사람들에 대해 생각할지 모른다. 만약 여러분이 이러한 인물들의 역사적 중요성과 광범위한 영향력을 고려한다면, 리더십은 고귀하고 높은 목표처럼 보일지도 모른다. 그러나 우리 모두와 마찬가지로, 이러한 인물들은 일상생활의 어느 측면이 더 큰 규모로 어떻게 개선될 수 있는지에 대한 생각을 가졌던 학생, 근로자, 그리고 시민으로 시작했다. 근면함과 경험을 통해, 그들은 자신의 생각을 다른 사람들과 공유하고, 그들의 의견과 반응을 구하며, 끊임없이 집단의 목표를 성취할 수 있는 가장 좋은 방법을 찾음으로써 자신의 생각을 발전시켰다. 그러므로 우리는 모두, 나이나 경험에 관계없이, 학교, 공동체, 그리고 일터에서 리더가 될 수 있는 잠재력을 가지고 있다.

23.
Crop rotation is the [**process / progress**]38) [**in which / which**]39) farmers change the crops they grow in their fields in a [**spatial / special**]40) order. For example, if a farmer has three fields, he or she may grow carrots in the first field, green beans in the second, and tomatoes in the third. The next year, green beans will be in the first field, tomatoes in the second field, and carrots will be in the third. In year three, the crops will rotate again. By the fourth year, the crops will go back [**in / to**]41) their original order. Each [**crop / crops**]42) enriches the soil for the next crop. This type of farming is [**suitable / sustainable**]43) [**because / because of**]44) the soil stays healthy.

윤작은 농부가 자신의 밭에서 재배하는 작물을 특별한 순서로 바꾸는 과정이다. 예를 들면, 만약 한 농부가 세 개의 밭을 가지고 있다면, 그들은 첫 번째 밭에는 당근을, 두 번째 밭에는 녹색 콩을, 세 번째 밭에는 토마토를 재배할 수 있다. 그 다음 해에 첫 번째 밭에는 녹색 콩을, 두 번째 밭에는 토마토를, 세 번째 밭에는 당근을 재배할 것이다. 3년 차에 작물은 다시 순환할 것이다. 4년째에 이르면 작물은 원래의 순서로 되돌아갈 것이다. 각각의 작물은 다음 작물을 위한 토양을 비옥하게 한다. 이 유형의 농업은 토양이 건강하게 유지되기 때문에 지속 가능하다.

24. Working around the whole painting, rather than [**concentrating** / **to concentrate**]45) on one area at a time, will mean you can stop at any point and the painting can be considered "finished." Artists often find [**it** / **that**]46) difficult to know when to stop [**painting** / **to paint**]47), and it can be tempting to keep on adding more to your work. It is important to take [**a few** / **few**]48) steps back from the painting from time to time to [**access** / **assess**]49) your progress. Putting too much into a painting can spoil its impact and leave it looking overworked. If you find yourself [**struggled** / **struggling**]50) to decide whether you have finished, [**take** / **taking**]51) a break and come back to it later with fresh eyes. Then you can decide whether any areas of your painting would benefit from [**farther** / **further**]52) refinement.

한 번에 한 영역에만 집중하기보다 전체 그림에 대해서 작업하는 것은 여러분이 어떤 지점에서도 멈출 수 있고 그림이 '완성'된 것으로 간주 될 수 있다는 것을 의미할 것이다. 화가인 여러분은 종종 언제 그림을 멈춰야 할지 알기 어렵다는 것을 발견하고, 자신의 그림에 계속해서 더 추가하고 싶은 유혹을 느낄 수도 있다. 때때로 자신의 진행 상황을 평가하기 위해 그림에서 몇 걸음 뒤로 물러나는 것이 중요하다. 한 그림에 너무 많은 것을 넣으면 그것의 영향력을 망칠 수 있고 그것이 과하게 작업된 것처럼 보이게 둘 수 있다. 만약 여러분이 끝냈는지를 결정하는 데 자신이 어려움을 겪고 있음을 알게 된다면, 잠시 휴식을 취하고 나중에 새로운 눈으로 그것(그림)으로 다시 돌아와라. 그러면 여러분은 더 정교하게 꾸며서 자신의 그림 어느 부분이 득을 볼지를 결정할 수 있다.

25. The above graph shows the [**extent** / **intent**]53) to which young people aged 16-25 in six countries had fear about climate change in 2021. The Philippines had the highest percentage of young people who said they were extremely or very worried, at 84 percent, [**followed** / **following**]54) by 67 percent in Brazil. More than 60 percent of young people in Portugal said they were extremely worried or very worried. In France, the percentage of young people who were extremely worried was lower than [**that** / **those**]55) of young people who were very worried. In the United Kingdom, the percentage of young generation who said that they were very worried was 29 percent. In the United States, the total percentage of extremely worried and very worried youth was the smallest among the six countries.

위 그래프는 2021년 6개국의 16세에서 25세 사이 젊은 사람들이 기후 변화에 대해 두려움을 갖는 정도를 보여 준다. 필리핀은 극도로 혹은 매우 걱정한다고 말한 젊은 사람들의 비율이 84퍼센트로 가장 높았으며, 브라질이 67퍼센트로 그 뒤를 이었다. 포르투갈은 60퍼센트 이상의 젊은 사람들이 극도로 혹은 매우 걱정하고 있다고 말했다. 프랑스는 극도로 걱정하는 젊은 사람들의 비율이 매우 걱정하는 젊은 사람들의 비율보다 낮았다. 영국은 매우 걱정한다고 말하는 젊은 세대의 비율이 29퍼센트였다. 미국은 극도로 걱정하거나 매우 걱정하는 젊은 사람들의 총비율이 6개국 중에서 가장 작았다.

26. Jaroslav Heyrovsky [**born** / **was born**]56) in Prague on December 20, 1890, as the fifth child of Leopold Heyrovsky. In 1901 Jaroslav went to a secondary school called the Akademicke Gymnasium. Rather than Latin and Greek, he showed a strong interest in the [**natural** / **nature**]57) sciences. At Czech University in Prague he studied chemistry, physics, and mathematics. From 1910 to 1914 he continued his studies at University College, London. Throughout the First World War, Jaroslav [**served** / **was served**]58) in a military hospital. In 1926, Jaroslav became the first Professor of Physical Chemistry at Charles University in Prague. He won the Nobel Prize in chemistry in 1959.

Jaroslav Heyrovsky는 1890년 12월 20일 Prague에서 Leopold Heyrovsky의 다섯째 자녀로 태어났다. 1901년 Jaroslav는 Akademicke Gymnasium이라고 불리는 중등학교에 다녔다. 그는 라틴어와 그리스어보다는 자연 과학에 강한 흥미를 보였다. Prague에 있는 Czech University에서 그는 화학, 물리학 및 수학을 공부했다. 1910년부터 1914년까지 그는 런던의 University College에서 학업을 이어 나갔다. 제1차 세계 대전 내내 Jaroslav는 군 병원에 복무했다. 1926년에 Jaroslav는 Prague에 있는 Charles University 최초의 물리화학 교수가 되었다. 그는 1959년에 노벨 화학상을 수상했다.

29. It would be hard to [**overstate / understate**]59) how important meaningful work is to human beings — work that provides a sense of fulfillment and empowerment. Those who have found deeper meaning in their careers find their days much more [**energized / energizing**]60) and [**satisfied / satisfying**]61), and [**count / counted**]62) their employment as one of their greatest sources of joy and pride. Sonya Lyubomirsky, professor of psychology at the University of California, has conducted numerous workplace studies showing [**that / in that**]63) when people are more fulfilled on the job, they not only produce higher quality work and a greater output, but also generally [**earn / earned**]64) higher [**incomes / outcomes**]65). Those most [**satisfied / satisfying**]66) with their work [**are / is**]67) also much more likely to be happier with their lives overall. For her book Happiness at Work, researcher Jessica Pryce-Jones conducted a study of 3,000 workers in seventy-nine countries, [**finding / found**]68) that those who took greater satisfaction from their work were 150 percent [**less / more**]69) likely to have a happier life overall.

인간에게 의미 있는 일, 즉 성취감과 권한을 제공하는 일이 얼마나 중요한지를 과장해서 말한다는 것은 어려울 것이다. 자신의 직업에서 더 깊은 의미를 찾은 사람은 자신의 하루하루가 훨씬 더 활기차고 만족감을 준다는 것을 발견하고, 자신의 직업을 기쁨과 자부심의 가장 큰 원천 중 하나로 꼽는다. University of California의 심리학 교수인 Sonya Lyubomirsky는 사람이 직업에 더 많은 성취감을 느낄 때 그들은 더 질 높은 업무와 더 큰 성과를 만들어 낼 뿐만 아니라 일반적으로 더 높은 수입을 거둔다는 것을 보여주는 수많은 업무 현장 연구를 수행했다. 자신의 일에 가장 만족하는 사람은 또한 전반적으로 자신의 삶에 더 행복해할 가능성이 훨씬 더 크다. 자신의 저서 'Happiness at Work'를 위해 연구자 Jessica Pryce-Jones는 79개 국가의 3,000명의 근로자에 대한 연구를 수행했고, 자신의 일로부터 더 큰 만족감을 갖는 사람이 전반적으로 더 행복한 삶을 살 가능성이 150퍼센트 더 크다는 것을 알아냈다.

30. The rate of speed [**at which / which**]70) one is traveling will greatly determine the ability to process detail in the environment. In [**evolutionary / revolutionary**]71) terms, human senses are [**adapted / adopted**]72) to the speed at which humans move through space under their own power [**during / while**]73) walking. Our ability to [**extinguish / distinguish**]74) detail in the environment is therefore ideally [**suit / suited**]75) to movement at speeds of perhaps five miles per hour and under. The fastest users of the street, motorists, therefore [**has / have**]76) a much more limited ability to process details along the street — a motorist simply has [**a little / little**]77) time or ability to appreciate design details. On the other hand, [**pedestrian / pediatrician**]78) travel, being much slower, [**allowing / allows**]79) for the appreciation of environmental detail. Joggers and bicyclists fall somewhere in between these [**bipolar / polar**]80) opposites; while they travel faster than pedestrians, their rate of speed is [**extraordinarily / ordinarily**]81) much slower than [**that / those**]82) of the [**atypical / typical**]83) motorist.

사람이 이동하는 속도의 빠르기는 환경 속 세세한 것을 처리하는 능력을 크게 결정할 것이다. 진화론적 관점에서, 인간의 감각은 그 자신의 힘으로 걸으며 공간을 이동하는 속도에 적응되어 있다. 환경 속에서 세세한 것을 구별하는 우리의 능력은 그래서 대략 시속 5마일 또는 그 속도 이하의 이동에 이상적으로 맞추어져 있다. 그러므로 도로의 가장 빠른 사용자인 운전자는 도로를 따라서 (이동하며) 세세한 것을 처리하는 훨씬 더 제한된 능력을 가지고 있고, 그래서 운전자는 단지 디자인의 세세한 것을 감상할 수 있는 적은 시간이나 능력이 있다. 반면에 보행자 이동은 훨씬 더 느려서, 환경의 세세한 것을 감상할 수 있도록 허용해 준다. 조깅하는 사람과 자전거를 타는 사람은 이러한 극과 극 사이의 어딘가에 해당한다. 그들은 보행자보다 더 빨리 이동하지만, 속도의 빠르기는 보통 전형적인 운전자의 그것보다 훨씬 더 느리다.

31.
Every species [**has / have**]84) certain climatic requirements — what degree of heat or cold it can endure, for example. When the climate changes, the places that [**satisfied / satisfy**]85) those requirements change, too. Species [**are forced / forced**]86) to follow. [**All / Some**]87) creatures are capable of [**all / some**]88) degree of movement. Even creatures that appear immobile, like trees and barnacles, are capable of [**dispersal / disposal**]89) at some stage of their life — as a seed, in the case of the tree, or as a larva, in the case of the barnacle. A creature must get from the place it is born — often occupied by [**its / their**]90) parent — to a place where it can survive, grow, and [**produce / reproduce**]91). From fossils, scientists know that even creatures like trees [**moved / moving**]92) with surprising speed [**during / while**]93) past periods of climate change.

모든 종은, 예를 들자면 어느 정도의 더위나 추위를 견딜 수 있는지와 같은, 특정한 기후 요건을 가지고 있다. 기후가 변할 때, 그러한 요건을 충족시키는 장소도 역시 변한다. 종은 따르도록 강요받는다. 모든 생명체는 어느 정도의 이동이 가능하다. 심지어 나무나 따개비처럼 움직이지 않는 것처럼 보이는 생명체도, 나무의 경우는 씨앗으로, 따개비의 경우는 유충으로, 그들 일생의 어느 단계에서 분산할 수 있다. 생명체는 종종 자신의 부모에 의해서 점유된, 그래서 자신이 태어난 장소로부터 생존하고 성장하며 번식할 수 있는 장소로 이동해야 한다. 화석으로부터, 과학자들은 심지어 나무와 같은 생명체는 기후 변화의 과거 시기 동안 놀라운 속도로 이동했다는 것을 알고 있다.

32. No [**respectable / respective**]94) boss would say, "I make it a point to discourage my staff from speaking up, and I [**maintain / oppose**]95) a culture that prevents [**agreeing / disagreeing**]96) viewpoints from ever getting aired." If anything, most bosses even say that they are pro-dissent. This idea can [**be found / found**]97) throughout the series of conversations with corporate, university, and nonprofit leaders, [**published / publishing**]98) weekly in the business sections of newspapers. In the interviews, the featured leaders [**asked / are asked**]99) about their management techniques, and regularly claim to continually [**discourage / encourage**]100) internal protest from more junior staffers. As Bot Pittman remarked in one of these conversations: "I want us to listen to these [**advocates / dissenters**]101) because they [**may / should**]102) intend to tell you why we can't do something, but if you listen hard, what they're really telling you is [**that / what**]103) you must do to get something done."

존경할 만한 상사라면 누구라도 '나는 반드시 내 직원이 자유롭게 의견을 내지 못하도록 하고, 동의하지 않는 관점이 언제든 공공연히 알려지는 것을 가로막는 문화를 유지한다.'라고 말하지는 않을 것이다. 오히려, 대부분의 상사는 심지어 자신은 반대에 찬성한다고 말한다. 이러한 생각은 매주 발행되는 신문의 경제란에 기업, 대학, 그리고 비영리 (단체의) 리더와의 일련의 대담을 통해서 발견될 수 있다. 인터뷰에서, (기사에) 다루어진 리더는 자신의 경영 기법에 대해 질문을 받고, 내부적인 저항이 더 많은 부하 직원에게서 (나오기를) 계속해서 장려하고 있다고 어김없이 주장한다. Bot Pittman은 이러한 대담 중 하나에서 "저는 우리가 이러한 반대자에게 귀 기울이기를 원합니다. 왜냐하면 그들은 여러분에게 우리가 무엇인가를 할 수 없는 이유를 말하려고 의도할 수 있겠지만, 그러나 만약에 여러분이 열심히 귀 기울이면, 그들이 정말로 여러분에게 말하고 있는 것은 어떤 일이 이루어지도록 하기 위해서 여러분이 무엇을 해야만 하는가이기 때문입니다." 라고 말했다.

33. One of the most striking characteristics of a sleeping animal or person is that they do not respond [**normal / normally**]104) to environmental stimuli. If you open the eyelids of a sleeping mammal the eyes will not see normally — they are functionally blind. Some visual information apparently gets in, but it is not normally [**possessed / processed**]105) as it is shortened or [**strengthened / weakened**]106) ; same with [**another / the other**]107) sensing systems. Stimuli [**are registered / registered**]108) but not processed normally and they fail to wake the individual. Perceptual disengagement probably [**serve / serves**]109) the function of protecting sleep, so some authors [**are / do**]110) not count it as part of the definition of sleep [**it / itself**]111). But as sleep would be impossible [**with / without**]112) it, it seems essential to its definition. Nevertheless, many animals (including humans) use the [**immediate / intermediate**]113) state of drowsiness to [**derive / drive**]114) some benefits of sleep without total perceptual [**disengagement / engagement**]115).

잠을 자고 있는 동물이나 사람의 가장 두드러진 특징 중 하나는 그들이 환경의 자극에 정상적으로 반응하지 않는다는 것이다. 만약 당신이 잠을 자고 있는 포유류의 눈꺼풀을 열면, 그 눈은 정상적으로 볼 수 없을 것인데, 즉 그 눈은 기능적으로는 실명 상태이다. 어떤 시각적 정보는 명백히 눈으로 들어오지만, 그것은 짧아지거나 약화되어서 정상적으로 처리되지 않는 데, 이는 다른 감각 체계도 마찬가지다. 자극은 등록되지만 정상적으로 처리되지 않고 사람을 깨우는 데 실패한다. 지각 이탈은 추측하건대 수면을 보호하는 기능을 제공해서 어떤 저자는 그것을 수면 자체의 정의의 일부로 여기지 않는다. 그러나 수면이 그것 없이는 불가능하기 때문에 그것(지각 이탈)은 그것(수면)의 정의에 필수적인 것으로 보여진다. 그럼에도 (인간을 포함한) 많은 동물은 완전한 지각 이탈 없이 수면의 일부 이득을 끌어내기 위해서 졸음이라는 중간 상태를 이용한다.

34. [**A** / **The**]116) number of research studies have shown how experts in a field often experience difficulties when [**introduced** / **introducing**]117) newcomers to that field. For example, in a genuine training situation, Dr Pamela Hinds found that people expert in using mobile phones were remarkably [**less** / **more**]118) accurate than novice phone users in judging how long [**it** / **that**]119) takes people to learn to use the phones. Experts can become [**insensitive** / **sensitive**]120) to how hard a task is for the beginner, an effect [**referred** / **referring**]121) to as the 'curse of [**ignorance** / **knowledge**]122)'. Dr Hinds was able to show that as people [**acquired** / **required**]123) the skill, they then began to underestimate the level of [**difficulty** / **familiarity**]124) of that skill. Her participants even [**overestimated** / **underestimated**]125) how long it had taken [**them** / **themselves**]126) to acquire that skill in an earlier session. Knowing that experts forget how hard it was for them to learn, we can understand the need to look at the learning process through students' eyes, rather than making [**assumptions** / **judgments**]127) about how students 'should be' learning.

많은 조사 연구는 한 분야의 전문가가 그 분야로 초보자를 입문시킬 때 어떻게 어려움을 종종 겪는지를 보여줬다. 예를 들어, 실제 교육 상황에서 Pamela Hinds 박사는 휴대 전화기를 사용하는 데 능숙한 사람들이 휴대 전화기 사용법을 배우는 것에 얼마나 오랜 시간이 걸리는지를 판단하는 데 있어서, 초보 휴대 전화기 사용자보다 놀랍도록 덜 정확하다는 것을 알아냈다. 전문가는 한 과업이 초보자에게 얼마나 어려운지에 대해 무감각해질 수 있는데, 즉 '지식의 저주'로 칭해지는 효과이다. Hinds 박사는 사람이 기술을 습득했을 때 그 이후에 그 기술의 어려움의 정도를 과소평가하기 시작했다는 것을 보여줄 수 있었다. 그녀의 참가자는 심지어 자신들이 이전 기간에 그 기술을 습득하는 데 얼마나 오래 걸렸는지를 과소평가했다. 전문가가 자신이 학습하는 것이 얼마나 어려웠는지를 잊어버린다는 것을 안다면, 우리는 학생이 어떻게 학습을 '해야 하는지'에 대한 (근거 없는) 추정을 하기보다 학생들의 눈을 통해 학습 과정을 바라봐야 할 필요성을 이해할 수 있을 것이다.

35. A group of psychologists studied individuals with severe mental illness who experienced weekly group music therapy, [**included** / **including**]128) singing familiar songs and composing original songs. The results showed that the group music therapy improved the [**qualify** / **quality**]129) of participants' life, with those participating in a greater number of sessions experiencing the greatest benefits. [**Focused** / **Focusing**]130) on singing, [**another** / **other**]131) group of psychologists reviewed articles on the efficacy of group singing as a mental health treatment for individuals living [**in** / **with**]132) a mental health condition in a community setting. The findings showed that, when people with mental health conditions participated in a [**choir** / **chore**]133), their mental health and wellbeing [**significant** / **significantly**]134) improved. Group singing provided enjoyment, improved emotional states, developed a sense of belonging and [**embraced** / **enhanced**]135) self-confidence.

한 심리학자 그룹이 친숙한 노래 부르기와 독창적인 작곡하기를 포함한 집단 음악 치료를 매주 경험한 심각한 정신 질환이 있는 사람들을 연구했다. 그 연구 결과는 참여자가 (치료) 활동에 참여한 횟수가 많을수록 가장 큰 효과를 경험했기에, 집단 음악 치료가 참여자의 삶의 질을 개선하였음을 보여주었다. 노래 부르기에 초점을 두고, 또 다른 그룹의 심리학자는 집단생활의 환경에서 정신적인 건강 문제를 가지고 살고 있는 이들에게 미치는 집단 가창의 효능에 대한 논문을 검토했다. 발견된 결과는, 정신적인 건강 문제를 가진 사람이 합창단에 참여했을 때, 정신 건강과 행복이 상당히 개선되었음을 보여주었다. 집단 가창은 즐거움을 제공했고 감정 상태를 개선하였으며 소속감을 키웠고 자신감을 강화하였다.

36. In many sports, people realized the difficulties and even [**impossibilities** / **possibilities**]136) of young children participating fully in many adult sport environments. They found the road to success for young children is [**likely** / **unlikely**]137) if they play on adult fields, courts or arenas with equipment that is too large, too heavy or too fast for them to handle [**during** / **while**]138) trying [**competing** / **to compete**]139) in adult-style competition. Common sense has prevailed: different sports have made [**adoptions** / **adaptations**]140) for children. As examples, baseball has T ball, football has flag football and junior soccer uses a [**bigger** / **smaller**]141) and [**heavier** / **lighter**]142) ball and (sometimes) a smaller field. All have junior competitive structures [**where** / **which**]143) children play for shorter time periods and often in smaller teams. In a similar way, tennis has adapted the court areas, balls and rackets to make [**it** / **them**]144) more appropriate for children under 10. The adaptations are [**aggressive** / **progressive**]145) and relate to the age of the child.

많은 스포츠에서 사람들은 어린아이들이 여러 성인 스포츠 환경에 완전히 참여하기란 어렵고 심지어 불가 능하다는 것을 깨달았다. 어린아이들이 너무 크거나 너무 무겁고 또는 너무 빨라서 그들(어린아이들)이 다룰 수 없는 장비를 가지고 성인 스타일의 시합에서 경쟁하려고 하면서 성인용 운동장, 코트 또는 경기장에서 운동한다면 그들(어린아이들)이 성공으로 가는 길이 있을 것 같지 않다는 것을 그들은 발견했다. 이러한 공통된 견해가 널리 퍼졌기에 여러 스포츠는 어린아이들을 위한 조정을 했다. 예를 들자면, 야구에는 티볼이 있고, 풋볼에는 플래그 풋볼이 있고, 유소년 축구는 더 작고 더 가벼운 공과 (가끔은) 더 작은 경기장을 사용한다. 모두가 어린아이들이 더 짧아진 경기 시간 동안 그리고 종종 더 작은 팀으로 경기하는 유소년 시합의 구조를 가진다. 비슷한 방식으로, 테니스는 코트 면적, 공, 라켓을 10세 미만의 어린아이에게 더 적합하도록 만들기 위해 조정했다. 이러한 조정은 점진적이고 어린아이의 연령과 관련이 있다.

37. With no horses available, the Inca empire [**excelled / was excelled**]146) at delivering messages on foot. The messengers [**stationed / were stationed**]147) on the royal roads to deliver the Inca king's orders and reports coming from his lands. Called Chasquis, they lived in groups of four to six in huts, [**placed / was placed**]148) from one to two miles apart along the roads. They were all young men and especially good runners who watched the road in both directions. If they caught sight of [**another / other**]149) messenger coming, they hurried out to meet [**them / themselves**]150). The Inca built the huts on high ground, in sight of one another. When a messenger neared the next hut, he began to call out and [**repeat / repeated**]151) the message three or four times to the one who was running out to meet him. The Inca empire could [**delay / relay**]152) messages 1,000 miles (1,610 km) in three or four days under good conditions.

구할 수 있는 말이 없어서, Inca 제국은 걸어서 메시지를 전달하는 데 탁월했다. 전령들은 Inca 왕의 명령과 그의 영토에서 오는 보고를 전달하기 위해 왕의 길에 배치되었다. Chasquis라고 불리는, 그들은 네 명에서 여섯 명의 집단을 이루어 길을 따라 1마일에서 2마일 간격으로 떨어져 배치된 오두막에서 생활했다. 그들은 모두 젊은 남자였고, 양방향으로 길을 주시하는 특히 잘 달리는 이들이었다. 그들은 다른 전령이 오는 것을 발견하면 그들을 맞이하기 위해 서둘러 나갔다. Inca 사람들은 서로를 볼 수 있는 높은 지대에 오두막을 지었다. 전령은 다음 오두막에 다가갈 때, 자신을 만나러 달려 나오고 있는 전령에게 소리치기 시작했고 메시지를 서너 번 반복했다. Inca 제국은 사정이 좋으면 사나흘 만에 1,000마일(1,610km) 정도 메시지를 이어 갈 수 있었다.

38.
The tongue [**mapped / was mapped**]153) into [**combined / separate**]154) areas where certain tastes were registered: sweetness at the tip, sourness on the sides, and bitterness at the back of the mouth. Research in the 1980s and 1990s, however, [**demonstrated / was demonstrated**]155) that the "tongue map" explanation of how we taste was, in fact, totally wrong. As it turns out, the map was a [**interpretation / misinterpretation**]156) and [**translation / mistranslation**]157) of research conducted in Germany at the turn of the twentieth century. Today, leading taste researchers believe that taste buds are not grouped according to specialty. Sweetness, saltiness, bitterness, and sourness can be tasted everywhere in the mouth, although they may be perceived at [**a little / little**]158) different intensities at different sites. Moreover, the mechanism at work is not place, but time. It's not [**that / what**]159) you taste sweetness at the tip of your tongue, but rather that you register that perception first.

혀는 특정 맛이 등록되는 개별적인 영역으로 구획되었는데, 즉, 끝에는 단맛, 측면에는 신맛, 그리고 입의 뒤쪽에는 쓴맛이 있었다. 그러나 1980년대와 1990년대의 연구는 우리가 맛을 느끼는 방식에 대한 '혀 지도' 설명이 사실은 완전히 틀렸다는 것을 보여주었다. 밝혀진 바와 같이, 그 지도는 20세기 초입 독일에서 수행된 연구를 오해하고 오역한 것이었다. 오늘날, 선도적인 미각 연구자는 미뢰가 맛을 느끼는 특화된 분야에 따라 분류되지 않는다고 믿는다. 비록 그것들이 여러 위치에서 조금씩 다른 강도로 지각될지도 모르겠지만, 단맛, 짠맛, 쓴맛 그리고 신맛은 입안 어디에서나 느낄 수 있다. 게다가, 작동 중인 기제는 위치가 아니라 시간이다. 여러분은 혀끝에서 단맛을 느낀다기보다 오히려 그 지각(단맛)을 '가장 먼저' 등록하는 것이다.

39. No two animals are alike. Animals from the same litter will display some of the same features, but will not be exactly the same as each other; therefore, they may not respond in entirely the same way [**during / while**]160) a healing session. Environmental factors can also determine [**how / when**]161) the animal will respond during the treatment. For instance, a cat in a rescue center will respond very [**different / differently**]162) than a cat within a [**domestic / exotic**]163) home environment. In addition, animals that experience healing for physical illness will react differently than [**that / those**]164) accepting healing for emotional confusion. With this in mind, every healing session needs to [**be explored / explore**]165) differently, and each healing [**treatment / treatments**]166) should be adjusted to suit the specific needs of the animal. You will learn as you go; healing is a constant learning process.

어떤 두 동물도 똑같지 않다. 한 배에서 태어난 동물은 똑같은 몇몇 특성을 보여 줄 수 있겠지만, 서로 정확히 같지는 않을 것이다. 그런 까닭에, 그들은 치료 활동 중에 완전히 똑같은 방식으로 반응하지 않을지도 모른다. 또한 환경적 요인은 치료 중에 동물이 어떻게 반응할지를 결정할 수 있다. 예를 들어, 구조 센터에 있는 고양이는 가정집 환경 내에 있는 고양이와는 매우 다르게 반응할 것이다. 게다가, 신체적 질병의 치료를 받는 동물은 감정적 동요의 치료를 받는 동물과는 다르게 반응할 것이다. 이를 염두에 두어, 모든 치료 활동은 다르게 탐구되어야 하고, 각각의 치료법은 동물의 특정한 필요에 맞도록 조정되어야 한다. 여러분은 치료가 끊임없는 학습의 과정인 것을 직접 겪으면서 배우게 될 것이다.

40. The mind has parts that [**are known / known**]167) as the conscious mind and the subconscious mind. The [**conscious / subconscious**]168) mind is very fast to act and [**does / doesn't**]169) deal with emotions. It deals with memories of your responses to life, your memories and recognition. However, the [**conscious / subconscious**]170) mind is the one that you have [**less / more**]171) control over. You think. You can choose whether to carry on a thought [**and / or**]172) to add emotion to it and this is the part of your mind that lets you down frequently [**because / because of**]173) — fueled by emotions — you make the wrong decisions time and time again. When your judgment is clouded by emotions, this puts in biases and all kinds of other negativities that hold [**back you / you back**]174). Scared of spiders? Scared of the dark? There are reasons for all of these fears, but they [**originate / were originated**]175) in the [**conscious / subconscious**]176) mind. They only become real fears when the subconscious mind [**record / records**]177) your reactions.

마음은 의식적 마음과 잠재의식적 마음이라고 알려진 부분을 갖고 있다. 잠재의식적 마음은 매우 빠르게 작동하며 감정을 다루지 않는다. 그것은 여러분의 삶에 대한 반응의 기억, 기억 및 인식을 다룬다. 그러나 의식적 마음은 여러분이 더 많은 통제력을 갖고 있는 부분이다. 여러분은 생각한다. 여러분은 생각을 계속할지 또는 그 생각에 감정을 더할지를 선택할 수 있다. 그리고 이것은 감정에 북받쳐 잘못된 결정을 반복해서 내리게 만들기 때문에 여러분을 빈번하게 낙담시키는 마음의 부분이기도 하다. 감정에 의해 여러분의 판단력이 흐려질 때 이것은 편견과 그 밖의 여러분을 억제하는 모든 종류의 부정성을 자리 잡게 만든다. 거미를 무서워하는가? 어둠을 무서워하는가? 이러한 두려움 전부 이유가 있지만 그것들은 의식적 마음에서 비롯된다. 그것들은 오직 잠재의식적 마음이 여러분의 반응을 기록할 때 실제 두려움이 된다.

41-42. Norms are everywhere, [**defined / defining**]178) what is "normal" and guiding our interpretations of social life at every turn. As a simple example, there is a norm in Anglo society to say Thank you to strangers who [**had / have**]179) just done something to help, such as open a door for you, [**point / pointing**]180) out that you've just dropped something, or give you directions. There is no law that [**forces / reinforces**]181) you to say Thank you. But if people don't say Thank you in these cases it is [**remarked / marked**]182). People expect that you will say it. You become [**irresponsible / responsible**]183). Failing to say it will be both surprising and [**worthy / worthy of**]184) criticism. Not knowing the norms of [**another / other**]185) community is the central problem of cross-cultural communication. To continue the Thank you example, even though another culture may have an expression that appears [**translatable / untranslatable**]186) (many don't), there may be [**different / similar**]187) norms for its usage, for example, such that you should say Thank you only when the cost someone has caused is [**considerable / considerate**]188). In such a case it would sound [**ridiculous / ridiculously**]189) (i.e., unexpected, surprising, and worthy of criticism) if you were to thank someone for something so [**major / minor**]190) as holding a door open for you.

규범은 무엇이 '정상적'인지를 규정하고 모든 순간 사회적 생활에 대한 우리의 해석을 안내해 주며 어디에나 존재한다. 간단한 예로, 문을 열어 주거나, 여러분이 물건을 방금 떨어뜨렸다는 것을 짚어 주거나, 길을 알려주는 것과 같이 도움을 줄 수 있는 무언가를 이제 막 해준 낯선 사람에게 '감사합니다'라고 말하는 규범이 Anglo 사회에 있다. 여러분이 '감사합니다'라고 말하도록 강요하는 법은 없다. 하지만 이런 상황에서 사람들이 '감사합니다'라고 말하지 않으면 그것은 눈에 띄게 된다. 사람들은 여러분이 그렇게 말하기를 기대한다. 여러분은 책임을 지게 되는 것이다. 그렇게 말하지 못하는 것은 (주변을) 놀라게 하기도 하고 비판을 받을 만하다. 다른 집단의 규범을 모른다는 것은 문화간 의사소통에서 중심적인 문제이다. '감사합니다'의 예를 이어 보자면, 비록 또 다른 문화권이 번역할 수 있는 것처럼 보이는 어떤 표현(다수는 그렇지 못하지만)을 가지고 있다 할지라도, 그것의 사용법에 대해, 예를 들어, 누군가가 초래한 대가가 상당할 때만 '감사합니다'라고 말해야 한다는 것처럼 다른 규범이 있을 수 있다. 그 같은 상황에서 만약 여러분이 혹시라도, 여러분을 위해 문을 잡아주는 것과 같이 아주 사소한 일에 대해 누군가에게 감사해한다면, 그것은 우스꽝스럽게(즉, 예상치 못하게, 놀랍게, 비판을 받을 만하게) 들릴 수 있을 것이다.

43-45.

Long ago, when the world was young, an old Native American spiritual leader Odawa had a dream on a high mountain. In his dream, Iktomi, the great spirit and searcher of wisdom, [appear / appeared]¹⁹¹⁾ to him in the form of a spider. Iktomi spoke to him in a holy language. Iktomi told Odawa about the cycles of life. He said, "We all begin our lives as babies, move on to childhood, and then to adulthood. Finally, we come to old age, where we must [be taken / take]¹⁹²⁾ care of as babies again." Iktomi also told him that there are good and bad forces in each [stage / stages]¹⁹³⁾ of life. "If we listen to the good forces, they will guide us in the right direction. But if we listen to the bad forces, they will lead us the wrong way and may harm us," Iktomi said. When Iktomi finished speaking, he [spins / spun]¹⁹⁴⁾ a web and gave it to Odawa. He said to Odawa, "The web is a perfect circle [with / without]¹⁹⁵⁾ a hole in the center. Use the web to help your people [reach / reach at]¹⁹⁶⁾ their goals. Make good use of their ideas, dreams, and visions. If you believe in the great spirit, the web will catch your good ideas and the bad ones will go through the hole." Right after Odawa woke up, he went back to his village. Odawa [shared / shares]¹⁹⁷⁾ Iktomi's lesson with his people. Today, many Native Americans have dream catchers hanging above their beds. Dream catchers [are believed / believed]¹⁹⁸⁾ to filter out bad dreams. The good dreams [are captured / captured]¹⁹⁹⁾ in the web of life and [are carried / carried]²⁰⁰⁾ with the people. The bad dreams pass through the hole in the web and are no longer a part of their lives.

오래전, 세상이 생겨난지 오래지 않을 무렵, 아메리카 원주민의 늙은 영적 지도자인 Odawa는 높은 산에서 꿈을 꾸었다. 자신의 꿈속에서 위대한 신령이자 지혜의 구도자인 Iktomi가 거미의 형태로 그에게 나타났다. Iktomi는 성스러운 언어로 그에게 말했다. Iktomi는 Odawa에게 삶의 순환에 관해서 말했 다. 그는 "우리는 모두 아기로 삶을 출발하고, 유년기를 거쳐 그다음 성년기에 이르게 된다. 결국 우리는 노년기에 도달하고, 거기서 우리는 다시 아기처럼 보살핌을 받아야 한다."라고 말했다. 또한 Iktomi는 삶의 각 단계에는 좋고 나쁜 힘이 있다고 그에게 말했다. "우리가 좋은 힘에 귀를 기울이면 그들은 우리를 올바른 방향으로 인도할 것이다. 하지만 만약 나쁜 힘에 귀를 기울이면 그들은 우리를 잘못된 길로 이끌고 우리를 해칠 수도 있다."라고 Iktomi는 말했다. Iktomi가 말을 끝냈을 때, 그는 거미집을 짜서 Odawa에게 주었다. 그가 Odawa에게 말하기를, "그 거미집은 가운데 구멍이 뚫린 완벽한 원이다. 너의 마을 사람들이 자신들의 목표에 도달할 수 있도록 거미집을 사용해라. 그들의 생각, 꿈, 비전을 잘 활용해라. 만약 네가 위대한 신령을 믿는다면 그 거미집이 네 좋은 생각을 붙잡아 줄 것이고 나쁜 생각은 구멍을 통해 빠져나갈 것이다." Odawa는 잠에서 깨자마자 자기 마을로 되돌아갔다. Odawa는 Iktomi의 교훈을 그의 마을 사람들과 나누었다. 오늘날 많은 미국 원주민은 침대 위에 드림 캐처를 건다. 드림캐처는 나쁜 꿈을 걸러 준다고 믿어진다. 좋은 꿈은 인생이라는 거미집에 걸리고 사람들과 동반하게 된다. 나쁜 꿈은 거미집의 구멍 사이로 빠져나가고 더 이상 그들의 삶의 한 부분이 되지 못한다.

18. Dear Ms. Jane Watson,
I am John Austin, a science teacher at Crestville High School. Recently I [**impressed / was impressed**]¹⁾ by the latest book you wrote about the environment. Also my students read your book and had a class discussion [**about / X**]²⁾ it. They are big fans of your book, so I'd like to [**ask / asking**]³⁾ you to visit our school and give a special lecture. We can set the date and time to suit your schedule. [**Have / Having**]⁴⁾ you at our school would be a fantastic experience for the students. We would be very grateful if you could come. / Best regards, John Austin

19. Marilyn and her three-year-old daughter, Sarah, took a trip to the beach, [**where / which**]⁵⁾ Sarah built her first sandcastle. Moments later, an enormous wave [**destroyed / was destroyed**]⁶⁾ Sarah's castle. In response to the loss of her sandcastle, tears streamed down Sarah's cheeks and her heart [**broken / was broken**]⁷⁾. She ran to Marilyn, saying she [**should / would**]⁸⁾ never build a sandcastle again. Marilyn said, "Part of the joy of building a sandcastle is that, in the end, we give [**it / them**]⁹⁾ as a gift to the ocean." Sarah loved this idea and responded with enthusiasm to the idea of building [**another / other**]¹⁰⁾ castle — this time, even closer to the water so the ocean would get [**its / their**]¹¹⁾ gift sooner!

20. Magic is [**that / what**]¹²⁾ we all wish for to happen in our life. Do you love the movie Cinderella like me? Well, in real life, you can also create magic. Here's the trick. Write down all the real-time challenges [**that / when**]¹³⁾ you face and deal with. Just change the challenge statement into positive statements. Let me give you an example here. If you struggle [**of / with**]¹⁴⁾ getting up early in the morning, then write a positive statement such as "I get up early in the morning at 5:00 am every day." [**Once / Otherwise**]¹⁵⁾ you write these statements, get ready to witness magic and [**confidence / confident**]¹⁶⁾. You will be surprised that just by writing these statements, there is a shift in the way you think and act. Suddenly you feel [**less / more**]¹⁷⁾ powerful and positive.

21. Consider the seemingly simple question How many senses are there? Around 2,370 years ago, Aristotle wrote [**that / what**]¹⁸⁾ there are five, in both humans [**and / or**]¹⁹⁾ animals — sight, hearing, smell, taste, and touch. However, according to the philosopher Fiona Macpherson, there are reasons to [**believe / doubt**]²⁰⁾ it. For a start, Aristotle missed a [**few / little**]²¹⁾ in humans: the perception of your own body which is different [**at / from**]²²⁾ touch and the sense of balance [**where / which**]²³⁾ has links to both touch and vision. [**Other / The other**]²⁴⁾ animals have senses that are even [**hard / harder**]²⁵⁾ to categorize. Many vertebrates have a different sense system for detecting odors. Some snakes can [**be detected / detect**]²⁶⁾ the body heat of their [**predator / prey**]²⁷⁾. These examples tell us that "senses cannot be clearly divided into a [**limited / limitless**]²⁸⁾ number of specific kinds," Macpherson wrote in The Senses. Instead of trying [**pushing / to push**]²⁹⁾ animal senses into Aristotelian buckets, we should study them for [**what / which**]³⁰⁾ they are.

22. When we think of leaders, we may [**think / think of**]³¹⁾ people such as Abraham Lincoln or Martin Luther King, Jr. If you consider the historical importance and [**far-reached / far-reaching**]³²⁾ influence of these individuals, leadership might seem like a noble and high goal. But like all of us, these people started out as students, workers, and citizens [**who / whose**]³³⁾ possessed ideas about how some aspect of daily life could be [**improved / involved**]³⁴⁾ on a larger scale. Through diligence and experience, they improved upon their ideas by sharing them with others, [**seeked / seeking**]³⁵⁾ their opinions and feedback and constantly looking for the best way to accomplish goals for a group. Thus we all [**has / have**]³⁶⁾ the potential to be leaders at school, in our communities, and [**at / in**]³⁷⁾ work, regardless of age or experience.

23. Crop rotation is the [**process / progress**]³⁸⁾ [**in which / which**]³⁹⁾ farmers change the crops they grow in their fields in a [**spatial / special**]⁴⁰⁾ order. For example, if a farmer has three fields, he or she may grow carrots in the first field, green beans in the second, and tomatoes in the third. The next year, green beans will be in the first field, tomatoes in the second field, and carrots will be in the third. In year three, the crops will rotate again. By the fourth year, the crops will go back [**in / to**]⁴¹⁾ their original order. Each [**crop / crops**]⁴²⁾ enriches the soil for the next crop. This type of farming is [**suitable / sustainable**]⁴³⁾ [**because / because of**]⁴⁴⁾ the soil stays healthy.

24. Working around the whole painting, rather than [**concentrating / to concentrate**]⁴⁵⁾ on one area at a time, will mean you can stop at any point and the painting can be considered "finished." Artists often find [**it / that**]⁴⁶⁾ difficult to know when to stop [**painting / to paint**]⁴⁷⁾, and it can be tempting to keep on adding more to your work. It is important to take [**a few / few**]⁴⁸⁾ steps back from the painting from time to time to [**access / assess**]⁴⁹⁾ your progress. Putting too much into a painting can spoil its impact and leave it looking overworked. If you find yourself [**struggled / struggling**]⁵⁰⁾ to decide whether you have finished, [**take / taking**]⁵¹⁾ a break and come back to it later with fresh eyes. Then you can decide whether any areas of your painting would benefit from [**farther / further**]⁵²⁾ refinement.

25. The above graph shows the [**extent / intent**]⁵³⁾ to which young people aged 16-25 in six countries had fear about climate change in 2021. The Philippines had the highest percentage of young people who said they were extremely or very worried, at 84 percent, [**followed / following**]⁵⁴⁾ by 67 percent in Brazil. More than 60 percent of young people in Portugal said they were extremely worried or very worried. In France, the percentage of young people who were extremely worried was lower than [**that / those**]⁵⁵⁾ of young people who were very worried. In the United Kingdom, the percentage of young generation who said that they were very worried was 29 percent. In the United States, the total percentage of extremely worried and very worried youth was the smallest among the six countries.

26. Jaroslav Heyrovsky [**born / was born**]⁵⁶⁾ in Prague on December 20, 1890, as the fifth child of Leopold Heyrovsky. In 1901 Jaroslav went to a secondary school called the Akademicke Gymnasium. Rather than Latin and Greek, he showed a strong interest in the [**natural / nature**]⁵⁷⁾ sciences. At Czech University in Prague he studied chemistry, physics, and mathematics. From 1910 to 1914 he continued his studies at University College, London. Throughout the First World War, Jaroslav [**served / was served**]⁵⁸⁾ in a military hospital. In 1926, Jaroslav became the first Professor of Physical Chemistry at Charles University in Prague. He won the Nobel Prize in chemistry in 1959.

29. It would be hard to [**overstate / understate**]⁵⁹⁾ how important meaningful work is to human beings — work that provides a sense of fulfillment and empowerment. Those who have found deeper meaning in their careers find their days much more [**energized / energizing**]⁶⁰⁾ and [**satisfied / satisfying**]⁶¹⁾, and [**count / counted**]⁶²⁾ their employment as one of their greatest sources of joy and pride. Sonya Lyubomirsky, professor of psychology at the University of California, has conducted numerous workplace studies showing [**that / in that**]⁶³⁾ when people are more fulfilled on the job, they not only produce higher quality work and a greater output, but also generally [**earn / earned**]⁶⁴⁾ higher [**incomes / outcomes**]⁶⁵⁾. Those most [**satisfied / satisfying**]⁶⁶⁾ with their work [**are / is**]⁶⁷⁾ also much more likely to be happier with their lives overall. For her book Happiness at Work, researcher Jessica Pryce-Jones conducted a study of 3,000 workers in seventy-nine countries, [**finding / found**]⁶⁸⁾ that those who took greater satisfaction from their work were 150 percent [**less / more**]⁶⁹⁾ likely to have a happier life overall.

30. The rate of speed [**at which / which**]⁷⁰⁾ one is traveling will greatly determine the ability to process detail in the environment. In [**evolutionary / revolutionary**]⁷¹⁾ terms, human senses are [**adapted / adopted**]⁷²⁾ to the speed at which humans move through space under their own power [**during / while**]⁷³⁾ walking. Our ability to [**extinguish / distinguish**]⁷⁴⁾ detail in the environment is therefore ideally [**suit / suited**]⁷⁵⁾ to movement at speeds of perhaps five miles per hour and under. The fastest users of the street, motorists, therefore [**has / have**]⁷⁶⁾ a much more limited ability to process details along the street — a motorist simply has [**a little / little**]⁷⁷⁾ time or ability to appreciate design details. On the other hand, [**pedestrian / pediatrician**]⁷⁸⁾ travel, being much slower, [**allowing / allows**]⁷⁹⁾ for the appreciation of environmental detail. Joggers and bicyclists fall somewhere in between these [**bipolar / polar**]⁸⁰⁾ opposites; while they travel faster than pedestrians, their rate of speed is [**extraordinarily / ordinarily**]⁸¹⁾ much slower than [**that / those**]⁸²⁾ of the [**atypical / typical**]⁸³⁾ motorist.

31. Every species [**has / have**]⁸⁴⁾ certain climatic requirements — what degree of heat or cold it can endure, for example. When the climate changes, the places that [**satisfied / satisfy**]⁸⁵⁾ those requirements change, too. Species [**are forced / forced**]⁸⁶⁾ to follow. [**All / Some**]⁸⁷⁾ creatures are capable of [**all / some**]⁸⁸⁾ degree of movement. Even creatures that appear immobile, like trees and barnacles, are capable of [**dispersal / disposal**]⁸⁹⁾ at some stage of their life — as a seed, in the case of the tree, or as a larva, in the case of the barnacle. A creature must get from the place it is born — often occupied by [**its / their**]⁹⁰⁾ parent — to a place where it can survive, grow, and [**produce / reproduce**]⁹¹⁾. From fossils, scientists know that even creatures like trees [**moved / moving**]⁹²⁾ with surprising speed [**during / while**]⁹³⁾ past periods of climate change.

32. No [**respectable / respective**]⁹⁴⁾ boss would say, "I make it a point to discourage my staff from speaking up, and I [**maintain / oppose**]⁹⁵⁾ a culture that prevents [**agreeing / disagreeing**]⁹⁶⁾ viewpoints from ever getting aired." If anything, most bosses even say that they are pro-dissent. This idea can [**be found / found**]⁹⁷⁾ throughout the series of conversations with corporate, university, and nonprofit leaders, [**published / publishing**]⁹⁸⁾ weekly in the business sections of newspapers. In the interviews, the featured leaders [**asked / are asked**]⁹⁹⁾ about their management techniques, and regularly claim to continually [**discourage / encourage**]¹⁰⁰⁾ internal protest from more junior staffers. As Bot Pittman remarked in one of these conversations: "I want us to listen to these [**advocates / dissenters**]¹⁰¹⁾ because they [**may / should**]¹⁰²⁾ intend to tell you why we can't do something, but if you listen hard, what they're really telling you is [**that / what**]¹⁰³⁾ you must do to get something done."

33. One of the most striking characteristics of a sleeping animal or person is that they do not respond [**normal / normally**]¹⁰⁴⁾ to environmental stimuli. If you open the eyelids of a sleeping mammal the eyes will not see normally — they are functionally blind. Some visual information apparently gets in, but it is not normally [**possessed / processed**]¹⁰⁵⁾ as it is shortened or [**strengthened / weakened**]¹⁰⁶⁾ ; same with [**another / the other**]¹⁰⁷⁾ sensing systems. Stimuli [**are registered / registered**]¹⁰⁸⁾ but not processed normally and they fail to wake the individual. Perceptual disengagement probably [**serve / serves**]¹⁰⁹⁾ the function of protecting sleep, so some authors [**are / do**]¹¹⁰⁾ not count it as part of the definition of sleep [**it / itself**]¹¹¹⁾. But as sleep would be impossible [**with / without**]¹¹²⁾ it, it seems essential to its definition. Nevertheless, many animals (including humans) use the [**immediate / intermediate**]¹¹³⁾ state of drowsiness to [**derive / drive**]¹¹⁴⁾ some benefits of sleep without total perceptual [**disengagement / engagement**]¹¹⁵⁾.

34. [**A / The**]¹¹⁶⁾ number of research studies have shown how experts in a field often experience difficulties when [**introduced / introducing**]¹¹⁷⁾ newcomers to that field. For example, in a genuine training situation, Dr Pamela Hinds found that people expert in using mobile phones were remarkably [**less / more**]¹¹⁸⁾ accurate than novice phone users in judging how long [**it / that**]¹¹⁹⁾ takes people to learn to use the phones. Experts can become [**insensitive / sensitive**]¹²⁰⁾ to how hard a task is for the beginner, an effect [**referred / referring**]¹²¹⁾ to as the 'curse of [**ignorance / knowledge**]¹²²⁾'. Dr Hinds was able to show that as people [**acquired / required**]¹²³⁾ the skill, they then

began to underestimate the level of [**difficulty / familiarity**]124) of that skill. Her participants even [**overestimated / underestimated**]125) how long it had taken [**them / themselves**]126) to acquire that skill in an earlier session. Knowing that experts forget how hard it was for them to learn, we can understand the need to look at the learning process through students' eyes, rather than making [**assumptions / judgments**]127) about how students 'should be' learning.

35. A group of psychologists studied individuals with severe mental illness who experienced weekly group music therapy, [**included / including**]128) singing familiar songs and composing original songs. The results showed that the group music therapy improved the [**qualify / quality**]129) of participants' life, with those participating in a greater number of sessions experiencing the greatest benefits. [**Focused / Focusing**]130) on singing, [**another / other**]131) group of psychologists reviewed articles on the efficacy of group singing as a mental health treatment for individuals living [**in / with**]132) a mental health condition in a community setting. The findings showed that, when people with mental health conditions participated in a [**choir / chore**]133), their mental health and wellbeing [**significant / significantly**]134) improved. Group singing provided enjoyment, improved emotional states, developed a sense of belonging and [**embraced / enhanced**]135) self-confidence.

36. In many sports, people realized the difficulties and even [**impossibilities / possibilities**]136) of young children participating fully in many adult sport environments. They found the road to success for young children is [**likely / unlikely**]137) if they play on adult fields, courts or arenas with equipment that is too large, too heavy or too fast for them to handle [**during / while**]138) trying [**competing / to compete**]139) in adult-style competition. Common sense has prevailed: different sports have made [**adoptions / adaptations**]140) for children. As examples, baseball has T ball, football has flag football and junior soccer uses a [**bigger / smaller**]141) and [**heavier / lighter**]142) ball and (sometimes) a smaller field. All have junior competitive structures [**where / which**]143) children play for shorter time periods and often in smaller teams. In a similar way, tennis has adapted the court areas, balls and rackets to make [**it / them**]144) more appropriate for children under 10. The adaptations are [**aggressive / progressive**]145) and relate to the age of the child.

37. With no horses available, the Inca empire [**excelled / was excelled**]146) at delivering messages on foot. The messengers [**stationed / were stationed**]147) on the royal roads to deliver the Inca king's orders and reports coming from his lands. Called Chasquis, they lived in groups of four to six in huts, [**placed / was placed**]148) from one to two miles apart along the roads. They were all young men and especially good runners who watched the road in both directions. If they caught sight of [**another / other**]149) messenger coming, they hurried out to meet [**them / themselves**]150). The Inca built the huts on high ground, in sight of one another. When a messenger neared the next hut, he began to call out and [**repeat / repeated**]151) the message three or four times to the one who was running out to meet him. The Inca empire could [**delay / relay**]152) messages 1,000 miles (1,610 km) in three or four days under good conditions.

38. The tongue [**mapped / was mapped**]153) into [**combined / separate**]154) areas where certain tastes were registered: sweetness at the tip, sourness on the sides, and bitterness at the back of the mouth. Research in the 1980s and 1990s, however, [**demonstrated / was demonstrated**]155) that the "tongue map" explanation of how we taste was, in fact, totally wrong. As it turns out, the map was a [**interpretation / misinterpretation**]156) and [**translation / mistranslation**]157) of research conducted in Germany at the turn of the twentieth century. Today, leading taste researchers believe that taste buds are not grouped according to specialty. Sweetness, saltiness, bitterness, and sourness can be tasted everywhere in the mouth, although they may be perceived at [**a little / little**]158) different intensities at different sites. Moreover, the mechanism at work is not place, but time. It's not [**that / what**]159) you taste sweetness at the tip of your tongue, but rather that you register that perception first.

39. No two animals are alike. Animals from the same litter will display some of the same features, but will not be exactly the same as each other; therefore, they may not respond in entirely the same way [**during / while**]¹⁶⁰⁾ a healing session. Environmental factors can also determine [**how / when**]¹⁶¹⁾ the animal will respond during the treatment. For instance, a cat in a rescue center will respond very [**different / differently**]¹⁶²⁾ than a cat within a [**domestic / exotic**]¹⁶³⁾ home environment. In addition, animals that experience healing for physical illness will react differently than [**that / those**]¹⁶⁴⁾ accepting healing for emotional confusion. With this in mind, every healing session needs to [**be explored / explore**]¹⁶⁵⁾ differently, and each healing [**treatment / treatments**]¹⁶⁶⁾ should be adjusted to suit the specific needs of the animal. You will learn as you go; healing is a constant learning process.

40. The mind has parts that [**are known / known**]¹⁶⁷⁾ as the conscious mind and the subconscious mind. The [**conscious / subconscious**]¹⁶⁸⁾ mind is very fast to act and [**does / doesn't**]¹⁶⁹⁾ deal with emotions. It deals with memories of your responses to life, your memories and recognition. However, the [**conscious / subconscious**]¹⁷⁰⁾ mind is the one that you have [**less / more**]¹⁷¹⁾ control over. You think. You can choose whether to carry on a thought [**and / or**]¹⁷²⁾ to add emotion to it and this is the part of your mind that lets you down frequently [**because / because of**]¹⁷³⁾ — fueled by emotions — you make the wrong decisions time and time again. When your judgment is clouded by emotions, this puts in biases and all kinds of other negativities that hold [**back you / you back**]¹⁷⁴⁾ . Scared of spiders? Scared of the dark? There are reasons for all of these fears, but they [**originate / were originated**]¹⁷⁵⁾ in the [**conscious / subconscious**]¹⁷⁶⁾ mind. They only become real fears when the subconscious mind [**record / records**]¹⁷⁷⁾ your reactions.

41-42. Norms are everywhere, [**defined / defining**]¹⁷⁸⁾ what is "normal" and guiding our interpretations of social life at every turn. As a simple example, there is a norm in Anglo society to say Thank you to strangers who [**had / have**]¹⁷⁹⁾ just done something to help, such as open a door for you, [**point / pointing**]¹⁸⁰⁾ out that you've just dropped something, or give you directions. There is no law that [**forces / reinforces**]¹⁸¹⁾ you to say Thank you. But if people don't say Thank you in these cases it is [**remarked / marked**]¹⁸²⁾. People expect that you will say it. You become [**irresponsible / responsible**]¹⁸³⁾. Failing to say it will be both surprising and [**worthy / worthy of**]¹⁸⁴⁾ criticism. Not knowing the norms of [**another / other**]¹⁸⁵⁾ community is the central problem of cross-cultural communication. To continue the Thank you example, even though another culture may have an expression that appears [**translatable / untranslatable**]¹⁸⁶⁾ (many don't), there may be [**different / similar**]¹⁸⁷⁾ norms for its usage, for example, such that you should say Thank you only when the cost someone has caused is [**considerable / considerate**]¹⁸⁸⁾. In such a case it would sound [**ridiculous / ridiculously**]¹⁸⁹⁾ (i.e., unexpected, surprising, and worthy of criticism) if you were to thank someone for something so [**major / minor**]¹⁹⁰⁾ as holding a door open for you.

43-45. Long ago, when the world was young, an old Native American spiritual leader Odawa had a dream on a high mountain. In his dream, Iktomi, the great spirit and searcher of wisdom, [**appear / appeared**]¹⁹¹⁾ to him in the form of a spider. Iktomi spoke to him in a holy language. Iktomi told Odawa about the cycles of life. He said, "We all begin our lives as babies, move on to childhood, and then to adulthood. Finally, we come to old age, where we must [**be taken / take**]¹⁹²⁾ care of as babies again." Iktomi also told him that there are good and bad forces in each [**stage / stages**]¹⁹³⁾ of life. "If we listen to the good forces, they will guide us in the right direction. But if we listen to the bad forces, they will lead us the wrong way and may harm us," Iktomi said. When Iktomi finished speaking, he [**spins / spun**]¹⁹⁴⁾ a web and gave it to Odawa. He said to Odawa, "The web is a perfect circle [**with / without**]¹⁹⁵⁾ a hole in the center. Use the web to help your people [**reach / reach at**]¹⁹⁶⁾ their goals. Make good use of their ideas, dreams, and visions. If you believe in the great spirit, the web will catch your good ideas and the bad ones will go through the hole." Right after Odawa woke up, he went back to his village. Odawa [**shared / shares**]¹⁹⁷⁾ Iktomi's lesson with his people. Today, many Native Americans have dream catchers hanging above their beds. Dream catchers [**are believed / believed**]¹⁹⁸⁾ to filter out bad dreams. The good dreams [**are captured / captured**]¹⁹⁹⁾ in the web of life and [**are carried / carried**]²⁰⁰⁾ with the people. The bad dreams pass through the hole in the web and are no longer a part of their lives.

2024 고1 3월 모의고사   ❶ 회차   :   점 / 335점

❶ voca   ❷ text   ❸ [/]   ❹ _____   ❺ quiz 1   ❻ quiz 2   ❼ quiz 3   ❽ quiz 4   ❾ quiz 5

18. Dear Ms. Jane Watson,

I am John Austin, a science teacher at Crestville High School. Recently I was i_____1) by the l_____2) book you wrote about the environment. Also my students read your book and had a class d_____3) about it. They are big fans of your book, so I'd like to ask you to visit our school and give a special lecture. We can set the date and time to s_____4) your schedule. Having you at our school would be a fantastic experience for the students. We would be very g_____5) if you could come.

Best regards, John Austin

친애하는 Jane Watson 씨, 저는 Crestville 고등학교의 과학 교사 John Austin입니다. 최근에, 저는 환경에 관해 당신이 쓴 최신 도서에 감명받았습니다. 또한 저의 학생들은 당신의 책을 읽었고 그것에 대해 토론 수업을 하였습니다. 그들은 당신의 책을 아주 좋아하고, 그래서 저는 당신이 우리 학교에 방문하여 특별 강연을 해주시기를 요청드리고 싶습니다. 우리는 당신의 일정에 맞춰 날짜와 시간을 정하겠습니다. 당신이 우리 학교에 와주신다면 학생들에게 멋진 경험이 될 것 같습니다. 우리는 당신이 와주신다면 정말 감사하겠습니다. 안부를 전하며, John Austin

19. Marilyn and her three-year-old daughter, Sarah, took a trip to the beach, w_____6) Sarah built her first sandcastle. Moments later, an e_____7) wave d_____8) Sarah's castle. In response to the l_____9) of her sandcastle, tears s_____10) down Sarah's cheeks and her heart was broken. She ran to Marilyn, saying she would never build a sandcastle again. Marilyn said, "Part of the joy of building a sandcastle is that, in the end, we give it as a gift to the ocean." Sarah loved this idea and responded with e_____11) to the idea of building another castle — this time, even closer to the water so the ocean would get its gift sooner!

Marilyn과 세 살 된 딸 Sarah는 해변으로 여행을 떠났고, 그곳에서 Sarah는 처음으로 모래성을 쌓았다. 잠시 후, 거대한 파도가 Sarah의 성을 무너뜨렸다. 모래성을 잃은 것에 반응하여 눈물이 Sarah의 뺨을 타고 흘러내렸고, 그녀의 마음은 무너졌다. 그녀는 다시는 모래성을 쌓지 않겠다고 말하며 Marilyn에게 달려갔다. Marilyn은 "모래성을 쌓는 즐거움 중 일부는 결국 에는 우리가 그것을 바다에게 선물로 주는 것이란다." 라고 말했다. Sarah는 이 생각이 마음에 들었고 또 다른 모래성을 만들 생각에 이번에는 바다와 훨씬 더 가까운 곳에서 바다가 그 선물을 더 빨리 받을 수 있도록 하겠다며 열정적으로 반응했다.

20. Magic is w_____12) we all wish for to h_____13) in our life. Do you love the movie Cinderella like me? Well, in real life, you can also create magic. Here's the trick. Write down all the real-time c_____14) that you face and deal w_____15) . Just c_____16) the challenge statement into p_____17) statements. Let me give you an example here. If you s_____18) with getting up early in the morning, then write a positive statement such as "I get up early in the morning at 5:00 am every day." Once you write these statements, get ready to w_____19) magic and c_____20) . You will be surprised that just by writing these statements, there is a s_____21) in the way you think and act. Suddenly you feel more powerful and positive.

마법은 우리 모두 자신의 삶에서 일어나기를 바라는 바이다. 여러분도 나처럼 신데렐라 영화를 사랑하는가? 그러면, 실제 삶에서, 여러분도 마법을 만들 수 있다. 여기 그 요령이 있다. 여러분이 직면하고 처리하는 모든 실시간의 어려움을 적어라. 그 어려움에 관한 진술을 긍정적인 진술로 바꾸어라. 여기서 여러분에게한 예시를 제시하겠다. 만약 여러분이 아침 일찍 일어나는 것에 어려움을 겪는다면, 그러면 '나는 매일 일찍 아침 5시에 일어난다.'와 같은 긍정적인 진술을 써라. 일단 여러분이 이러한 진술을 적는다면, 마법과 자신감을 목격할 준비를 하라. 여러분은 단지 이러한 진술을 적음으로써 여러분이 생각하고 행동하는 방식에 변화가 있다는 것에 놀랄 것이다. 어느 순간 여러분은 더 강력하고 긍정적이라고 느끼게 된다.

21. Consider the seemingly s_____ 22) question How many s_____ 23) are there? Around 2,370 years ago, Aristotle wrote that there are five, in both humans and animals — sight, hearing, smell, taste, and touch. However, according to the philosopher Fiona Macpherson, there are r_____ 24) to d_____ 25) it. For a start, Aristotle m_____ 26) a few in humans: the p_____ 27) of your own body which is different from t_____ 28) and the sense of b_____ 29) which has l_____ 30) to both touch and vision. Other animals have senses that are even harder to c_____ 31) . Many v_____ 32) have a different sense system for d_____ 33) o_____ 34) . Some snakes can d_____ 35) the body heat of their prey. These examples tell us that "senses cannot be clearly d_____ 36) into a l_____ 37) number of specific kinds," Macpherson wrote in The Senses. Instead of trying to push animal senses into Aristotelian b_____ 38) , we should study them for what they are.

'얼마나 많은 감각이 존재하는가?'라는 겉으로 보기에 단순한 질문을 고려해 봐라. 약 2,370년 전 Aristotle은 인간과 동물 둘 다에게 시각, 청각, 후각, 미각, 그리고 촉각의 다섯(감각)이 있다고 썼다. 그러나, 철학자 Fiona Macpherson에 따르면, 그것을 의심할 이유가 존재한다. 우선, Aristotle은 인간에게서 몇 가지를 빠뜨렸는데, 그것은 촉각과는 다른 여러분 자신의 신체에 대한 인식과, 촉각과 시각 모두에 관련되어 있는 균형 감각이었다. 다른 동물들은 훨씬 더 범주화하기 어려운 감각을 가지고 있다. 많은 척추동물은 냄새를 탐지하기 위한 다른 감각 체계를 가지고 있다. 어떤 뱀은 그들의 먹잇감의 체열을 감지할 수 있다. Macpherson이 'The Senses'에서 쓰기를, 이러한 사례는 우리에게 '감각은 제한된 수의 특정한 종류로 명확하게 나누어지지 않을 수 있다.'라는 것을 알려 준다. 동물의 감각을 Aristotle의 양동이로 밀어 넣는 대신, 우리는 그것들을 존재하는 그대로 연구해야 한다.

22. When we think of leaders, we may think of people such as Abraham Lincoln or Martin Luther King, Jr. If you consider the h_____ 39) importance and f_____ 40) i_____ 41) of these individuals, leadership might seem like a n_____ 42) and high goal. But like all of us, these people started out as students, workers, and citizens who p_____ 43) ideas about how some aspect of daily life could be improved on a larger scale. Through d_____ 44) and experience, they improved upon their ideas by s_____ 45) them with others, s_____ 46) their opinions and feedback and c_____ 47) looking for the best way to a_____ 48) goals for a group. Thus we all have the p_____ 49) to be leaders at school, in our communities, and at work, regardless of age or experience.

우리가 리더에 대해 생각할 때, 우리는 Abraham Lincoln 혹은 Martin Luther King, Jr. 와 같은 사람들에 대해 생각할지 모른다. 만약 여러분이 이러한 인물들의 역사적 중요성과 광범위한 영향력을 고려한다면, 리더십은 고귀하고 높은 목표처럼 보일지도 모른다. 그러나 우리 모두와 마찬가지로, 이러한 인물들은 일상생활의 어느 측면이 더 큰 규모로 어떻게 개선될 수 있는지에 대한 생각을 가졌던 학생, 근로자, 그리고 시민으로 시작했다. 근면함과 경험을 통해, 그들은 자신의 생각을 다른 사람들과 공유하고, 그들의 의견과 반응을 구하며, 끊임없이 집단의 목표를 성취할 수 있는 가장 좋은 방법을 찾음으로써 자신의 생각을 발전시켰다. 그러므로 우리는 모두, 나이나 경험에 관계없이, 학교, 공동체, 그리고 일터에서 리더가 될 수 있는 잠재력을 가지고 있다.

23. Crop r_____ 50) is the process in which farmers change the crops they grow in their fields in a special order. For example, if a farmer has three fields, he or she may grow carrots in the first field, green beans in the second, and tomatoes in the third. The next year, green beans will be in the first field, tomatoes in the second field, and carrots will be in the third. In year three, the crops will r_____ 51) again. By the fourth year, the crops will go back to their o_____ 52) order. Each crop e_____ 53) the soil for the next crop. This type of f_____ 54) is s_____ 55) because the soil stays h_____ 56) .

윤작은 농부가 자신의 밭에서 재배하는 작물을 특별한 순서로 바꾸는 과정이다. 예를 들면, 만약 한 농부가 세 개의 밭을 가지고 있다면, 그들은 첫 번째 밭에는 당근을, 두 번째 밭에는 녹색 콩을, 세 번째 밭에는 토마토를 재배할 수 있다. 그 다음 해에 첫 번째 밭에는 녹색 콩을, 두 번째 밭에는 토마토를, 세 번째 밭에는 당근을 재배할 것이다. 3년 차에 작물은 다시 순환할 것이다. 4년째에 이르면 작물은 원래의 순서로 되돌아갈 것이다. 각각의 작물은 다음 작물을 위한 토양을 비옥하게 한다. 이 유형의 농업은 토양이 건강하게 유지되기 때문에 지속 가능하다.

24. Working around the w_____57) painting, rather than c_____58) on one area at a time, will mean you can stop at any point and the painting can be c_____59) "finished." Artists often find it d_____60) to know when to stop p_____61), and it can be t_____62) to keep on a_____63) more to your work. It is important to take a few steps b_____64) from the painting from time to time to a_____65) your progress. Putting too much into a painting can s_____66) its impact and leave it looking o_____67). If you find yourself s_____68) to decide whether you have finished, take a break and come back to it later with fresh eyes. Then you can decide whether any areas of your painting would benefit from further r_____69).

한 번에 한 영역에만 집중하기보다 전체 그림에 대해서 작업하는 것은 여러분이 어떤 지점에서도 멈출 수 있고 그림이 '완성'된 것으로 간주 될 수 있다는 것을 의미할 것이다. 화가인 여러분은 종종 언제 그림을 멈춰야 할지 알기 어렵다는 것을 발견하고, 자신의 그림에 계속해서 더 추가하고 싶은 유혹을 느낄 수도 있다. 때때로 자신의 진행 상황을 평가하기 위해 그림에서 몇 걸음 뒤로 물러나는 것이 중요하다. 한 그림에 너무 많은 것을 넣으면 그것의 영향력을 망칠 수 있고 그것이 과하게 작업된 것처럼 보이게 둘 수 있다. 만약 여러분이 끝냈는지를 결정하는 데 자신이 어려움을 겪고 있음을 알게 된다면, 잠시 휴식을 취하고 나중에 새로운 눈으로 그것(그림)으로 다시 돌아와라. 그러면 여러분은 더 정교하게 꾸며서 자신의 그림 어느 부분이 득을 볼지를 결정할 수 있다.

26. Jaroslav Heyrovsky was born in Prague on December 20, 1890, as the f_____70) child of Leopold Heyrovsky. In 1901 Jaroslav went to a secondary school called the Akademicke Gymnasium. R_____71) than Latin and Greek, he showed a strong i_____72) in the natural sciences. At Czech University in Prague he studied c_____73), p_____74), and m_____75). From 1910 to 1914 he continued his studies at University College, London. Throughout the First World War, Jaroslav s_____76) in a military hospital. In 1926, Jaroslav became the first Professor of P_____77) Chemistry at Charles University in Prague. He w_____78) the Nobel Prize in chemistry in 1959.

Jaroslav Heyrovsky는 1890년 12월 20일 Prague에서 Leopold Heyrovsky의 다섯째 자녀로 태어났다. 1901년 Jaroslav는 Akademicke Gymnasium이라고 불리는 중등학교에 다녔다. 그는 라틴어와 그리스어보다는 자연 과학에 강한 흥미를 보였다. Prague에 있는 Czech University에서 그는 화학, 물리학 및 수학을 공부했다. 1910년부터 1914년까지 그는 런던의 University College에서 학업을 이어 나갔다. 제1차 세계 대전 내내 Jaroslav는 군 병원에 복무했다. 1926년에 Jaroslav는 Prague에 있는 Charles University 최초의 물리화학 교수가 되었다. 그는 1959년에 노벨 화학상을 수상했다.

29. It would be hard to o_____79) how important m_____80) work is to human beings — work that provides a sense of f_____81) and e_____82). Those who have found deeper meaning in their c_____83) find their days much more e_____84) and s_____85), and c_____86) their employment as one of their greatest sources of joy and pride. Sonya Lyubomirsky, professor of p_____87) at the University of California, has c_____88) numerous workplace studies showing that when people are more f_____89) on the job, they not only produce higher q_____90) work and a greater o_____91), but also generally earn higher i_____92). Those most s_____93) with their work are also much more likely to be happier with their lives overall. For her book Happiness at Work, researcher Jessica Pryce-Jones conducted a study of 3,000 workers in seventy-nine countries, finding that those who took greater s_____94) from their work were 150 percent more l_____95) to have a happier life overall.

인간에게 의미 있는 일, 즉 성취감과 권한을 제공하는 일이 얼마나 중요한지를 과장해서 말한다는 것은 어려울 것이다. 자신의 직업에서 더 깊은 의미를 찾은 사람은 자신의 하루하루가 훨씬 더 활기차고 만족감을 준다는 것을 발견하고, 자신의 직업을 기쁨과 자부심의 가장 큰 원천 중 하나로 꼽는다. University of California의 심리학 교수인 Sonya Lyubomirsky는 사람이 직업에 더 많은 성취감을 느낄 때 그들은 더 질 높은 업무와 더 큰 성과를 만들어 낼 뿐만 아니라 일반적으로 더 높은 수입을 거둔다는 것을 보여주는 수많은 업무 현장 연구를 수행했다. 자신의 일에 가장 만족하는 사람은 또한 전반적으로 자신의 삶에 더 행복해할 가능성이 훨씬 더 크다. 자신의 저서 'Happiness at Work'를 위해 연구자 Jessica Pryce-Jones는 79개 국가의 3,000명의 근로자에 대한 연구를 수행했고, 자신의 일로부터 더 큰 만족감을 갖는 사람이 전반적으로 더 행복한 삶을 살 가능성이 150퍼센트 더 크다는 것을 알아냈다.

30. The r_____96) of speed at which one is traveling will greatly d_____97) the ability to process d_____98) in the environment. In e_____99) terms, human senses are a_____100) to the speed at which humans move through space under their own p_____101) while walking. Our ability to d_____102) d_____103) in the environment is therefore ideally s_____104) to movement at speeds of perhaps five miles per hour and under. The fastest users of the street, motorists, therefore have a much more l_____105) ability to p_____106) d_____107) along the street — a motorist simply has l_____108) time or ability to a_____109) design details. On the other hand, p_____110) travel, being much s_____111) , allows for the a_____112) of environmental d_____113) . Joggers and bicyclists fall somewhere in between these p_____114) opposites; while they travel f_____115) than pedestrians, their rate of speed is ordinarily much s_____116) than that of the typical motorist.

사람이 이동하는 속도의 빠르기는 환경 속 세세한 것을 처리하는 능력을 크게 결정할 것이다. 진화론적 관점에서, 인간의 감각은 그 자신의 힘으로 걸으며 공간을 이동하는 속도에 적응되어 있다. 환경 속에서 세세한 것을 구별하는 우리의 능력은 그래서 대략 시속 5마일 또는 그 속도 이하의 이동에 이상적으로 맞추어져 있다. 그러므로 도로의 가장 빠른 사용자인 운전자는 도로를 따라서 (이동하며) 세세한 것을 처리하는 훨씬 더 제한된 능력을 가지고 있고, 그래서 운전자는 단지 디자인의 세세한 것을 감상할 수 있는 적은 시간이나 능력이 있다. 반면에 보행자 이동은 훨씬 더 느려서, 환경의 세세한 것을 감상할 수 있도록 허용해 준다. 조깅하는 사람과 자전거를 타는 사람은 이러한 극과 극 사이의 어딘가에 해당한다. 그들은 보행자보다 더 빨리 이동하지만, 속도의 빠르기는 보통 전형적인 운전자의 그것보다 훨씬 더 느리다.

31. Every species has certain c_____117) r_____118) — what degree of heat or cold it can e_____119) , for example. When the climate c_____120) , the p_____121) that s_____122) those r_____123) change, too. Species are f_____124) to f_____125) . All creatures are capable of some degree of m_____126) . Even creatures that appear i_____127) , like trees and barnacles, are capable of d_____128) at some stage of their life — as a seed, in the case of the tree, or as a larva, in the case of the barnacle. A creature must get from the p_____129) it is b_____130) — often o_____131) by its parent — to a place where it can survive, grow, and reproduce. From fossils, scientists know that even creatures like trees m_____132) with surprising speed during past periods of climate change.

모든 종은, 예를 들자면 어느 정도의 더위나 추위를 견딜 수 있는지와 같은, 특정한 기후 요건을 가지고 있다. 기후가 변할 때, 그러한 요건을 충족시키는 장소도 역시 변한다. 종은 따르도록 강요받는다. 모든 생명체는 어느 정도의 이동이 가능하다. 심지어 나무나 따개비처럼 움직이지 않는 것처럼 보이는 생명체도, 나무의 경우는 씨앗으로, 따개비의 경우는 유충으로, 그들 일생의 어느 단계에서 분산할 수 있다. 생명체는 종종 자신의 부모에 의해서 점유된, 그래서 자신이 태어난 장소로부터 생존하고 성장하며 번식할 수 있는 장소로 이동해야 한다. 화석으로부터, 과학자들은 심지어 나무와 같은 생명체는 기후 변화의 과거 시기 동안 놀라운 속도로 이동했다는 것을 알고 있다.

32. No r_____133) boss would say, "I make it a point to d_____134) my staff from s_____135) up, and I maintain a culture that p_____136) d_____137) viewpoints from ever getting a_____138) ." If anything, most bosses even say that they are p_____139) . This idea can be found throughout the series of c_____140) with corporate, university, and nonprofit leaders, published weekly in the business sections of newspapers. In the interviews, the f_____141) leaders are asked about their management techniques, and regularly claim to continually e_____142) internal p_____143) from more junior staffers. As Bot Pittman remarked in one of these conversations: "I want us to listen to these d_____144) because they may intend to tell you why we can't do something, but if you listen hard, what they're really telling you is what you must do to get something done."

존경할 만한 상사라면 누구라도 '나는 반드시 내 직원이 자유롭게 의견을 내지 못하도록 하고, 동의하지 않는 관점이 언제든 공공연히 알려지는 것을 가로막는 문화를 유지한다.'라고 말하지는 않을 것이다. 오히려, 대부분의 상사는 심지어 자신은 반대에 찬성한다고 말한다. 이러한 생각은 매주 발행되는 신문의 경제란에 기업, 대학, 그리고 비영리 (단체의) 리더와의 일련의 대담을 통해서 발견될 수 있다. 인터뷰에서, (기사에) 다루어진 리더는 자신의 경영 기법에 대해 질문을 받고, 내부적인 저항이 더 많은 부하 직원에게서 (나오기를) 계속해서 장려하고 있다고 어김없이 주장한다. Bot Pittman은 이러한 대담 중 하나에서 "저는 우리가 이러한 반대자에게 귀 기울이기를 원합니다. 왜냐하면 그들은 여러분에게 우리가 무엇인가를 할 수 없는 이유를 말하려고 의도할 수 있겠지만, 그러나 만약에 여러분이 열심히 귀 기울이면, 그들이 정말로 여러분에게 말하고 있는 것은 어떤 일이 이루어지도록 하기 위해서 여러분이 무엇을 해야만 하는가이기 때문입니다."라고 말했다.

33. One of the most striking characteristics of a s_____145) animal or person is that they do not r_____146) normally to environmental s_____147) . If you open the e_____148) of a sleeping mammal the eyes will not see normally — they are functionally b_____149) . Some v_____150) information apparently gets in, but it is not normally p_____151) as it is s_____152) or w_____153) ; same with the other s_____154) systems. Stimuli are r_____155) but not p_____156) normally and they f_____157) to wake the individual. P_____158) d_____159) probably s_____160) the f_____161) of p_____162) sleep, so some authors do not c_____163) it as part of the d_____164) of sleep itself. But as sleep would be i_____165) without it, it seems essential to its d_____166) . Nevertheless, many animals (including humans) use the i_____167) state of d_____168) to d_____169) some b_____170) of sleep without total p_____171) d_____172) .

잠을 자고 있는 동물이나 사람의 가장 두드러진 특징 중 하나는 그들이 환경의 자극에 정상적으로 반응하지 않는다는 것이다. 만약 당신이 잠을 자고 있는 포유류의 눈꺼풀을 열면, 그 눈은 정상적으로 볼 수 없을 것인데, 즉 그 눈은 기능적으로는 실명 상태이다. 어떤 시각적 정보는 명백히 눈으로 들어오지만, 그것은 짧아지거나 약화되어서 정상적으로 처리되지 않는데, 이는 다른 감각 체계도 마찬가지이다. 자극은 등록되지만 정상적으로 처리되지 않고 사람을 깨우는 데 실패한다. 지각 이탈은 추측하건대 수면을 보호하는 기능을 제공해서 어떤 저자는 그것을 수면 자체의 정의의 일부로 여기지 않는다. 그러나 수면이 그것 없이는 불가능하기 때문에 그것(지각 이탈)은 그것(수면)의 정의에 필수적인 것으로 보여진다. 그럼에도 (인간을 포함한) 많은 동물은 완전한 지각 이탈 없이 수면의 일부 이득을 끌어내기 위해서 졸음이라는 중간 상태를 이용한다.

34. A number of research studies have shown how e_____173) in a field often experience d_____174) when introducing n_____175) to that field. For example, in a g_____176) training situation, Dr Pamela Hinds found that people expert in using mobile phones were remarkably less a_____177) than n_____178) phone users in j_____179) how long it takes people to learn to use the phones. Experts can become i_____180) to how hard a task is for the beginner, an effect r_____181) to as the '_____182) of knowledge'. Dr Hinds was able to show that as people a_____183) the skill, they then began to u_____184) the level of d_____185) of that skill. Her participants even u_____186) how long it had taken themselves to a_____187) that skill in an earlier session. Knowing that experts forget how hard it was for them to learn, we can understand the need to look at the learning process through s_____188) eyes, rather than making a_____189) about how students 'should be' learning.

많은 조사 연구는 한 분야의 전문가가 그 분야로 초보자를 입문시킬 때 어떻게 어려움을 종종 겪는지를 보여줬다. 예를 들어, 실제 교육 상황에서 Pamela Hinds 박사는 휴대 전화기를 사용하는 데 능숙한 사람들이 휴대 전화기 사용법을 배우는 것에 얼마나 오랜 시간이 걸리는지를 판단하는 데 있어서, 초보 휴대 전화기 사용자보다 놀랍도록 덜 정확하다는 것을 알아냈다. 전문가는 한 과업이 초보자에게 얼마나 어려운지에 대해 무감각해질 수 있는데, 즉 '지식의 저주'로 칭해지는 효과이다. Hinds 박사는 사람이 기술을 습득했을 때 그 이후에 그 기술의 어려움의 정도를 과소평가하기 시작했다는 것을 보여줄 수 있었다. 그녀의 참가자는 심지어 자신들이 이전 기간에 그 기술을 습득하는 데 얼마나 오래 걸렸는지를 과소평가했다. 전문가가 자신이 학습하는 것이 얼마나 어려웠는지를 잊어버린다는 것을 안다면, 우리는 학생이 어떻게 학습을 '해야 하는지'에 대한 (근거 없는) 추정을 하기보다 학생들의 눈을 통해 학습 과정을 바라봐야 할 필요성을 이해할 수 있을 것이다.

35. A group of psychologists studied individuals with severe **m**_____190) illness who experienced weekly group music therapy, including singing familiar songs and **c**_____191) original songs. The results showed that the group music therapy improved the quality of participants' life, with those **p**_____192) in a greater number of sessions **e**_____193) the greatest benefits. **F**_____194) on singing, another group of psychologists reviewed articles on the **e**_____195) of group singing as a mental health treatment for individuals **l**_____196) with a mental health condition in a community setting. The findings showed that, when people with mental health conditions **p**_____197) in a choir, their mental health and wellbeing significantly **i**_____198) . Group singing provided enjoyment, improved emotional states, developed a sense of **b**_____199) and **e**_____200) self-confidence.

한 심리학자 그룹이 친숙한 노래 부르기와 독창적인 작곡하기를 포함한 집단 음악 치료를 매주 경험한 심각한 정신 질환이 있는 사람들을 연구했다. 그 연구 결과는 참여자가 (치료) 활동에 참여한 횟수가 많을수록 가장 큰 효과를 경험했기에, 집단 음악 치료가 참여자의 삶의 질을 개선하였음을 보여주었다. 노래 부르기에 초점을 두고, 또 다른 그룹의 심리학자는 집단생활의 환경에서 정신적인 건강 문제를 가지고 살고 있는 이들에게 미치는 집단 가창의 효능에 대한 논문을 검토했다. 발견된 결과는, 정신적인 건강 문제를 가진 사람이 합창단에 참여했을 때, 정신 건강과 행복이 상당히 개선되었음을 보여주었다. 집단 가창은 즐거움을 제공했고 감정 상태를 개선하였으며 소속감을 키웠고 자신감을 강화하였다.

36. In many sports, people realized the **d**_____201) and even impossibilities of young children **p**_____202) fully in many adult sport environments. They found the road to **s**_____203) for young children is **u**_____204) if they play on adult fields, courts or arenas with **e**_____205) that is too large, too heavy or too fast for them to **h**_____206) while trying to compete in adult-style **c**_____207) . Common sense has **p**_____208) : different sports have made **a**_____209) for children. As examples, baseball has T ball, football has flag football and **j**_____210) soccer uses a smaller and lighter ball and (sometimes) a smaller field. All have junior **c**_____211) structures where children play for **s**_____212) time periods and often in **s**_____213) teams. In a similar way, tennis has **a**_____214) the court areas, balls and **r**_____215) to make them more **a**_____216) for children under 10. The **a**_____217) are **p**_____218) and **r**_____219) to the age of the child.

많은 스포츠에서 사람들은 어린아이들이 여러 성인 스포츠 환경에 완전히 참여하기란 어렵고 심지어 불가 능하다는 것을 깨달았다. 어린아이들이 너무 크거나 너무 무겁고 또는 너무 빨라서 그들(어린아이들)이 다룰 수 없는 장비를 가지고 성인 스타일의 시합에서 경쟁하려고 하면서 성인용 운동장, 코트 또는 경기장에서 운동한다면 그들(어린아이들)이 성공으로 가 는 길이 있을 것 같지 않다는 것을 그들은 발견했다. 이러한 공통된 견해가 널리 퍼졌기에 여러 스포츠는 어린아이들을 위 한 조정을 했다. 예를 들자면, 야구에는 티볼이 있고, 풋볼에는 플래그 풋볼이 있고, 유소년 축구는 더 작고 더 가벼운 공 과 (가끔은) 더 작은 경기장을 사용한다. 모두가 어린아이들이 더 짧아진 경기 시간 동안 그리고 종종 더 작은 팀으로 경 기하는 유소년 시합의 구조를 가진다. 비슷한 방식으로, 테니스는 코트 면적, 공, 라켓을 10세 미만의 어린아이에게 더 적 합하도록 만들기 위해 조정했다. 이러한 조정은 점진적이고 어린아이의 연령과 관련이 있다.

37. With no **h**_____220) available, the Inca empire **e**_____221) at **d**_____222) messages on foot. The messengers were **s**_____223) on the royal roads to deliver the Inca king's **o**_____224) and **r**_____225) coming from his lands. Called Chasquis, they lived in groups of four to six in huts, **p**_____226) from one to two miles **a**_____227) **a**_____228) the roads. They were all young men and especially good runners who watched the road in both directions. If they **c**_____229) sight of another messenger **c**_____230) , they **h**_____231) out to meet them. The Inca **b**_____232) the huts on high ground, in sight of one another. When a messenger **n**_____233) the next hut, he began to **c**_____234) out and **r**_____235) the message three or four times to the one who was running out to meet him. The Inca empire could **r**_____236) messages 1,000 miles (1,610 km) in three or four days under good **c**_____237) .

구할 수 있는 말이 없어서, Inca 제국은 걸어서 메시지를 전달하는 데 탁월했다. 전령들은 Inca 왕의 명령과 그의 영토에서 오는 보고를 전달하기 위해 왕의 길에 배치되었다. Chasquis라고 불리는, 그들은 네 명에서 여섯 명의 집단을 이루어 길을 따라 1마일에서 2마일 간격으로 떨어져 배치된 오두막에서 생활했다. 그들은 모두 젊은 남자였고, 양방향으로 길을 주시하는 특히 잘 달리는 이들이었다. 그들은 다른 전령이 오는 것을 발견하면 그들을 맞이하기 위해 서둘러 나갔다. Inca 사람들은 서로를 볼 수 있는 높은 지대에 오두막을 지었다. 전령은 다음 오두막에 다가갈 때, 자신을 만나러 달려 나오고 있는 전령에게 소리치기 시작했고 메시지를 서너 번 반복했다. Inca 제국은 사정이 좋으면 사나흘 만에 1,000마일(1,610km) 정도 메시지를 이어 갈 수 있었다.

38. The tongue was **m**_____ 238) into **s**_____ 239) areas **w**_____ 240) certain tastes were **r**_____ _241) : sweetness at the tip, sourness on the sides, and **b**_____ 242) at the back of the mouth. Research in the 1980s and 1990s, however, **d**_____ 243) that the "tongue map" **e**_____ 244) of how we taste was, in fact, totally **w**_____ 245) . As it turns out, the map was a **m**_____ 246) and **m**_____ 247) of research **c**_____ 248) in Germany at the turn of the twentieth century. Today, leading taste researchers believe that taste **b**_____ 249) are not **g**_____ 250) according to **s**_____ 251) . Sweetness, saltiness, bitterness, and **s**_____ 252) can be tasted **e**_____ 253) in the mouth, although they may be **p**_____ 254) at a little different **i**_____ 255) at **d**_____ 256) sites. Moreover, the **m**_____ 257) at work is not place, but **t**_____ 258) . It's not that you taste sweetness at the tip of your tongue, but rather that you **r**_____ 259) that **p**_____ 260) **f**_____ 261) .

혀는 특정 맛이 등록되는 개별적인 영역으로 구획되었는데, 즉, 끝에는 단맛, 측면에는 신맛, 그리고 입의 뒤쪽에는 쓴맛이 있었다. 그러나 1980년대와 1990년대의 연구는 우리가 맛을 느끼는 방식에 대한 '혀 지도' 설명이 사실은 완전히 틀렸다는 것을 보여주었다. 밝혀진 바와 같이, 그 지도는 20세기 초입 독일에서 수행된 연구를 오해하고 오역한 것이었다. 오늘날, 선도적인 미각 연구자는 미뢰가 맛을 느끼는 특화된 분야에 따라 분류되지 않는다고 믿는다. 비록 그것들이 여러 위치에서 조금씩 다른 강도로 지각될지도 모르겠지만, 단맛, 짠맛, 쓴맛 그리고 신맛은 입안 어디에서나 느낄 수 있다. 게다가, 작동 중인 기제는 위치가 아니라 시간이다. 여러분은 혀끝에서 단맛을 느낀다기보다 오히려 그 지각(단맛)을 '가장 먼저' 등록하는 것이다.

39. No two animals are **a**_____ 262) . Animals from the same **l**_____ 263) will display some of the same **f**_____ 264) , but will not be exactly the **s**_____ 265) as each other; therefore, they may not **r**_____ _266) in entirely the same way **d**_____ 267) a **h**_____ 268) session. **E**_____ 269) factors can also **d**_____ 270) how the animal will **r**_____ 271) during the **t**_____ 272) . For instance, a cat in a rescue center will respond very **d**_____ 273) than a cat within a **d**_____ 274) home environment. In addition, animals that experience healing for **p**_____ 275) illness will react differently than those **a**_____ 276) healing for **e**_____ 277) confusion. With this in mind, every healing session needs to be **e**_____ 278) differently, and each healing treatment should be **a**_____ 279) to suit the specific **n**_____ 280) of the animal. You will learn as you go; healing is a **c**_____ 281) **l**_____ 282) process.

어떤 두 동물도 똑같지 않다. 한 배에서 태어난 동물은 똑같은 몇몇 특성을 보여 줄 수 있겠지만, 서로 정확히 같지는 않을 것이다. 그런 까닭에, 그들은 치료 활동 중에 완전히 똑같은 방식으로 반응하지 않을지도 모른다. 또한 환경적 요인은 치료 중에 동물이 어떻게 반응할지를 결정할 수 있다. 예를 들어, 구조 센터에 있는 고양이는 가정집 환경 내에 있는 고양이와는 매우 다르게 반응할 것이다. 게다가, 신체적 질병의 치료를 받는 동물은 감정적 동요의 치료를 받는 동물과는 다르게 반응할 것이다. 이를 염두에 두어, 모든 치료 활동은 다르게 탐구되어야 하고, 각각의 치료법은 동물의 특정 필요에 맞도록 조정되어야 한다. 여러분은 치료가 끊임없는 학습의 과정인 것을 직접 겪으면서 배우게 될 것이다.

40. The mind has parts that are known as the conscious mind and the s_____ 283) mind. The subconscious mind is very fast to act and doesn't deal with e_____ 284) . It deals with m_____ 285) of your responses to life, your memories and r_____ 286) . However, the conscious mind is the one that you have more c_____ 287) over. You think. You can c_____ 288) whether to carry on a t_____ 289) or to add e_____ 290) to it and this is the part of your mind that lets you d_____ 291) frequently because — f_____ 292) by e_____ 293) — you make the w_____ 294) decisions time and time again. When your j_____ 295) is c_____ 296) by emotions, this puts in b_____ 297) and all kinds of other n_____ _298) that hold you back. Scared of spiders? Scared of the dark? There are reasons for all of these fears, but they o_____ 299) in the c_____ 300) mind. They only become real f_____ 301) when the s_____ 302) mind records your reactions.

마음은 의식적 마음과 잠재의식적 마음이라고 알려진 부분을 갖고 있다. 잠재의식적 마음은 매우 빠르게 작동하며 감정을 다루지 않는다. 그것은 여러분의 삶에 대한 반응의 기억, 기억 및 인식을 다룬다. 그러나 의식적 마음은 여러분이 더 많은 통제력을 갖고 있는 부분이다. 여러분은 생각한다. 여러분은 생각을 계속할지 또는 그 생각에 감정을 더할지를 선택할 수 있다. 그리고 이것은 감정에 북받쳐 잘못된 결정을 반복해서 내리게 만들기 때문에 여러분을 빈번하게 낙담시키는 마음의 부분이기도 하다. 감정에 의해 여러분의 판단력이 흐려질 때 이것은 편견과 그 밖의 여러분을 억제하는 모든 종류의 부정성을 자리 잡게 만든다. 거미를 무서워하는가? 어둠을 무서워하는가? 이러한 두려움 전부 이유가 있지만 그것들은 의식적 마음에서 비롯된다. 그것들은 오직 잠재의식적 마음이 여러분의 반응을 기록할 때 실제 두려움이 된다.

41-42. N_____ 303) are everywhere, d_____ 304) what is "normal" and g_____ 305) our i_____ _306) of s_____ 307) life at every turn. As a simple example, there is a n_____ 308) in Anglo society to say Thank you to strangers who have just done something to help, such as open a door for you, point out that you've just dropped something, or give you directions. There is no l_____ 309) that f_____ 310) you to say Thank you. But if people don't say Thank you in these cases it is m_____ 311) . People expect that you will say it. You become r_____ 312) . Failing to say it will be both s_____ 313) and w_____ 314) of c_____ 315) . Not k_____ 316) the n_____ 317) of another community is the central problem of c_____ 318) communication. To continue the Thank you example, even though another culture may have an expression that appears t_____ 319) (many don't), there may be different n_____ 320) for its usage, for example, such that you should say Thank you only when the cost someone has c_____ 321) is c_____ 322) . In such a case it would sound r_____ 323) (i.e., unexpected, surprising, and worthy of criticism) if you w_____ 324) to thank someone for something so m_____ 325) as holding a door open for you.

규범은 무엇이 '정상적'인지를 규정하고 모든 순간 사회적 생활에 대한 우리의 해석을 안내해 주며 어디에나 존재한다. 간단한 예로, 문을 열어 주거나, 여러분이 물건을 방금 떨어뜨렸다는 것을 짚어 주거나, 길을 알려주는 것과 같이 도움을 줄 수 있는 무언가를 이제 막 해준 낯선 사람에게 '감사합니다'라고 말하는 규범이 Anglo 사회에 있다. 여러분이 '감사합니다'라고 말하도록 강요하는 법은 없다. 하지만 이런 상황에서 사람들이 '감사합니다'라고 말하지 않으면 그것은 눈에 띄게 된다. 사람들은 여러분이 그렇게 말하기를 기대한다. 여러분은 책임을 지게 되는 것이다. 그렇게 말하지 못하는 것은 (주변을) 놀라게 하기도 하고 비판을 받을 만하다. 다른 집단의 규범을 모른다는 것은 문화간 의사소통에서 중심적인 문제이다. '감사합니다'의 예를 이어 보자면, 비록 또 다른 문화권이 번역할 수 있는 것처럼 보이는 어떤 표현(다수는 그렇게 못하지만)을 가지고 있다 할지라도, 그것의 사용법에 대해, 예를 들어, 누군가가 초래한 대가가 상당할 때만 '감사합니다'라고 말해야 한다는 것처럼 다른 규범이 있을 수 있다. 그 같은 상황에서 만약 여러분이 혹시라도, 여러분을 위해 문을 잡아주는 것과 같이 아주 사소한 일에 대해 누군가에게 감사해한다면, 그것은 우스꽝스럽게(즉, 예상치 못하게, 놀랍게, 비판을 받을 만하게) 들릴 수 있을 것이다.

43-45. Long ago, when the world was y_____326) , an old Native American s_____327) leader Odawa had a dream on a high mountain. In his dream, Iktomi, the great spirit and searcher of wisdom, a_____328) to him in the form of a spider. Iktomi spoke to him in a holy language. Iktomi told Odawa about the cycles of life. He said, "We all begin our lives as babies, move on to childhood, and then to adulthood. Finally, we come to old age, where we must be taken care of as babies again." Iktomi also told him that there are good and bad f_____329) in each stage of life. "If we listen to the good forces, they will g_____330) us in the right direction. But if we listen to the bad forces, they will lead us the wrong way and may h_____331) us," Iktomi said. When Iktomi finished s_____332) he spun a web and gave it to Odawa. He said to Odawa, "The web is a perfect circle with a hole in the center. Use the web to help your people r_____333) their goals. Make good use of their ideas, dreams, and visions. If you believe in the great spirit, the web will catch your good ideas and the bad ones will go through the hole." Right after Odawa woke up, he went back to his village. Odawa s_____334) Iktomi's lesson with his people. Today, many Native Americans have dream catchers hanging above their beds. Dream catchers are believed to f_____335) out bad dreams. The good dreams are captured in the web of life and carried with the people. The bad dreams pass through the hole in the web and are no longer a part of their lives.

오래전, 세상이 생겨난지 오래지 않을 무렵, 아메리카 원주민의 늙은 영적 지도자인 Odawa는 높은 산에서 꿈을 꾸었다. 자신의 꿈속에서 위대한 신령이자 지혜의 구도자인 Iktomi가 거미의 형태로 그에게 나타났다. Iktomi는 성스러운 언어로 그에게 말했다. Iktomi는 Odawa에게 삶의 순환에 관해서 말했 다. 그는 "우리는 모두 아기로 삶을 출발하고, 유년기를 거쳐 그다음 성년기에 이르게 된다. 결국 우리는 노년기에 도달하고, 거기서 우리는 다시 아기처럼 보살핌을 받아야 한다."라고 말했다. 또한 Iktomi는 삶의 각 단계에는 좋고 나쁜 힘이 있다고 그에게 말했다. "우리가 좋은 힘에 귀를 기울이면 그들은 우리를 올바른 방향으로 인도할 것이다. 하지만 만약 나쁜 힘에 귀를 기울이면 그들은 우리를 잘못된 길로 이끌고 우리를 해칠 수도 있다."라고 Iktomi는 말했다. Iktomi가 말을 끝냈을 때, 그는 거미집을 짜서 Odawa에게 주었다. 그가 Odawa에게 말하기를, "그 거미집은 가운데 구멍이 뚫린 완벽한 원이다. 너의 마을 사람들이 자신들의 목표에 도달할 수 있도록 거미집을 사용해라. 그들의 생각, 꿈, 비전을 잘 활용해라. 만약 네가 위대한 신령을 믿는다면 그 거미집이 네 좋은 생각을 붙잡아 줄 것이고 나쁜 생각은 구멍을 통해 빠져나갈 것이다." Odawa는 잠에서 깨자마자 자기 마을로 되돌아갔다. Odawa는 Iktomi의 교훈을 그의 마을 사람들과 나누었다. 오늘날 많은 미국 원주민은 침대 위에 드림 캐처를 건다. 드림캐처는 나쁜 꿈을 걸러 준다고 믿어진다. 좋은 꿈은 인생이라는 거미집에 걸리고 사람들과 동반하게 된다. 나쁜 꿈은 거미집의 구멍 사이로 빠져나가고 더 이상 그들의 삶의 한 부분이 되지 못한다.

2024 고1 3월 모의고사　　　❷ 회차　:　　　점 / 335점

❶ voca　　❷ text　　❸ [/]　　④ _____　　❺ quiz 1　　❻ quiz 2　　❼ quiz 3　　❽ quiz 4　　❾ quiz 5

18. Dear Ms. Jane Watson,

I am John Austin, a science teacher at Crestville High School. Recently I was i_____ 1) by the l_____ 2) book you wrote about the environment. Also my students read your book and had a class d_____ 3) about it. They are big fans of your book, so I'd like to ask you to visit our school and give a special lecture. We can set the date and time to s_____ 4) your schedule. Having you at our school would be a fantastic experience for the students. We would be very g_____ 5) if you could come.

Best regards, John Austin

19. Marilyn and her three-year-old daughter, Sarah, took a trip to the beach, w_____ 6) Sarah built her first sandcastle. Moments later, an e_____ 7) wave d_____ 8) Sarah's castle. In response to the l_____ 9) of her sandcastle, tears s_____ 10) down Sarah's cheeks and her heart was broken. She ran to Marilyn, saying she would never build a sandcastle again. Marilyn said, "Part of the joy of building a sandcastle is that, in the end, we give it as a gift to the ocean." Sarah loved this idea and responded with e_____ 11) to the idea of building another castle — this time, even closer to the water so the ocean would get its gift sooner!

20. Magic is w_____ 12) we all wish for to h_____ 13) in our life. Do you love the movie Cinderella like me? Well, in real life, you can also create magic. Here's the trick. Write down all the real-time c_____ 14) that you face and deal w_____ 15) . Just c_____ 16) the challenge statement into p_____ 17) statements. Let me give you an example here. If you s_____ 18) with getting up early in the morning, then write a positive statement such as "I get up early in the morning at 5:00 am every day." Once you write these statements, get ready to w_____ 19) magic and c_____ 20) . You will be surprised that just by writing these statements, there is a s_____ 21) in the way you think and act. Suddenly you feel more powerful and positive.

21. Consider the seemingly s_____ 22) question How many s_____ 23) are there? Around 2,370 years ago, Aristotle wrote that there are five, in both humans and animals — sight, hearing, smell, taste, and touch. However, according to the philosopher Fiona Macpherson, there are r_____ 24) to d_____ 25) it. For a start, Aristotle m_____ 26) a few in humans: the p_____ 27) of your own body which is different from t_____ 28) and the sense of b_____ 29) which has l_____ 30) to both touch and vision. Other animals have senses that are even harder to c_____ 31) . Many v_____ 32) have a different sense system for d_____ 33) o_____ 34) . Some snakes can d_____ 35) the body heat of their prey. These examples tell us that "senses cannot be clearly d_____ 36) into a l_____ 37) number of specific kinds," Macpherson wrote in The Senses. Instead of trying to push animal senses into Aristotelian b_____ 38) , we should study them for what they are.

22. When we think of leaders, we may think of people such as Abraham Lincoln or Martin Luther King, Jr. If you consider the h_____ 39) importance and f_____ 40) i_____ 41) of these individuals, leadership might seem like a n_____ 42) and high goal. But like all of us, these people started out as students, workers, and citizens who **p**_____ 43) ideas about how some aspect of daily life could be improved on a larger scale. Through **d**_____ 44) and experience, they improved upon their ideas by **s**_____ 45) them with others, **s**_____ 46) their opinions and feedback and **c**_____ 47) looking for the best way to **a**_____ 48) goals for a group. Thus we all have the **p**_____ 49) to be leaders at school, in our communities, and at work, regardless of age or experience.

23. Crop **r**_____ 50) is the process in which farmers change the crops they grow in their fields in a special order. For example, if a farmer has three fields, he or she may grow carrots in the first field, green beans in the second, and tomatoes in the third. The next year, green beans will be in the first field, tomatoes in the second field, and carrots will be in the third. In year three, the crops will **r**_____ 51) again. By the fourth year, the crops will go back to their **o**_____ 52) order. Each crop **e**_____ 53) the soil for the next crop. This type of **f**_____ 54) is **s**_____ 55) because the soil stays **h**_____ 56) .

24. Working around the **w**_____ 57) painting, rather than **c**_____ 58) on one area at a time, will mean you can stop at any point and the painting can be **c**_____ 59) "finished." Artists often find it **d**_____ 60) to know when to stop **p**_____ 61) , and it can be **t**_____ 62) to keep on **a**_____ 63) more to your work. It is important to take a few steps **b**_____ 64) from the painting from time to time to **a**_____ 65) your progress. Putting too much into a painting can **s**_____ 66) its impact and leave it looking **o**_____ 67) . If you find yourself **s**_____ 68) to decide whether you have finished, take a break and come back to it later with fresh eyes. Then you can decide whether any areas of your painting would benefit from further **r**_____ 69) .

26. Jaroslav Heyrovsky was born in Prague on December 20, 1890, as the **f**_____ 70) child of Leopold Heyrovsky. In 1901 Jaroslav went to a secondary school called the Akademicke Gymnasium. **R**_____ 71) than Latin and Greek, he showed a strong **i**_____ 72) in the natural sciences. At Czech University in Prague he studied **c**_____ 73) , **p**_____ 74) , and **m**_____ 75) . From 1910 to 1914 he continued his studies at University College, London. Throughout the First World War, Jaroslav **s**_____ 76) in a military hospital. In 1926, Jaroslav became the first Professor of **P**_____ 77) Chemistry at Charles University in Prague. He **w**_____ 78) the Nobel Prize in chemistry in 1959.

29. It would be hard to **o**_____ 79) how important **m**_____ 80) work is to human beings — work that provides a sense of **f**_____ 81) and **e**_____ 82) . Those who have found deeper meaning in their **c**_____ 83) find their days much more **e**_____ 84) and **s**_____ 85) , and **c**_____ 86) their employment as one of their greatest sources of joy and pride. Sonya Lyubomirsky, professor of **p**_____ 87) at the University of California, has **c**_____ 88) numerous workplace studies showing that when people are more **f**_____ 89) on the job, they not only produce higher **q**_____ 90) work and a greater **o**_____ 91) , but also generally earn higher **i**_____ 92) . Those most **s**_____ 93) with their work are also much more likely to be happier with their lives overall. For her book Happiness at Work, researcher Jessica Pryce-Jones conducted a study of 3,000 workers in seventy-nine countries, finding that those who took greater **s**_____ 94) from their work were 150 percent more **l**_____ 95) to have a happier life overall.

30. The **r**_____96) of speed at which one is traveling will greatly **d**_____97) the ability to process **d**_____98) in the environment. In **e**_____99) terms, human senses are **a**_____100) to the speed at which humans move through space under their own **p**_____101) while walking. Our ability to **d**_____102) **d**_____103) in the environment is therefore ideally **s**_____104) to movement at speeds of perhaps five miles per hour and under. The fastest users of the street, motorists, therefore have a much more **l**_____105) ability to **p**_____106) **d**_____107) along the street — a motorist simply has **l**_____108) time or ability to **a**_____109) design details. On the other hand, **p**_____110) travel, being much **s**_____111) , allows for the **a**_____112) of environmental **d**_____113) . Joggers and bicyclists fall somewhere in between these **p**_____114) opposites; while they travel **f**_____115) than pedestrians, their rate of speed is ordinarily much **s**_____116) than that of the typical motorist.

31. Every species has certain **c**_____117) **r**_____118) — what degree of heat or cold it can **e**_____119) , for example. When the climate **c**_____120) , the **p**_____121) that **s**_____122) those **r**_____123) change, too. Species are **f**_____124) to **f**_____125) . All creatures are capable of some degree of **m**_____126) . Even creatures that appear **i**_____127) , like trees and barnacles, are capable of **d**_____128) at some stage of their life — as a seed, in the case of the tree, or as a larva, in the case of the barnacle. A creature must get from the **p**_____129) it is **b**_____130) — often **o**_____131) by its parent — to a place where it can survive, grow, and reproduce. From fossils, scientists know that even creatures like trees **m**_____132) with surprising speed during past periods of climate change.

32. No **r**_____133) boss would say, "I make it a point to **d**_____134) my staff from **s**_____135) up, and I maintain a culture that **p**_____136) **d**_____137) viewpoints from ever getting **a**_____138) ." If anything, most bosses even say that they are **p**_____139) . This idea can be found throughout the series of **c**_____140) with corporate, university, and nonprofit leaders, published weekly in the business sections of newspapers. In the interviews, the **f**_____141) leaders are asked about their management techniques, and regularly claim to continually **e**_____142) internal **p**_____143) from more junior staffers. As Bot Pittman remarked in one of these conversations: "I want us to listen to these **d**_____144) because they may intend to tell you why we can't do something, but if you listen hard, what they're really telling you is what you must do to get something done."

33. One of the most striking characteristics of a **s**_____145) animal or person is that they do not **r**_____146) normally to environmental **s**_____147) . If you open the **e**_____148) of a sleeping mammal the eyes will not see normally — they are functionally **b**_____149) . Some **v**_____150) information apparently gets in, but it is not normally **p**_____151) as it is **s**_____152) or **w**_____153) ; same with the other **s**_____154) systems. Stimuli are **r**_____155) but not **p**_____156) normally and they **f**_____157) to wake the individual. **P**_____158) **d**_____159) probably **s**_____160) the **f**_____161) of **p**_____162) sleep, so some authors do not **c**_____163) it as part of the **d**_____164) of sleep itself. But as sleep would be **i**_____165) without it, it seems essential to its **d**_____166) . Nevertheless, many animals (including humans) use the **i**_____167) state of **d**_____168) to **d**_____169) some **b**_____170) of sleep without total **p**_____171) **d**_____172) .

34. A number of research studies have shown how e_____173) in a field often experience d_____174) when introducing n_____175) to that field. For example, in a g_____176) training situation, Dr Pamela Hinds found that people expert in using mobile phones were remarkably less a_____177) than n_____178) phone users in j_____179) how long it takes people to learn to use the phones. Experts can become i_____180) to how hard a task is for the beginner, an effect r_____181) to as the '_____182) of knowledge'. Dr Hinds was able to show that as people a_____183) the skill, they then began to u_____ _184) the level of d_____185) of that skill. Her participants even u_____186) how long it had taken themselves to a_____187) that skill in an earlier session. Knowing that experts forget how hard it was for them to learn, we can understand the need to look at the learning process through s_____188) eyes, rather than making a_____189) about how students 'should be' learning.

35. A group of psychologists studied individuals with severe m_____190) illness who experienced weekly group music therapy, including singing familiar songs and c_____191) original songs. The results showed that the group music therapy improved the quality of participants' life, with those p_____192) in a greater number of sessions e_____193) the greatest benefits. F_____194) on singing, another group of psychologists reviewed articles on the e_____195) of group singing as a mental health treatment for individuals l_____196) with a mental health condition in a community setting. The findings showed that, when people with mental health conditions p_____197) in a choir, their mental health and wellbeing significantly i_____198) . Group singing provided enjoyment, improved emotional states, developed a sense of b_____199) and e_____200) self-confidence.

36. In many sports, people realized the d_____201) and even impossibilities of young children p_____202) fully in many adult sport environments. They found the road to s_____203) for young children is u_____ _204) if they play on adult fields, courts or arenas with e_____205) that is too large, too heavy or too fast for them to h_____206) while trying to compete in adult-style c_____207) . Common sense has p_____ _208) : different sports have made a_____209) for children. As examples, baseball has T ball, football has flag football and j_____210) soccer uses a smaller and lighter ball and (sometimes) a smaller field. All have junior c_____211) structures where children play for s_____212) time periods and often in s_____213) teams. In a similar way, tennis has a_____214) the court areas, balls and r_____215) to make them more a_____216) for children under 10. The a_____217) are p_____218) and r_____219) to the age of the child.

37. With no h_____220) available, the Inca empire e_____221) at d_____222) messages on foot. The messengers were s_____223) on the royal roads to deliver the Inca king's o_____224) and r_____ _225) coming from his lands. Called Chasquis, they lived in groups of four to six in huts, p_____226) from one to two miles a_____227) a_____228) the roads. They were all young men and especially good runners who watched the road in both directions. If they **c**_____229) sight of another messenger **c**_____230) , they **h**_____231) out to meet them. The Inca **b**_____232) the huts on high ground, in sight of one another. When a messenger **n**_____233) the next hut, he began to **c**_____234) out and **r**_____235) the message three or four times to the one who was running out to meet him. The Inca empire could **r**_____236) messages 1,000 miles (1,610 km) in three or four days under good **c**_____237) .

38. The tongue was **m**_____238) into **s**_____239) areas **w**_____240) certain tastes were **r**_____241) : sweetness at the tip, sourness on the sides, and **b**_____242) at the back of the mouth. Research in the 1980s and 1990s, however, **d**_____243) that the "tongue map" **e**_____244) of how we taste was, in fact, totally **w**_____245) . As it turns out, the map was a **m**_____246) and **m**_____247) of research **c**_____248) in Germany at the turn of the twentieth century. Today, leading taste researchers believe that taste **b**_____249) are not **g**_____250) according to **s**_____251) . Sweetness, saltiness, bitterness, and **s**_____252) can be tasted **e**_____253) in the mouth, although they may be **p**_____254) at a little different **i**_____255) at **d**_____256) sites. Moreover, the **m**_____257) at work is not place, but **t**_____258) . It's not that you taste sweetness at the tip of your tongue, but rather that you **r**_____259) that **p**_____260) **f**_____261) .

39. No two animals are **a**_____262) . Animals from the same **l**_____263) will display some of the same **f**_____264) , but will not be exactly the **s**_____265) as each other; therefore, they may not **r**_____266) in entirely the same way **d**_____267) a **h**_____268) session. **E**_____269) factors can also **d**_____270) how the animal will **r**_____271) during the **t**_____272) . For instance, a cat in a rescue center will respond very **d**_____273) than a cat within a **d**_____274) home environment. In addition, animals that experience healing for **p**_____275) illness will react differently than those **a**_____276) healing for **e**_____277) confusion. With this in mind, every healing session needs to be **e**_____278) differently, and each healing treatment should be **a**_____279) to suit the specific **n**_____280) of the animal. You will learn as you go; healing is a **c**_____281) **l**_____282) process.

40. The mind has parts that are known as the conscious mind and the **s**_____283) mind. The subconscious mind is very fast to act and doesn't deal with **e**_____284) . It deals with **m**_____285) of your responses to life, your memories and **r**_____286) . However, the conscious mind is the one that you have more **c**_____287) over. You think. You can **c**_____288) whether to carry on a **t**_____289) or to add **e**_____290) to it and this is the part of your mind that lets you **d**_____291) frequently because — **f**_____292) by **e**_____293) — you make the **w**_____294) decisions time and time again. When your **j**_____295) is **c**_____296) by emotions, this puts in **b**_____297) and all kinds of other **n**_____298) that hold you back. Scared of spiders? Scared of the dark? There are reasons for all of these fears, but they **o**_____299) in the **c**_____300) mind. They only become real **f**_____301) when the **s**_____302) mind records your reactions.

41-42. N_____303) are everywhere, d_____304) what is "normal" and g_____305) our i_____ _306) of s_____307) life at every turn. As a simple example, there is a n_____308) in Anglo society to say Thank you to strangers who have just done something to help, such as open a door for you, point out that you've just dropped something, or give you directions. There is no l_____309) that f_____310) you to say Thank you. But if people don't say Thank you in these cases it is m_____311) . People expect that you will say it. You become r_____312) . Failing to say it will be both s_____313) and w_____314) of c_____315) . Not k_____316) the n_____317) of another community is the central problem of c_____318) communication. To continue the Thank you example, even though another culture may have an expression that appears t_____319) (many don't), there may be different n_____320) for its usage, for example, such that you should say Thank you only when the cost someone has c_____321) is c_____322) . In such a case it would sound r_____323) (i.e., unexpected, surprising, and worthy of criticism) if you w_____324) to thank someone for something so m_____325) as holding a door open for you.

43-45. Long ago, when the world was y_____326) , an old Native American s_____327) leader Odawa had a dream on a high mountain. In his dream, Iktomi, the great spirit and searcher of wisdom, a_____328) to him in the form of a spider. Iktomi spoke to him in a holy language. Iktomi told Odawa about the cycles of life. He said, "We all begin our lives as babies, move on to childhood, and then to adulthood. Finally, we come to old age, where we must be taken care of as babies again." Iktomi also told him that there are good and bad f_____329) in each stage of life. "If we listen to the good forces, they will g_____330) us in the right direction. But if we listen to the bad forces, they will lead us the wrong way and may h_____331) us," Iktomi said. When Iktomi finished s_____332) he spun a web and gave it to Odawa. He said to Odawa, "The web is a perfect circle with a hole in the center. Use the web to help your people r_____333) their goals. Make good use of their ideas, dreams, and visions. If you believe in the great spirit, the web will catch your good ideas and the bad ones will go through the hole." Right after Odawa woke up, he went back to his village. Odawa s_____334) Iktomi's lesson with his people. Today, many Native Americans have dream catchers hanging above their beds. Dream catchers are believed to f_____335) out bad dreams. The good dreams are captured in the web of life and carried with the people. The bad dreams pass through the hole in the web and are no longer a part of their lives.

2024 고1 3월 모의고사

☑ 다음 글을 읽고 물음에 답하시오. (18)

> Also my students read your book and had a class discussion about it.

Dear Ms. Jane Watson,I am John Austin, a science teacher at Crestville High School. (①) Recently I was impressed by the latest book you wrote about the environment. (②) They are big fans of your book, so I'd like to ask you to visit our school and give a special lecture. (③) We can set the date and time to suit your schedule. (④) Having you at our school would be a fantastic experience for the students. (⑤) We would be very grateful if you could come.   Best regards, John Austin

1. ¹⁾글의 흐름으로 보아, 주어진 문장이 들어가기에 가장 적절한 곳은?

☑ 다음 글을 읽고 물음에 답하시오. (19)

> Sarah loved this idea and responded with enthusiasm to the idea of building another castle.

Marilyn and her three-year-old daughter, Sarah, took a trip to the beach, where Sarah built her first sandcastle. (①) Moments later, an enormous wave destroyed Sarah's castle. (②) In response to the loss of her sandcastle, tears streamed down Sarah's cheeks and her heart was broken. (③) She ran to Marilyn, saying she would never build a sandcastle again. (④) Marilyn said, "Part of the joy of building a sandcastle is that, in the end, we give it as a gift to the ocean". (⑤) This time, it was even closer to the water so the ocean would get its gift sooner!

2. ²⁾글의 흐름으로 보아, 주어진 문장이 들어가기에 가장 적절한 곳은?

☑ 다음 글을 읽고 물음에 답하시오. (20)

> If you struggle with getting up early in the morning, then write a positive statement such as "I get up early in the morning at 5:00 am every day". Once you write these statements, get ready to witness magic and confidence.

Magic is what we all wish for to happen in our life. Do you love the movie Cinderella like me? Well, in real life, you can also create magic. Here's the trick. (①) Write down all the real-time challenges that you face and deal with. (②) Just change the challenge statement into positive statements. (③) Let me give you an example here. (④) You will be surprised that just by writing these statements, there is a shift in the way you think and act. (⑤) Suddenly you feel more powerful and positive.

3. ³⁾글의 흐름으로 보아, 주어진 문장이 들어가기에 가장 적절한 곳은?

☑ 다음 글을 읽고 물음에 답하시오. (21)

> However, according to the philosopher Fiona Macpherson, there are reasons to doubt it. For a start, Aristotle missed a few in humans: the perception of your own body which is different from touch and the sense of balance which has links to both touch and vision.

Consider the seemingly simple question How many senses are there? Around 2,370 years ago, Aristotle wrote that there are five, in both humans and animals — sight, hearing, smell, taste, and touch. (①) Other animals have senses that are even harder to categorize. (②) Many vertebrates have a different sense system for detecting odors. (③) Some snakes can detect the body heat of their prey. (④) These examples tell us that "senses cannot be clearly divided into a limited number of specific kinds", Macpherson wrote in The Senses. (⑤) Instead of trying to push animal senses into Aristotelian buckets, we should study them for what they are.

4. ⁴⁾글의 흐름으로 보아, 주어진 문장이 들어가기에 가장 적절한 곳은?

☑ **다음 글을 읽고 물음에 답하시오.** (22)

> But like all of us, these people started out as students, workers, and citizens who possessed ideas about how some aspect of daily life could be improved on a larger scale.

When we think of leaders, we may think of people such as Abraham Lincoln or Martin Luther King, Jr. (①) If you consider the historical importance and far-reaching influence of these individuals, leadership might seem like a noble and high goal. (②) Through diligence and experience, they improved upon their ideas by sharing them with others. (③) At the same time, they were seeking their opinions and feedback and constantly looking for the best way to accomplish goals for a group. (④) Thus we all have the potential to be leaders at school, in our communities, and at work, regardless of age or experience. (⑤)

5. 5)글의 흐름으로 보아, 주어진 문장이 들어가기에 <u>가장 적절한</u> 곳은?

☑ **다음 글을 읽고 물음에 답하시오.** (23)

> Each crop enriches the soil for the next crop.

Crop rotation is the process in which farmers change the crops they grow in their fields in a special order. (①) For example, if a farmer has three fields, he or she may grow carrots in the first field, green beans in the second, and tomatoes in the third. (②) The next year, green beans will be in the first field, tomatoes in the second field, and carrots will be in the third. (③) In year three, the crops will rotate again. (④) By the fourth year, the crops will go back to their original order. (⑤) This type of farming is sustainable because the soil stays healthy.

6. 6)글의 흐름으로 보아, 주어진 문장이 들어가기에 <u>가장 적절한</u> 곳은?

☑ **다음 글을 읽고 물음에 답하시오.** (24)

> If you find yourself struggling to decide whether you have finished, take a break and come back to it later with fresh eyes.

Working around the whole painting, rather than concentrating on one area at a time, will mean you can stop at any point and the painting can be considered "finished". (①) Artists often find it difficult to know when to stop painting, and it can be tempting to keep on adding more to your work. (②) It is important to take a few steps back from the painting from time to time to assess your progress. (③) Putting too much into a painting can spoil its impact and leave it looking overworked. (④) Then you can decide whether any areas of your painting would benefit from further refinement. (⑤)

7. 7)글의 흐름으로 보아, 주어진 문장이 들어가기에 <u>가장 적절한</u> 곳은?

☑ **다음 글을 읽고 물음에 답하시오.** (26)

> Rather than Latin and Greek, he showed a strong interest in the natural sciences.

Jaroslav Heyrovsky was born in Prague on December 20, 1890, as the fifth child of Leopold Heyrovsky. In 1901 Jaroslav went to a secondary school called the Akademicke Gymnasium. (①) At Czech University in Prague he studied chemistry, physics, and mathematics. (②) From 1910 to 1914 he continued his studies at University College, London. (③) Throughout the First World War, Jaroslav served in a military hospital. (④) In 1926, Jaroslav became the first Professor of Physical Chemistry at Charles University in Prague. (⑤) He won the Nobel Prize in chemistry in 1959.

8. 8)글의 흐름으로 보아, 주어진 문장이 들어가기에 <u>가장 적절한</u> 곳은?

☑ **다음 글을 읽고 물음에 답하시오.** (29)

> Those most satisfied with their work are also much more likely to be happier with their lives overall.

It would be hard to overstate how important meaningful work is to human beings — work that provides a sense of fulfillment and empowerment. (①) Those who have found deeper meaning in their careers find their days much more energizing and satisfying, and count their employment as one of their greatest sources of joy and pride. (②) Sonya Lyubomirsky, professor of psychology at the University of California, has conducted numerous workplace studies showing that when people are more fulfilled on the job, they not only produce higher quality work and a greater output, but also generally earn higher incomes. (③) For her book Happiness at Work, researcher Jessica Pryce-Jones conducted a study of 3,000 workers in seventy-nine countries. (④) She found that those who took greater satisfaction from their work were 150 percent more likely to have a happier life overall. (⑤)

9. 9)글의 흐름으로 보아, 주어진 문장이 들어가기에 <u>가장 적절한</u> 곳은?

☑ **다음 글을 읽고 물음에 답하시오.** (30)

> On the other hand, pedestrian travel, being much slower, allows for the appreciation of environmental detail.

The rate of speed at which one is traveling will greatly determine the ability to process detail in the environment. (①) In evolutionary terms, human senses are adapted to the speed at which humans move through space under their own power while walking. (②) Our ability to distinguish detail in the environment is therefore ideally suited to movement at speeds of perhaps five miles per hour and under. (③) The fastest users of the street, motorists, therefore have a much more limited ability to process details along the street — a motorist simply has little time or ability to appreciate design details. (④) Joggers and bicyclists fall somewhere in between these polar opposites; while they travel faster than pedestrians, their rate of speed is ordinarily much slower than that of the typical motorist. (⑤)

10. 10)글의 흐름으로 보아, 주어진 문장이 들어가기에 <u>가장 적절한</u> 곳은?

☑ **다음 글을 읽고 물음에 답하시오.** (31)

> Even creatures that appear immobile, like trees and barnacles, are capable of dispersal at some stage of their life — as a seed, in the case of the tree, or as a larva, in the case of the barnacle.

Every species has certain climatic requirements — what degree of heat or cold it can endure, for example. When the climate changes, the places that satisfy those requirements change, too. (①) Species are forced to follow. (②) All creatures are capable of some degree of movement. (③) A creature must get from the place it is born — often occupied by its parent — to a place where it can survive, grow, and reproduce. (④) From fossils, scientists know that even creatures like trees moved with surprising speed during past periods of climate change. (⑤)

11. 11)글의 흐름으로 보아, 주어진 문장이 들어가기에 <u>가장 적절한</u> 곳은?

☑ **다음 글을 읽고 물음에 답하시오.** (32)

> It's because they may intend to tell you why we can't do something, but if you listen hard, what they're really telling you is what you must do to get something done".

No respectable boss would say, "I make it a point to discourage my staff from speaking up, and I maintain a culture that prevents disagreeing viewpoints from ever getting aired". (①) If anything, most bosses even say that they are pro-dissent. (②) This idea can be found throughout the series of conversations with corporate, university, and nonprofit leaders, published weekly in the business sections of newspapers. (③) In the interviews, the featured leaders are asked about their management techniques, and regularly claim to continually encourage internal protest from more junior staffers. (④) As Bot Pittman remarked in one of these conversations: "I want us to listen to these dissenters. (⑤)

12. 12)글의 흐름으로 보아, 주어진 문장이 들어가기에 <u>가장 적절한</u> 곳은?

☑ **다음 글을 읽고 물음에 답하시오.** (33)

> But as sleep would be impossible without it, it seems essential to its definition.

One of the most striking characteristics of a sleeping animal or person is that they do not respond normally to environmental stimuli. If you open the eyelids of a sleeping mammal the eyes will not see normally — they are functionally blind. (①) Some visual information apparently gets in, but it is not normally processed as it is shortened or weakened; same with the other sensing systems. (②) Stimuli are registered but not processed normally and they fail to wake the individual. (③) Perceptual disengagement probably serves the function of protecting sleep, so some authors do not count it as part of the definition of sleep itself. (④) Nevertheless, many animals (including humans) use the intermediate state of drowsiness to derive some benefits of sleep without total perceptual disengagement. (⑤)

13. 13)글의 흐름으로 보아, 주어진 문장이 들어가기에 가장 적절한 곳은?

☑ **다음 글을 읽고 물음에 답하시오.** (34)

> Her participants even underestimated how long it had taken themselves to acquire that skill in an earlier session.

A number of research studies have shown how experts in a field often experience difficulties when introducing newcomers to that field. (①) For example, in a genuine training situation, Dr Pamela Hinds found that people expert in using mobile phones were remarkably less accurate than novice phone users in judging how long it takes people to learn to use the phones. (②) Experts can become insensitive to how hard a task is for the beginner, an effect referred to as the 'curse of knowledge'. (③) Dr Hinds was able to show that as people acquired the skill, they then began to underestimate the level of difficulty of that skill. (④) Knowing that experts forget how hard it was for them to learn, we can understand the need to look at the learning process through students' eyes, rather than making assumptions about how students 'should be' learning. (⑤)

14. 14)글의 흐름으로 보아, 주어진 문장이 들어가기에 가장 적절한 곳은?

☑ **다음 글을 읽고 물음에 답하시오.** (35)

> The findings showed that, when people with mental health conditions participated in a choir, their mental health and wellbeing significantly improved.

A group of psychologists studied individuals with severe mental illness who experienced weekly group music therapy. (①) It included singing familiar songs and composing original songs. (②) The results showed that the group music therapy improved the quality of participants' life, with those participating in a greater number of sessions experiencing the greatest benefits. (③) Focusing on singing, another group of psychologists reviewed articles on the efficacy of group singing as a mental health treatment for individuals living with a mental health condition in a community setting. (④) Group singing provided enjoyment, improved emotional states, developed a sense of belonging and enhanced self-confidence. (⑤)

15. 15)글의 흐름으로 보아, 주어진 문장이 들어가기에 가장 적절한 곳은?

☑ **다음 글을 읽고 물음에 답하시오.** (36)

> As examples, baseball has T ball, football has flag football and junior soccer uses a smaller and lighter ball and (sometimes) a smaller field.

In many sports, people realized the difficulties and even impossibilities of young children participating fully in many adult sport environments. (①) They found the road to success for young children is unlikely if they play on adult fields, courts or arenas with equipment that is too large, too heavy or too fast for them to handle while trying to compete in adult-style competition. (②) Common sense has prevailed: different sports have made adaptations for children. (③) All have junior competitive structures where children play for shorter time periods and often in smaller teams. (④) In a similar way, tennis has adapted the court areas, balls and rackets to make them more appropriate for children under 10. (⑤) The adaptations are progressive and relate to the age of the child.

16. 16)글의 흐름으로 보아, 주어진 문장이 들어가기에 가장 적절한 곳은?

☑ **다음 글을 읽고 물음에 답하시오.** (37)

When a messenger neared the next hut, he began to call out and repeated the message three or four times to the one who was running out to meet him.

With no horses available, the Inca empire excelled at delivering messages on foot. The messengers were stationed on the royal roads to deliver the Inca king's orders and reports coming from his lands. (①) Called Chasquis, they lived in groups of four to six in huts, placed from one to two miles apart along the roads. (②) They were all young men and especially good runners who watched the road in both directions. (③) If they caught sight of another messenger coming, they hurried out to meet them. (④) The Inca built the huts on high ground, in sight of one another. (⑤) The Inca empire could relay messages 1,000 miles (1,610 km) in three or four days under good conditions.

17. 17)글의 흐름으로 보아, 주어진 문장이 들어가기에 <u>가장 적절한</u> 곳은?

☑ **다음 글을 읽고 물음에 답하시오.** (38)

Today, leading taste researchers believe that taste buds are not grouped according to specialty.

The tongue was mapped into separate areas where certain tastes were registered: sweetness at the tip, sourness on the sides, and bitterness at the back of the mouth. (①) Research in the 1980s and 1990s, however, demonstrated that the "tongue map" explanation of how we taste was, in fact, totally wrong. (②) As it turns out, the map was a misinterpretation and mistranslation of research conducted in Germany at the turn of the twentieth century. (③) Sweetness, saltiness, bitterness, and sourness can be tasted everywhere in the mouth, although they may be perceived at a little different intensities at different sites. (④) Moreover, the mechanism at work is not place, but time. (⑤) It's not that you taste sweetness at the tip of your tongue, but rather that you register that perception first.

18. 18)글의 흐름으로 보아, 주어진 문장이 들어가기에 <u>가장 적절한</u> 곳은?

☑ **다음 글을 읽고 물음에 답하시오.** (39)

With this in mind, every healing session needs to be explored differently, and each healing treatment should be adjusted to suit the specific needs of the animal.

No two animals are alike. (①) Animals from the same litter will display some of the same features, but will not be exactly the same as each other; therefore, they may not respond in entirely the same way during a healing session. (②) Environmental factors can also determine how the animal will respond during the treatment. (③) For instance, a cat in a rescue center will respond very differently than a cat within a domestic home environment. (④) In addition, animals that experience healing for physical illness will react differently than those accepting healing for emotional confusion. (⑤) You will learn as you go; healing is a constant learning process.

19. 19)글의 흐름으로 보아, 주어진 문장이 들어가기에 <u>가장 적절한</u> 곳은?

☑ **다음 글을 읽고 물음에 답하시오.** (40)

When your judgment is clouded by emotions, this puts in biases and all kinds of other negativities that hold you back.

The mind has parts that are known as the conscious mind and the subconscious mind. The subconscious mind is very fast to act and doesn't deal with emotions. It deals with memories of your responses to life, your memories and recognition. However, the conscious mind is the one that you have more control over. (①) You think. (②) You can choose whether to carry on a thought or to add emotion to it and this is the part of your mind that lets you down frequently because — fueled by emotions — you make the wrong decisions time and time again. (③) Scared of spiders? Scared of the dark? There are reasons for all of these fears, but they originate in the conscious mind. (④) They only become real fears when the subconscious mind records your reactions. (⑤)

20. 20)글의 흐름으로 보아, 주어진 문장이 들어가기에 <u>가장 적절한</u> 곳은?

☑ **다음 글을 읽고 물음에 답하시오.** (41-42)

Not knowing the norms of another community is the central problem of cross-cultural communication.

Norms are everywhere, defining what is "normal" and guiding our interpretations of social life at every turn. As a simple example, there is a norm in Anglo society to say Thank you to strangers who have just done something to help, such as open a door for you, point out that you've just dropped something, or give you directions. There is no law that forces you to say Thank you. But if people don't say Thank you in these cases it is marked. (①) People expect that you will say it. (②) You become responsible. (③) Failing to say it will be both surprising and worthy of criticism. (④) To continue the Thank you example, even though another culture may have an expression that appears translatable (many don't), there may be different norms for its usage, for example, such that you should say Thank you only when the cost someone has caused is considerable. (⑤) In such a case it would sound ridiculous (i.e., unexpected, surprising, and worthy of criticism) if you were to thank someone for something so minor as holding a door open for you.

21. 21)글의 흐름으로 보아, 주어진 문장이 들어가기에 <u>가장 적절한</u> 곳은?

☑ **다음 글을 읽고 물음에 답하시오.** (43-45)

Use the web to help your people reach their goals. Make good use of their ideas, dreams, and visions.

Long ago, when the world was young, an old Native American spiritual leader Odawa had a dream on a high mountain. In his dream, Iktomi, the great spirit and searcher of wisdom, appeared to him in the form of a spider. Iktomi spoke to him in a holy language. Iktomi told Odawa about the cycles of life. He said, "We all begin our lives as babies, move on to childhood, and then to adulthood. (①) Finally, we come to old age, where we must be taken care of as babies again". Iktomi also told him that there are good and bad forces in each stage of life. (②) "If we listen to the good forces, they will guide us in the right direction. (③) But if we listen to the bad forces, they will lead us the wrong way and may harm us", Iktomi said. (④) When Iktomi finished speaking, he spun a web and gave it to Odawa. He said to Odawa, "The web is a perfect circle with a hole in the center. (⑤) If you believe in the great spirit, the web will catch your good ideas and the bad ones will go through the hole". Right after Odawa woke up, he went back to his village. Odawa shared Iktomi's lesson with his people. Today, many Native Americans have dream catchers hanging above their beds. Dream catchers are believed to filter out bad dreams. The good dreams are captured in the web of life and carried with the people. The bad dreams pass through the hole in the web and are no longer a part of their lives.

22. 22)글의 흐름으로 보아, 주어진 문장이 들어가기에 <u>가장 적절한</u> 곳은?

23. 23) 18

Dear Ms. Jane Watson, I am John Austin, a science teacher at Crestville High School.

(A) They are big fans of your book, so I'd like to ask you to visit our school and give a special lecture. We can set the date and time to suit your schedule.

(B) We would be very grateful if you could come. Best regards, John Austin

(C) Having you at our school would be a fantastic experience for the students.

(D) Recently I was impressed by the latest book you wrote about the environment. Also my students read your book and had a class discussion about it.

24. 24) 19

Marilyn and her three-year-old daughter, Sarah, took a trip to the beach, where Sarah built her first sandcastle.

(A) She ran to Marilyn, saying she would never build a sandcastle again. Marilyn said, "Part of the joy of building a sandcastle is that, in the end, we give it as a gift to the ocean."

(B) Sarah loved this idea and responded with enthusiasm to the idea of building another castle — this time, even closer to the water so the ocean would get its gift sooner!

(C) Moments later, an enormous wave destroyed Sarah's castle. In response to the loss of her sandcastle, tears streamed down Sarah's cheeks and her heart was broken.

25. 25) 20

Magic is what we all wish for to happen in our life.

(A) If you struggle with getting up early in the morning, then write a positive statement such as "I get up early in the morning at 5:00 am every day." Once you write these statements, get ready to witness magic and confidence.

(B) Do you love the movie Cinderella like me? Well, in real life, you can also create magic.

(C) Just change the challenge statement into positive statements. Let me give you an example here.

(D) You will be surprised that just by writing these statements, there is a shift in the way you think and act. Suddenly you feel more powerful and positive.

(E) Here's the trick. Write down all the real-time challenges that you face and deal with.

26. 26) 21

Consider the seemingly simple question How many senses are there?

(A) These examples tell us that "senses cannot be clearly divided into a limited number of specific kinds," Macpherson wrote in The Senses. Instead of trying to push animal senses into Aristotelian buckets, we should study them for what they are.

(B) Around 2,370 years ago, Aristotle wrote that there are five, in both humans and animals — sight, hearing, smell, taste, and touch. However, according to the philosopher Fiona Macpherson, there are reasons to doubt it. For a start, Aristotle missed a few in humans: the perception of your own body which is different from touch and the sense of balance which has links to both touch and vision.

(C) Other animals have senses that are even harder to categorize. Many vertebrates have a different sense system for detecting odors. Some snakes can detect the body heat of their prey.

27. 27) 22

When we think of leaders, we may think of people such as Abraham Lincoln or Martin Luther King, Jr.

(A) Through diligence and experience, they improved upon their ideas by sharing them with others, seeking their opinions and feedback and constantly looking for the best way to accomplish goals for a group.

(B) Thus we all have the potential to be leaders at school, in our communities, and at work, regardless of age or experience.

(C) If you consider the historical importance and far-reaching influence of these individuals, leadership might seem like a noble and high goal. But like all of us, these people started out as students, workers, and citizens who possessed ideas about how some aspect of daily life could be improved on a larger scale.

28. 28) 23

Crop rotation is the process in which farmers change the crops they grow in their fields in a special order.

(A) Each crop enriches the soil for the next crop.

(B) For example, if a farmer has three fields, he or she may grow carrots in the first field, green beans in the second, and tomatoes in the third. The next year, green beans will be in the first field, tomatoes in the second field, and carrots will be in the third.

(C) In year three, the crops will rotate again. By the fourth year, the crops will go back to their original order.

(D) This type of farming is sustainable because the soil stays healthy.

29. 29) 24

Working around the whole painting, rather than concentrating on one area at a time, will mean you can stop at any point and the painting can be considered "finished."

(A) Putting too much into a painting can spoil its impact and leave it looking overworked.

(B) If you find yourself struggling to decide whether you have finished, take a break and come back to it later with fresh eyes.

(C) It is important to take a few steps back from the painting from time to time to assess your progress.

(D) Then you can decide whether any areas of your painting would benefit from further refinement.

(E) Artists often find it difficult to know when to stop painting, and it can be tempting to keep on adding more to your work.

30. 30) 25

The above graph shows the extent to which young people aged 16-25 in six countries had fear about climate change in 2021.

(A) The Philippines had the highest percentage of young people who said they were extremely or very worried, at 84 percent, followed by 67 percent in Brazil. More than 60 percent of young people in Portugal said they were extremely worried or very worried.

(B) In France, the percentage of young people who were extremely worried was lower than that of young people who were very worried. In the United Kingdom, the percentage of young generation who said that they were very worried was 29 percent.

(C) In the United States, the total percentage of extremely worried and very worried youth was the smallest among the six countries.

31. 31) 26

Jaroslav Heyrovsky was born in Prague on December 20, 1890, as the fifth child of Leopold Heyrovsky.

(A) In 1926, Jaroslav became the first Professor of Physical Chemistry at Charles University in Prague. He won the Nobel Prize in chemistry in 1959.

(B) From 1910 to 1914 he continued his studies at University College, London. Throughout the First World War, Jaroslav served in a military hospital.

(C) In 1901 Jaroslav went to a secondary school called the Akademicke Gymnasium. Rather than Latin and Greek, he showed a strong interest in the natural sciences. At Czech University in Prague he studied chemistry, physics, and mathematics.

32. 32) 29

It would be hard to overstate how important meaningful work is to human beings — work that provides a sense of fulfillment and empowerment.

(A) Those most satisfied with their work are also much more likely to be happier with their lives overall.

(B) Those who have found deeper meaning in their careers find their days much more energizing and satisfying, and count their employment as one of their greatest sources of joy and pride.

(C) For her book Happiness at Work, researcher Jessica Pryce-Jones conducted a study of 3,000 workers in seventy-nine countries, finding that those who took greater satisfaction from their work were 150 percent more likely to have a happier life overall.

(D) Sonya Lyubomirsky, professor of psychology at the University of California, has conducted numerous workplace studies showing that when people are more fulfilled on the job, they not only produce higher quality work and a greater output, but also generally earn higher incomes.

33. 33) 30

The rate of speed at which one is traveling will greatly determine the ability to process detail in the environment.

(A) The fastest users of the street, motorists, therefore have a much more limited ability to process details along the street — a motorist simply has little time or ability to appreciate design details.

(B) Joggers and bicyclists fall somewhere in between these polar opposites; while they travel faster than pedestrians, their rate of speed is ordinarily much slower than that of the typical motorist.

(C) Our ability to distinguish detail in the environment is therefore ideally suited to movement at speeds of perhaps five miles per hour and under.

(D) In evolutionary terms, human senses are adapted to the speed at which humans move through space under their own power while walking.

(E) On the other hand, pedestrian travel, being much slower, allows for the appreciation of environmental detail.

34. 34) 31

Every species has certain climatic requirements — what degree of heat or cold it can endure, for example.

(A) All creatures are capable of some degree of movement.

(B) A creature must get from the place it is born — often occupied by its parent — to a place where it can survive, grow, and reproduce.

(C) From fossils, scientists know that even creatures like trees moved with surprising speed during past periods of climate change.

(D) Even creatures that appear immobile, like trees and barnacles, are capable of dispersal at some stage of their life — as a seed, in the case of the tree, or as a larva, in the case of the barnacle.

(E) When the climate changes, the places that satisfy those requirements change, too. Species are forced to follow.

35. 35) 32

No respectable boss would say, "I make it a point to discourage my staff from speaking up, and I maintain a culture that prevents disagreeing viewpoints from ever getting aired."

(A) In the interviews, the featured leaders are asked about their management techniques, and regularly claim to continually encourage internal protest from more junior staffers.

(B) This idea can be found throughout the series of conversations with corporate, university, and nonprofit leaders, published weekly in the business sections of newspapers.

(C) As Bot Pittman remarked in one of these conversations: "I want us to listen to these dissenters because they may intend to tell you why we can't do something, but if you listen hard, what they're really telling you is what you must do to get something done."

(D) If anything, most bosses even say that they are pro-dissent.

36. 36) ³³

One of the most striking characteristics of a sleeping animal or person is that they do not respond normally to environmental stimuli.

(A) If you open the eyelids of a sleeping mammal the eyes will not see normally — they are functionally blind. Some visual information apparently gets in, but it is not normally processed as it is shortened or weakened; same with the other sensing systems.

(B) But as sleep would be impossible without it, it seems essential to its definition. Nevertheless, many animals (including humans) use the intermediate state of drowsiness to derive some benefits of sleep without total perceptual disengagement.

(C) Stimuli are registered but not processed normally and they fail to wake the individual. Perceptual disengagement probably serves the function of protecting sleep, so some authors do not count it as part of the definition of sleep itself.

37. 37) ³⁴

A number of research studies have shown how experts in a field often experience difficulties when introducing newcomers to that field.

(A) Experts can become insensitive to how hard a task is for the beginner, an effect referred to as the 'curse of knowledge'.

(B) Her participants even underestimated how long it had taken themselves to acquire that skill in an earlier session.

(C) Knowing that experts forget how hard it was for them to learn, we can understand the need to look at the learning process through students' eyes, rather than making assumptions about how students 'should be' learning.

(D) For example, in a genuine training situation, Dr Pamela Hinds found that people expert in using mobile phones were remarkably less accurate than novice phone users in judging how long it takes people to learn to use the phones.

(E) Dr Hinds was able to show that as people acquired the skill, they then began to underestimate the level of difficulty of that skill.

38. 38) ³⁵

A group of psychologists studied individuals with severe mental illness who experienced weekly group music therapy, including singing familiar songs and composing original songs.

(A) The results showed that the group music therapy improved the quality of participants' life, with those participating in a greater number of sessions experiencing the greatest benefits.

(B) Group singing provided enjoyment, improved emotional states, developed a sense of belonging and enhanced self-confidence.

(C) The findings showed that, when people with mental health conditions participated in a choir, their mental health and wellbeing significantly improved.

(D) Focusing on singing, another group of psychologists reviewed articles on the efficacy of group singing as a mental health treatment for individuals living with a mental health condition in a community setting.

39. 39) ³⁶

In many sports, people realized the difficulties and even impossibilities of young children participating fully in many adult sport environments.

(A) They found the road to success for young children is unlikely if they play on adult fields, courts or arenas with equipment that is too large, too heavy or too fast for them to handle while trying to compete in adult-style competition. Common sense has prevailed: different sports have made adaptations for children.

(B) As examples, baseball has T ball, football has flag football and junior soccer uses a smaller and lighter ball and (sometimes) a smaller field. All have junior competitive structures where children play for shorter time periods and often in smaller teams.

(C) In a similar way, tennis has adapted the court areas, balls and rackets to make them more appropriate for children under 10. The adaptations are progressive and relate to the age of the child.

40. 40) 37

With no horses available, the Inca empire excelled at delivering messages on foot.

(A) When a messenger neared the next hut, he began to call out and repeated the message three or four times to the one who was running out to meet him. The Inca empire could relay messages 1,000 miles (1,610 km) in three or four days under good conditions.

(B) The messengers were stationed on the royal roads to deliver the Inca king's orders and reports coming from his lands. Called Chasquis, they lived in groups of four to six in huts, placed from one to two miles apart along the roads. They were all young men and especially good runners who watched the road in both directions.

(C) If they caught sight of another messenger coming, they hurried out to meet them. The Inca built the huts on high ground, in sight of one another.

41. 41) 38

The tongue was mapped into separate areas where certain tastes were registered: sweetness at the tip, sourness on the sides, and bitterness at the back of the mouth.

(A) Moreover, the mechanism at work is not place, but time. It's not that you taste sweetness at the tip of your tongue, but rather that you register that perception first.

(B) Today, leading taste researchers believe that taste buds are not grouped according to specialty. Sweetness, saltiness, bitterness, and sourness can be tasted everywhere in the mouth, although they may be perceived at a little different intensities at different sites.

(C) Research in the 1980s and 1990s, however, demonstrated that the "tongue map" explanation of how we taste was, in fact, totally wrong. As it turns out, the map was a misinterpretation and mistranslation of research conducted in Germany at the turn of the twentieth century.

42. 42) 39

No two animals are alike.

(A) With this in mind, every healing session needs to be explored differently, and each healing treatment should be adjusted to suit the specific needs of the animal.

(B) For instance, a cat in a rescue center will respond very differently than a cat within a domestic home environment. In addition, animals that experience healing for physical illness will react differently than those accepting healing for emotional confusion.

(C) Animals from the same litter will display some of the same features, but will not be exactly the same as each other; therefore, they may not respond in entirely the same way during a healing session. Environmental factors can also determine how the animal will respond during the treatment.

(D) You will learn as you go; healing is a constant learning process.

43. 43) 40

The mind has parts that are known as the conscious mind and the subconscious mind.

(A) You can choose whether to carry on a thought or to add emotion to it and this is the part of your mind that lets you down frequently because — fueled by emotions — you make the wrong decisions time and time again. When your judgment is clouded by emotions, this puts in biases and all kinds of other negativities that hold you back.

(B) There are reasons for all of these fears, but they originate in the conscious mind. They only become real fears when the subconscious mind records your reactions.

(C) Scared of spiders? Scared of the dark?

(D) However, the conscious mind is the one that you have more control over. You think.

(E) The subconscious mind is very fast to act and doesn't deal with emotions. It deals with memories of your responses to life, your memories and recognition.

44. 44) ⁴¹⁻⁴²

Norms are everywhere, defining what is "normal" and guiding our interpretations of social life at every turn.

(A) In such a case it would sound ridiculous (i.e., unexpected, surprising, and worthy of criticism) if you were to thank someone for something so minor as holding a door open for you.

(B) You become responsible. Failing to say it will be both surprising and worthy of criticism.

(C) Not knowing the norms of another community is the central problem of cross-cultural communication. To continue the Thank you example, even though another culture may have an expression that appears translatable (many don't), there may be different norms for its usage, for example, such that you should say Thank you only when the cost someone has caused is considerable.

(D) But if people don't say Thank you in these cases it is marked. People expect that you will say it.

(E) As a simple example, there is a norm in Anglo society to say Thank you to strangers who have just done something to help, such as open a door for you, point out that you've just dropped something, or give you directions. There is no law that forces you to say Thank you.

45. 45) ⁴³⁻⁴⁵

Long ago, when the world was young, an old Native American spiritual leader Odawa had a dream on a high mountain.

(A) Right after Odawa woke up, he went back to his village. Odawa shared Iktomi's lesson with his people. Today, many Native Americans have dream catchers hanging above their beds. Dream catchers are believed to filter out bad dreams. The good dreams are captured in the web of life and carried with the people. The bad dreams pass through the hole in the web and are no longer a part of their lives.

(B) But if we listen to the bad forces, they will lead us the wrong way and may harm us," Iktomi said. When Iktomi finished speaking, he spun a web and gave it to Odawa. He said to Odawa, "The web is a perfect circle with a hole in the center. Use the web to help your people reach their goals. Make good use of their ideas, dreams, and visions. If you believe in the great spirit, the web will catch your good ideas and the bad ones will go through the hole."

(C) In his dream, Iktomi, the great spirit and searcher of wisdom, appeared to him in the form of a spider. Iktomi spoke to him in a holy language. Iktomi told Odawa about the cycles of life. He said, "We all begin our lives as babies, move on to childhood, and then to adulthood. Finally, we come to old age, where we must be taken care of as babies again." Iktomi also told him that there are good and bad forces in each stage of life. "If we listen to the good forces, they will guide us in the right direction.

2024 고1 3월 모의고사

❶ voca   ❷ text   ❸ [/]   ❹ _____   ❺ quiz 1   ❻ quiz 2   ❼ quiz 3   ❽ quiz 4   ❾ quiz 5

1. 1)밑줄 친 부분 중, 어법, 혹은 문맥상 어색한 곳을 고르시오. 18

Dear Ms. Jane Watson, I am John Austin, a science teacher at Crestville High School. Recently I was impressed by the ① **latest** book you wrote about the environment. Also my students read your book and had a class discussion about it. They are big fans of your book, so I'd like to ask you to visit our school and give a special lecture. We can ② **set** the date and time to ③ **suiting** your schedule. ④ **Having** you at our school would be a fantastic experience for the students. We would be very ⑤ **grateful** if you could come. Best regards, John Austin

2. 2)밑줄 친 부분 중, 어법, 혹은 문맥상 어색한 곳을 고르시오. 19

Marilyn and her three-year-old daughter, Sarah, took a trip to the beach, ① **where** Sarah built her first sandcastle. Moments later, an enormous wave ② **destroyed** Sarah's castle. In response to the ③ **loss** of her sandcastle, tears streamed down Sarah's cheeks and her heart was broken. She ran to Marilyn, saying she would never build a sandcastle again. Marilyn said, "Part of the joy of building a sandcastle is ④ **what** , in the end, we give it as a gift to the ocean". Sarah loved this idea and responded with enthusiasm to the idea of building ⑤ **another** castle — this time, even closer to the water so the ocean would get its gift sooner!

3. 3)밑줄 친 부분 중, 어법, 혹은 문맥상 어색한 곳을 고르시오. 20

Magic is what we all wish for to happen in our life. Do you love the movie Cinderella like me? Well, in real life, you can also create magic. Here's the trick. ① **Write** down all the real-time challenges ② **that** you face and ③ **deal**. Just change the challenge statement into positive statements. Let me give you an example here. If you struggle with getting up early in the morning, then write a positive statement such as "I get up early in the morning at 5:00 am every day". Once you write these statements, get ready to witness magic and ④ **confidence** . You will be surprised that just by writing these statements, there is a shift in the way you think and act. Suddenly you feel ⑤ **more** powerful and positive.

4. 4)밑줄 친 부분 중, 어법, 혹은 문맥상 어색한 곳을 고르시오. 21

Consider the seemingly simple question How many senses ① **are** there? Around 2,370 years ago, Aristotle wrote that there are five, in both humans and animals — sight, hearing, smell, taste, and touch. ② **However** , according to the philosopher Fiona Macpherson, there are reasons to doubt it. For a start, Aristotle missed a few in humans: the perception of your own body which is different from touch and the sense of balance which has links to both touch and vision. Other animals have senses that are even harder to categorize. Many vertebrates have a different sense system for detecting odors. Some snakes can detect the body heat of their prey. These examples tell us that "senses ③ **cannot** be clearly divided into a limited number of ④ **vague** kinds", Macpherson wrote in The Senses. Instead of trying to push animal senses into Aristotelian buckets, we should study them for ⑤ **what** they are .

5. 5)밑줄 친 부분 중, 어법, 혹은 문맥상 어색한 곳을 고르시오. 22

When we think of leaders, we may think of people such as Abraham Lincoln or Martin Luther King, Jr. If you consider the historical importance and far-reaching influence of these individuals, leadership might seem like a noble and high goal. But like all of us, these people started out as students, workers, and citizens who ① **possessed** ideas about ② **how** some aspect of daily life could be improved on a larger scale. Through diligence and experience, they improved upon their ideas by sharing them with others, ③ **sought** their opinions and feedback and constantly looking for the best way to ④ **accomplish** goals for a group. Thus we all have the potential to be leaders at school, in our communities, and at work, ⑤ **regardless of** age or experience.

6. 6)**밑줄 친 부분 중, 어법, 혹은 문맥상 어색한 곳을 고르시오.** 23

Crop rotation is the process ① **in which** farmers change the crops they grow in their fields in a special order. For example, if a farmer ② **has** three fields, he or she may grow carrots in the first field, green beans in the second, and tomatoes in the third. The next year, green beans will be in the first field, tomatoes in the second field, and carrots ③ **will** be in the third. In year three, the crops will rotate again. By the fourth year, the crops will go back to their original order. Each ④ **crop** enriches the soil for the next crop. This type of farming is ⑤ **consuming** because the soil stays healthy .

7. 7)**밑줄 친 부분 중, 어법, 혹은 문맥상 어색한 곳을 고르시오.** 24

① **Working** around the whole painting, rather than concentrating on one area at a time, will mean you can stop at any point and the painting can be considered "finished". Artists often find ② **them** difficult to know when to stop painting , and it can be ③ **tempting** to keep on adding more to your work. It is important to take a few steps back from the painting from time to time to assess your progress. Putting too much into a painting can ④ **spoil** its impact and leave it looking ⑤ **overworked** . If you find yourself struggling to decide whether you have finished, take a break and come back to it later with fresh eyes. Then you can decide whether any areas of your painting would benefit from further refinement.

8. 8)**밑줄 친 부분 중, 어법, 혹은 문맥상 어색한 곳을 고르시오.** 26

Jaroslav Heyrovsky was born in Prague on December 20, 1890, as the ① **fifth** child of Leopold Heyrovsky. In 1901 Jaroslav went to a secondary school ② **called** the Akademicke Gymnasium. Rather ③ **then** Latin and Greek, he showed a strong interest in the ④ **natural** sciences. At Czech University in Prague he studied chemistry, physics, and mathematics. From 1910 to 1914 he continued his studies at University College, London. Throughout the First World War, Jaroslav served in a military hospital. In 1926, Jaroslav became the first Professor of Physical Chemistry at Charles University in Prague. He ⑤ **won** the Nobel Prize in chemistry in 1959.

9. 9)**밑줄 친 부분 중, 어법, 혹은 문맥상 어색한 곳을 고르시오.** 29

It would be ① **hard** to overstate how important meaningful work is to human beings — work that provides a sense of fulfillment and empowerment. Those who have found deeper meaning in their careers find their days much ② **more** energizing and satisfying, and count their employment as one of their greatest sources of joy and pride. Sonya Lyubomirsky, professor of psychology at the University of California, has conducted numerous workplace studies showing that when people are ③ **more** fulfilled on the job, they not only produce higher quality work and a greater output, but also generally earn higher incomes. Those most ④ **satisfying** their work are also much more likely to be happier with their lives overall. For her book Happiness at Work, researcher Jessica Pryce-Jones conducted a study of 3,000 workers in seventy-nine countries, finding that those who took greater satisfaction from their work were 150 percent ⑤ **more** likely to have a happier life overall.

10. 10)**밑줄 친 부분 중, 어법, 혹은 문맥상 어색한 곳을 고르시오.** 30

The rate of speed at which one is traveling will greatly determine the ability to process detail in the environment. In evolutionary terms, human senses are ① **adopted** to the speed at which humans move through space under their own power ② **while** walking. Our ability to distinguish detail in the environment is therefore ideally suited to movement at speeds of perhaps five miles per hour and under. The fastest users of the street, motorists, therefore have a much more limited ability to process details along the street — a motorist simply has ③ **little** time or ability to appreciate design details. On the other hand, pedestrian travel, being much slower, allows for the ④ **appreciation** of environmental detail. Joggers and bicyclists fall somewhere in between these polar opposites; while they travel ⑤ **faster** than pedestrians, their rate of speed is ordinarily much slower than that of the typical motorist.

11. ¹¹⁾밑줄 친 부분 중, 어법, 혹은 문맥상 어색한 곳을 고르시오. ³¹

Every species has certain climatic requirements — ① **that** degree of heat or cold it can endure, for example. When the climate changes, the places that satisfy those requirements change, too. Species are forced to follow. All creatures are ② **capable** of some degree of movement. Even creatures that appear ③ **immobile** , like trees and barnacles, are capable of ④ **dispersal** at some stage of their life — as a seed, in the case of the tree, or as a larva, in the case of the barnacle. A creature must get from the place it is born — often occupied by its parent — to a place ⑤ **where** it can survive, grow, and reproduce. From fossils, scientists know that even creatures like trees moved with surprising speed during past periods of climate change.

12. ¹²⁾밑줄 친 부분 중, 어법, 혹은 문맥상 어색한 곳을 고르시오. ³²

No ① **respectable** boss would say, "I make it a point to discourage my staff from speaking up, and I maintain a culture that prevents disagreeing viewpoints from ever getting aired ". If anything, most bosses even say that they are ② **pro-assent** . This idea can be found throughout the series of conversations with corporate, university, and nonprofit leaders, published weekly in the business sections of newspapers. In the interviews, the featured leaders are asked about their management techniques, and regularly claim to continually encourage internal protest from ③ **more** junior staffers. As Bot Pittman remarked in one of these conversations: "I want us to listen to these ④ **dissenters** because they may intend to tell you why we can't do something, but if you listen ⑤ **hard** , what they're really telling you is what you must do to get something done ".

13. ¹³⁾밑줄 친 부분 중, 어법, 혹은 문맥상 어색한 곳을 고르시오. ³³

One of the most striking characteristics of a sleeping animal or person is that they do not respond normally to environmental stimuli. If you open the eyelids of a sleeping mammal the eyes will not see normally — they are functionally ① **blind**. Some visual information ② **apparent** gets in, but it is not normally ③ **processed** as it is shortened or weakened; same with the other sensing systems. Stimuli ④ **are** registered but not processed normally and they fail ⑤ **to wake** the individual. Perceptual disengagement probably serves the function of protecting sleep, so some authors do not count it as part of the definition of sleep itself . But as sleep would be impossible without it, it seems essential to its definition. Nevertheless, many animals (including humans) use the intermediate state of drowsiness to derive some benefits of sleep without total perceptual disengagement.

14. ¹⁴⁾밑줄 친 부분 중, 어법, 혹은 문맥상 어색한 곳을 고르시오. ³⁴

A number of research studies have shown how experts in a field often experience difficulties when ① **introducing** newcomers to that field. For example, in a genuine training situation, Dr Pamela Hinds found that people expert in using mobile phones were remarkably ② **less** accurate than novice phone users in judging how long it takes people to learn to use the phones. Experts can become insensitive to how hard a task is for the beginner, an effect referred to as the 'curse of knowledge'. Dr Hinds was able to show that as people acquired the skill, they then began to underestimate the level of difficulty of that skill. Her participants even underestimated how long it had taken themselves to ③ **acquire** that skill in an earlier session. Knowing that experts ④ **forget** how hard ⑤ **that** was for them to learn, we can understand the need to look at the learning process through students' eyes, rather than making assumptions about how students 'should be' learning.

15. 15)밑줄 친 부분 중, 어법, 혹은 문맥상 어색한 곳을 고르시오. 35

A group of psychologists studied individuals with severe mental illness who experienced weekly group music therapy, including singing familiar songs and composing ① **original** songs. The results showed that the group music therapy improved the quality of participants' life, with those participating in a greater number of sessions ② **experiencing** the greatest benefits. Focusing on singing, another group of psychologists reviewed articles on the ③ **efficacy** of group singing as a mental health treatment for individuals living with a mental health condition in a community setting. The findings showed that, when people with mental health conditions ④ **participating** in a choir, their mental health and wellbeing significantly improved. Group singing provided enjoyment, improved emotional states, developed a sense of belonging and ⑤ **enhanced** self-confidence.

16. 16)밑줄 친 부분 중, 어법, 혹은 문맥상 어색한 곳을 고르시오. 36

In many sports, people realized the difficulties and even impossibilities of young children participating fully in many adult sport environments. They found the road to success for young children is ① **unlikely** ② **if** they play on adult fields, courts or arenas with equipment that is too large, too heavy or too fast for them to handle while trying to compete in adult-style competition. Common sense has prevailed : different sports have made adaptations for children. As examples, baseball has T ball, football has flag football and junior soccer uses a smaller and lighter ball and (sometimes) a smaller field. All have junior competitive structures ③ **where** children play for shorter time periods and often in smaller teams. In a similar way, tennis has ④ **adapted** the court areas, balls and rackets to make them more appropriate for children under 10. The ⑤ **adoptions** are progressive and relate to the age of the child.

17. 17)밑줄 친 부분 중, 어법, 혹은 문맥상 어색한 곳을 고르시오. 37

With no horses ① **available** , the Inca empire excelled at delivering messages on foot. The messengers were stationed on the ② **royal** roads to deliver the Inca king's orders and reports coming from his lands. Called Chasquis, they lived in groups of four to six in huts, placed from one to two miles apart along the roads. They were all young men and especially good runners who watched the road in both directions. If they ③ **were caught** sight of another messenger coming , they hurried out to meet them. The Inca built the huts on high ground, in sight of one ④ **another** . When a messenger neared the next hut, he began to call out and repeated the message three or four times to the one who was running out to meet him. The Inca empire could relay messages 1,000 miles (1,610 km) in three or four days ⑤ **under** good conditions.

18. 18)밑줄 친 부분 중, 어법, 혹은 문맥상 어색한 곳을 고르시오. 38

The tongue was mapped into separate areas where certain tastes were registered: sweetness at the tip, sourness on the sides, and bitterness at the back of the mouth. Research in the 1980s and 1990s, however , demonstrated that the "tongue map" explanation of how we taste ① **was** , in fact, totally wrong. As it turns out, the map was a misinterpretation and ② **translation** of research conducted in Germany at the turn of the twentieth century. Today, ③ **leading** taste researchers believe that taste buds are not grouped according to specialty. Sweetness, saltiness, bitterness, and sourness can be tasted everywhere in the mouth, although they may be perceived at a little different intensities at different sites. ④ **Moreover,** the mechanism at work is not place , but ⑤ **time** . It's not that you taste sweetness at the tip of your tongue, but rather that you register that perception first.

19. ¹⁹⁾밑줄 친 부분 중, 어법, 혹은 문맥상 어색한 곳을 고르시오. ³⁹

No two animals are ① **alike** . Animals from the ② **same** litter will display some of the same features, but will not be exactly the same as each other; therefore, they may not respond in entirely the same way during a healing session. Environmental factors can also determine how the animal will respond during the treatment. For instance, a cat in a rescue center will respond very differently than a cat within a domestic home environment. In ③ **contrast** , animals that experience healing for physical illness will react differently than those accepting healing for emotional confusion. With this in mind, every healing session needs to ④ **be explored** differently, and each healing treatment should ⑤ **be adjusted** to suit the specific needs of the animal. You will learn as you go; healing is a constant learning process.

20. ²⁰⁾밑줄 친 부분 중, 어법, 혹은 문맥상 어색한 곳을 고르시오. ⁴⁰

The mind has parts ① **that** are known as the conscious mind and the subconscious mind. The subconscious mind is very fast to act and doesn't deal with emotions. It deals with memories of your responses to life, your memories and recognition. However, the conscious mind is the one that you have ② **more** control over. You think. You can choose whether to carry on a thought or to add emotion to it and this is the part of your mind that lets you down ③ **frequently** because — ④ **fueled** by emotions — you make the wrong decisions time and time again. When your judgment is clouded by emotions, this puts in biases and all kinds of other negativities that hold you back. Scared of spiders? Scared of the dark? There are reasons for all of these fears, but they originate in the conscious mind. They only become real fears when the ⑤ **conscious** mind records your reactions.

21. ²¹⁾밑줄 친 부분 중, 어법, 혹은 문맥상 어색한 곳을 고르시오. ⁴¹⁻⁴²

① **Norms** are everywhere, defining ② **what** is "normal" and guiding our interpretations of social life at every turn. As a simple example, there is a norm in Anglo society to say Thank you to strangers who have just done something to help, such as open a door for you, point out that you've just dropped something, or give you directions. There is no law that forces you to say

Thank you. But if people don't say Thank you in these cases it is marked. People expect that you will say it. You become ③ **responsibility** . Failing to say it will be both surprising and worthy of criticism. Not knowing the ④ **norms** of another community is the central problem of cross-cultural communication. To continue the Thank you example, even though another culture may have an expression that appears translatable (many don't), there may be different norms for its usage, for example, such that you should say Thank you only when the cost someone has caused is considerable. In such a case it would sound ⑤ **ridiculous** (i.e., unexpected, surprising, and worthy of criticism) if you were to thank someone for something so minor as holding a door open for you.

22. ²²⁾밑줄 친 부분 중, 어법, 혹은 문맥상 어색한 곳을 고르시오. ⁴³⁻⁴⁵

Long ago, when the world was young, an old Native American spiritual leader Odawa had a dream on a high mountain. In his dream, Iktomi, the great spirit and searcher of wisdom, appeared to him in the form of a spider. Iktomi spoke to him in a holy language. Iktomi told Odawa about the cycles of life. He said, "We all begin our lives as babies, move on to childhood, and then to adulthood. Finally, we come to old age, ① **which** we must be taken care of as babies again". Iktomi also told him ② **that** there are good and bad forces in each ③ **stage** of life. "If we listen to the good forces, they will guide us in the right direction. But if we listen to the bad forces, they will lead us the wrong way and may harm us", Iktomi said. When Iktomi finished speaking , he spun a web and gave it to Odawa. He said to Odawa, "The web is a perfect circle with a hole in the center. Use the web to help your people ④ **reach** their goals. Make good use of their ideas, dreams, and visions. If you believe in the great spirit, the web will catch your good ideas and the bad ones will go through the hole". Right after Odawa woke up, he went back to his village. Odawa shared Iktomi's lesson with his people. Today, many Native Americans have dream catchers hanging above their beds. Dream catchers are believed to filter out bad dreams. The good dreams are captured in the web of life and carried with the people. The bad dreams pass through the hole in the web and ⑤ **are** no longer a part of their lives.

2024 고1 3월 모의고사

❶ voca ❷ text ❸ [/] ❹ _____ ❺ quiz 1 ❻ quiz 2 ❼ quiz 3 ❽ quiz 4 ❾ quiz 5

---

1. 1)밑줄 친 ⓐ~ⓖ 중 어법, 혹은 문맥상 어휘의 사용이 <u>어색한</u> 것끼리 짝지어진 것을 고르시오. 18

Dear Ms. Jane Watson, I am John Austin, a science teacher at Crestville High School. Recently I was ⓐ **impressing** by the ⓑ **latest** book you wrote about the environment. Also my students read your book and had a class discussion about it. They are big fans of your book, so I'd like to ask you ⓒ **visiting** our school and give a special lecture. We can ⓓ **set to** the date and time to ⓔ **suit** your schedule. ⓕ **Having** you at our school would be a fantastic experience for the students. We would be very ⓖ **graceful** if you could come. Best regards, John Austin

① ⓑ, ⓒ, ⓖ   ② ⓔ, ⓕ, ⓖ   ③ ⓐ, ⓒ, ⓓ, ⓕ
④ ⓐ, ⓒ, ⓓ, ⓖ   ⑤ ⓑ, ⓒ, ⓔ, ⓖ

---

2. 2)밑줄 친 ⓐ~ⓔ 중 어법, 혹은 문맥상 어휘의 사용이 <u>어색한</u> 것끼리 짝지어진 것을 고르시오. 19

Marilyn and her three-year-old daughter, Sarah, took a trip to the beach, ⓐ **which** Sarah built her first sandcastle. Moments later, an enormous wave ⓑ **destroying** Sarah's castle. In response to the ⓒ **lose** of her sandcastle, tears streamed down Sarah's cheeks and her heart was broken. She ran to Marilyn, saying she would never build a sandcastle again. Marilyn said, "Part of the joy of building a sandcastle is ⓓ **what** , in the end, we give it as a gift to the ocean". Sarah loved this idea and responded with enthusiasm to the idea of building ⓔ **another** castle — this time, even closer to the water so the ocean would get its gift sooner!

① ⓐ, ⓔ   ② ⓑ, ⓔ   ③ ⓑ, ⓒ, ⓔ
④ ⓑ, ⓓ, ⓔ   ⑤ ⓐ, ⓑ, ⓒ, ⓓ

---

3. 3)밑줄 친 ⓐ~ⓗ 중 어법, 혹은 문맥상 어휘의 사용이 <u>어색한</u> 것끼리 짝지어진 것을 고르시오. 20

Magic is ⓐ **that** we all wish for to happen in our life. Do you love the movie Cinderella like me? Well, in real life, you can also create magic. Here's the trick. ⓑ **Writing** down all the real-time challenges ⓒ **that** you face and ⓓ **deal**. Just change the challenge statement into ⓔ **positive** statements. Let me give you an example here. If you struggle with getting up early in the morning, then write a positive statement such as "I get up early in the morning at 5:00 am every day". Once you write these statements, get ready to witness magic and ⓕ **confidence** . You will be surprised ⓖ **to** just by writing these statements, there is a shift in the way you think and act. Suddenly you feel ⓗ **more** powerful and positive.

① ⓐ, ⓑ, ⓒ   ② ⓑ, ⓕ, ⓗ   ③ ⓐ, ⓑ, ⓒ, ⓗ
④ ⓐ, ⓑ, ⓓ, ⓖ   ⑤ ⓓ, ⓕ, ⓖ, ⓗ

---

4. 4)밑줄 친 ⓐ~ⓙ 중 어법, 혹은 문맥상 어휘의 사용이 <u>어색한</u> 것끼리 짝지어진 것을 고르시오. 21

Consider the seemingly simple question How many senses ⓐ **are** there? Around 2,370 years ago, Aristotle wrote that there are five, in both humans and animals — sight, hearing, smell, taste, and touch. ⓑ **So** , according to the philosopher Fiona Macpherson, there are reasons to ⓒ **doubt** it. For a start, Aristotle missed a few in humans: the ⓓ **deception** of your own body which is different from touch and the sense of balance which has links to both touch and vision. Other animals have senses that are even harder to categorize. Many vertebrates have a different sense system for ⓔ **detecting** odors. Some snakes can detect the body heat of their prey. These examples tell us that "senses ⓕ **cannot** be clearly divided into a ⓖ **limited** number of ⓗ **specific** kinds", Macpherson wrote in The Senses. Instead of trying to push animal senses into Aristotelian buckets, we should study them for ⓘ **what** they ⓙ **are** .

① ⓐ, ⓓ   ② ⓐ, ⓗ   ③ ⓑ, ⓓ   ④ ⓓ, ⓗ   ⑤ ⓓ, ⓖ, ⓗ

---

5. 5)**밑줄 친 ⓐ~ⓘ 중 어법, 혹은 문맥상 어휘의 사용이 어색한 것끼리 짝지어진 것을 고르시오.** 22

When we think of leaders, we may think of people such as Abraham Lincoln or Martin Luther King, Jr. ⓐ **If** you consider the historical importance and far-reaching influence of these individuals, leadership might seem like a ⓑ **novel** and high goal. But like all of us, these people started out as students, workers, and citizens who ⓒ **possessed** ideas about ⓓ **how** some aspect of daily life could be improved on a larger scale. Through ⓔ **diligence** and experience, they improved upon their ideas by ⓕ **sharing** them with others, ⓖ **sought** their opinions and feedback and constantly looking for the best way to ⓗ **abandon** goals for a group. Thus we all have the potential to be leaders at school, in our communities, and at work, ⓘ **along with** age or experience.

① ⓐ, ⓓ, ⓗ   ② ⓑ, ⓔ, ⓘ   ③ ⓒ, ⓓ, ⓗ
④ ⓐ, ⓓ, ⓔ, ⓗ   ⑤ ⓑ, ⓖ, ⓗ, ⓘ

6. 6)**밑줄 친 ⓐ~ⓜ 중 어법, 혹은 문맥상 어휘의 사용이 어색한 것끼리 짝지어진 것을 고르시오.** 23

Crop rotation is the ⓐ **process** ⓑ **in which** farmers change the crops they grow in their fields in a special order. For example, ⓒ **if** a farmer ⓓ **has** three fields, he or she may grow carrots in the first field, green beans in the second, and tomatoes in the third. The next year, green beans ⓔ **will** be in the first field, tomatoes in the second field, and carrots ⓕ **will** be in the third. In year three, the crops ⓖ **will** rotate again. By the ⓗ **fourth** year, the crops will go back to their ⓘ **previous** order. Each ⓙ **crop** ⓚ **are enriched by** the soil for the next crop. This type of farming is ⓛ **sustainable** because the soil stays ⓜ **healthy** .

① ⓕ, ⓚ   ② ⓘ, ⓚ   ③ ⓙ, ⓚ
④ ⓙ, ⓜ   ⑤ ⓚ, ⓜ

7. 7)**밑줄 친 ⓐ~ⓜ 중 어법, 혹은 문맥상 어휘의 사용이 어색한 것끼리 짝지어진 것을 고르시오.** 24

ⓐ **Work** around the whole painting, rather ⓑ **than** concentrating on one area at a time, will mean you can stop at any point and the painting can be considered "finished". Artists often find ⓒ **it** difficult to know when to stop ⓓ **painting** , and it can be ⓔ **tempting** to keep on adding ⓕ **more** to your work. It is important to take a few steps back from the painting from time to time to ⓖ **assess** your ⓗ **progress**. Putting too much into a painting can ⓘ **enhance** its impact and leave it looking ⓙ **overworked** . If you find yourself ⓚ **struggle** to decide whether you have finished, take a break and come back to it later with fresh eyes. Then you can decide ⓛ **if** any areas of your painting would ⓜ **benefit from** further refinement.

① ⓑ, ⓛ, ⓜ   ② ⓓ, ⓙ, ⓚ   ③ ⓗ, ⓘ, ⓛ
④ ⓐ, ⓘ, ⓙ, ⓛ   ⑤ ⓐ, ⓘ, ⓚ, ⓛ

8. 8)**밑줄 친 ⓐ~ⓔ 중 어법, 혹은 문맥상 어휘의 사용이 어색한 것끼리 짝지어진 것을 고르시오.** 26

Jaroslav Heyrovsky was born in Prague on December 20, 1890, as the ⓐ **fifth** child of Leopold Heyrovsky. In 1901 Jaroslav went to a secondary school ⓑ **was called** the Akademicke Gymnasium. Rather ⓒ **then** Latin and Greek, he showed a strong interest in the ⓓ **natural** sciences. At Czech University in Prague he studied chemistry, physics, and mathematics. From 1910 to 1914 he continued his studies at University College, London. Throughout the First World War, Jaroslav served in a military hospital. In 1926, Jaroslav became the first Professor of Physical Chemistry at Charles University in Prague. He ⓔ **won** the Nobel Prize in chemistry in 1959.

① ⓐ, ⓒ   ② ⓑ, ⓒ   ③ ⓑ, ⓓ
④ ⓐ, ⓑ, ⓔ   ⑤ ⓐ, ⓒ, ⓓ

9. 9)밑줄 친 ⓐ~ⓚ 중 어법, 혹은 문맥상 어휘의 사용이 어색한 것끼리 짝지어진 것을 고르시오. 29

It would be ⓐ **hard** to overstate how ⓑ **important** meaningful work is to human beings — work that provides a sense of fulfillment and empowerment. Those who have found deeper meaning in their careers find their days much ⓒ **more** energizing and satisfying, and count their employment as one of their greatest sources of joy and pride. Sonya Lyubomirsky, professor of psychology at the University of California, has ⓓ **deducted** numerous workplace studies showing that when people are ⓔ **less** fulfilled on the job, they not only produce ⓕ **higher** quality work and a greater output, but also generally earn ⓖ **higher** incomes. Those most ⓗ **satisfied with** their work are also much ⓘ **less** likely to be happier with their lives overall. For her book Happiness at Work, researcher Jessica Pryce-Jones conducted a study of 3,000 workers in seventy-nine countries, finding ⓙ **that** those who took greater satisfaction from their work were 150 percent ⓚ **less** likely to have a happier life overall.

① ⓑ, ⓓ, ⓚ   ② ⓓ, ⓕ, ⓖ   ③ ⓔ, ⓕ, ⓘ
④ ⓑ, ⓒ, ⓕ, ⓚ   ⑤ ⓓ, ⓔ, ⓘ, ⓚ

10. 10)밑줄 친 ⓐ~ⓝ 중 어법, 혹은 문맥상 어휘의 사용이 어색한 것끼리 짝지어진 것을 고르시오. 30

The rate of speed ⓐ **at which** one is traveling will greatly determine the ability to ⓑ **procedure** detail in the environment. In evolutionary terms, human senses are ⓒ **adapted** to the speed at which humans move through space under their own power ⓓ **while** walking. Our ability to ⓔ **distinguish** detail in the environment is therefore ideally suited to movement at speeds of perhaps five miles per hour and under. The fastest users of the street, motorists, therefore have a much ⓕ **more** ⓖ **limitless** ability to process details along the street — a motorist simply has ⓗ **little** time or ability to appreciate design details. On the other hand, pedestrian travel, ⓘ **being** much slower, allows for the ⓙ **appreciation** of environmental detail. Joggers and bicyclists fall somewhere in between these ⓚ **polar** opposites; while they travel ⓛ **slower** than pedestrians, their rate of speed is ordinarily much ⓜ **faster** than ⓝ **that** of the typical motorist.

① ⓐ, ⓜ   ② ⓑ, ⓓ, ⓛ   ③ ⓑ, ⓕ, ⓖ
④ ⓑ, ⓖ, ⓘ, ⓜ   ⑤ ⓓ, ⓖ, ⓘ, ⓜ

11. 11)밑줄 친 ⓐ~ⓛ 중 어법, 혹은 문맥상 어휘의 사용이 어색한 것끼리 짝지어진 것을 고르시오. 31

Every species ⓐ **has** certain ⓑ **climatic** requirements — ⓒ **what** degree of heat or cold it can endure, for example. When the climate changes, the places that satisfy those requirements change, too. Species are ⓓ **forced** to follow. All creatures are ⓔ **capable** of some degree of movement. Even creatures that appear ⓕ **immobile**, like trees and barnacles, are ⓖ **capable** of ⓗ **dispersal** at some stage of their life — as a seed, in the case of the tree, or as a larva, in the case of the barnacle. A creature must get from the place it is born — often occupied by its parent — to a place ⓘ **which** it can survive, grow, and reproduce. From fossils, scientists know ⓙ **that** even creatures like trees ⓚ **moved** with surprising speed ⓛ **while** past periods of climate change.

① ⓑ, ⓛ   ② ⓓ, ⓛ   ③ ⓗ, ⓘ
④ ⓘ, ⓛ   ⑤ ⓒ, ⓖ, ⓘ

12. 12)밑줄 친 ⓐ~ⓚ 중 어법, 혹은 문맥상 어휘의 사용이 어색한 것끼리 짝지어진 것을 고르시오. 32

No ⓐ **respectable** boss would say, "I make it a point to ⓑ **encourage** my staff ⓒ **from speaking** up, and I maintain a culture that prevents disagreeing viewpoints from ever getting ⓓ **aired** ". If anything, most bosses even say that they are ⓔ **pro-assent** . This idea can be found throughout the series of conversations with corporate, university, and nonprofit leaders, published weekly in the business sections of newspapers. In the interviews, the featured leaders ⓕ **asked** about their management techniques, and regularly claim to continually encourage ⓖ **internal** protest from ⓗ **more** junior staffers. As Bot Pittman remarked in one of these conversations: "I want us to listen to these ⓘ **assentors** because they may intend to tell you why we can't do something, but if you listen ⓙ **hard** , what they're really telling you is what you must do to get something ⓚ **done** ".

① ⓑ, ⓔ, ⓙ   ② ⓕ, ⓖ, ⓘ   ③ ⓐ, ⓑ, ⓓ, ⓕ
④ ⓑ, ⓒ, ⓓ, ⓘ   ⑤ ⓑ, ⓔ, ⓕ, ⓘ

13. 13)밑줄 친 ⓐ~ⓛ 중 어법, 혹은 문맥상 어휘의 사용이 어색한 것끼리 짝지어진 것을 고르시오. 33

One of the most striking characteristics of a sleeping animal or person is ⓐ **what** they do not respond normally to environmental stimuli. If you open the eyelids of a sleeping mammal the eyes will not see normally — they are functionally ⓑ **blind**. Some visual information ⓒ **apparently** gets in, but it is not normally ⓓ **processed** as it is shortened or weakened; ⓔ **same** with the other sensing systems. Stimuli ⓕ **is** registered but not processed normally and they fail ⓖ **to wake** the individual. Perceptual ⓗ **disengagement** probably serves the function of protecting sleep, so some authors do not count it as part of the definition of sleep ⓘ **themselves** . But as sleep would be impossible ⓙ **without** it, it seems essential to its definition. Nevertheless, many animals (including humans) use the intermediate state of drowsiness to ⓚ **thrive** some benefits of sleep ⓛ **without** total perceptual disengagement.

① ⓐ, ⓗ, ⓘ   ② ⓓ, ⓗ, ⓘ   ③ ⓐ, ⓕ, ⓘ, ⓚ
④ ⓑ, ⓗ, ⓙ, ⓛ   ⑤ ⓒ, ⓖ, ⓗ, ⓛ

14. 14)밑줄 친 ⓐ~ⓞ 중 어법, 혹은 문맥상 어휘의 사용이 어색한 것끼리 짝지어진 것을 고르시오. 34

A number of research ⓐ **studies** have shown how experts in a field often experience difficulties when ⓑ **introducing** newcomers to that field. For example, in a ⓒ **genuine** training situation, Dr Pamela Hinds found that people expert in using mobile phones were remarkably ⓓ **less** accurate ⓔ **than** ⓕ **novice** phone users in judging how long it takes people to learn to use the phones. Experts can become ⓖ **insensitive** to how ⓗ **hard** a task is for the beginner, an effect ⓘ **is referred** to as the 'curse of knowledge'. Dr Hinds was able to show that as people ⓙ **acquired** the skill, they then began to ⓚ **underestimate** the level of difficulty of that skill. Her participants even ⓛ **underestimated** how long it had taken themselves to ⓜ **acquire** that skill in an earlier session. Knowing that experts ⓝ **recognize** how hard ⓞ **it** was for them to learn, we can understand the need to look at the learning process through students' eyes, rather than making assumptions about how students 'should be' learning.

① ⓒ, ⓘ   ② ⓗ, ⓝ   ③ ⓘ, ⓛ
④ ⓘ, ⓝ   ⑤ ⓓ, ⓖ, ⓛ, ⓜ

15. 15)밑줄 친 ⓐ~ⓙ 중 어법, 혹은 문맥상 어휘의 사용이 어색한 것끼리 짝지어진 것을 고르시오. 35

A group of psychologists studied individuals with severe ⓐ **physical** illness who experienced weekly group music therapy, including singing familiar songs and composing ⓑ **stereotype** songs. The results showed that the group music therapy improved the quality of participants' life, with those ⓒ **participated** in a greater number of ⓓ **sessions** ⓔ **experiencing** the greatest benefits. ⓕ **Focusing** on singing, another group of psychologists reviewed articles on the ⓖ **efficacy** of group singing as a mental health treatment for individuals living with a mental health condition in a community setting. The findings showed that, when people with mental health conditions ⓗ **participating** in a choir, their mental health and wellbeing ⓘ **significantly** improved. Group singing provided enjoyment, improved emotional states, developed a sense of belonging and ⓙ **enhanced** self-confidence.

① ⓐ, ⓘ   ② ⓐ, ⓗ, ⓙ   ③ ⓔ, ⓕ, ⓖ
④ ⓐ, ⓑ, ⓒ, ⓗ   ⑤ ⓑ, ⓒ, ⓗ, ⓘ

16. 16)밑줄 친 ⓐ~ⓜ 중 어법, 혹은 문맥상 어휘의 사용이 어색한 것끼리 짝지어진 것을 고르시오. 36

In many sports, people realized the difficulties and even impossibilities of young children ⓐ **participating** fully in many adult sport environments. They found the road to ⓑ **success** for young children is ⓒ **unlikely** ⓓ **if** they play on adult fields, courts or arenas with equipment that is too large, too heavy or too fast for them to handle ⓔ **during** trying to ⓕ **compete** in adult-style competition. Common sense has ⓖ **prevailed** : different sports have made ⓗ **adaptations** for children. As examples, baseball has T ball, football has flag football and junior soccer uses a smaller and lighter ball and (sometimes) a smaller field. All have ⓘ **junior** competitive structures ⓙ **where** children play for shorter time periods and often in smaller teams. In a similar way, tennis has ⓚ **been adapted** the court areas, balls and rackets to make them more appropriate for children under 10. The ⓛ **adoptions** are ⓜ **progressive** and relate to the age of the child.

① ⓗ, ⓛ   ② ⓔ, ⓙ, ⓚ   ③ ⓔ, ⓚ, ⓛ
④ ⓒ, ⓔ, ⓕ, ⓖ   ⑤ ⓖ, ⓗ, ⓚ, ⓜ

17. 17)**밑줄 친 ⓐ~ⓚ 중 어법, 혹은 문맥상 어휘의 사용이 어색한 것끼리 짝지어진 것을 고르시오.** 37

With no horses ⓐ **available** , the Inca empire ⓑ **failed** at delivering messages on foot. The messengers were ⓒ **stationed** on the ⓓ **loyal** roads to deliver the Inca king's orders and reports ⓔ **coming** from his lands. ⓕ **Calling** Chasquis, they lived in groups of four to six in huts, ⓖ **placed** from one to two miles apart along the roads. They were all young men and especially good runners who watched the road in both directions. If they ⓗ **caught** sight of another messenger ⓘ **coming** , they hurried out to meet them. The Inca built the huts on high ground, in sight of one ⓙ **another** . When a messenger neared the next hut, he began to call out and repeated the message three or four times to the one who was running out to meet him. The Inca empire could relay messages 1,000 miles (1,610 km) in three or four days ⓚ **under** good conditions.

① ⓐ, ⓓ   ② ⓑ, ⓒ, ⓕ   ③ ⓑ, ⓓ, ⓕ
④ ⓑ, ⓕ, ⓚ   ⑤ ⓑ, ⓒ, ⓓ, ⓙ

18. 18)**밑줄 친 ⓐ~ⓝ 중 어법, 혹은 문맥상 어휘의 사용이 어색한 것끼리 짝지어진 것을 고르시오.** 38

The tongue was mapped into ⓐ **separate** areas ⓑ **where** certain tastes were registered: sweetness at the tip, sourness on the sides, and bitterness at the back of the mouth. Research in the 1980s and 1990s, ⓒ **however** , demonstrated that the "tongue map" explanation of how we taste ⓓ **was** , in fact, totally wrong. As it turns out, the map was a ⓔ **interpretation** and ⓕ **translation** of research ⓖ **conducted** in Germany at the turn of the twentieth century. Today, ⓗ **leading** taste researchers believe ⓘ **what** taste buds are not grouped according to specialty. Sweetness, saltiness, bitterness, and sourness can be tasted everywhere in the mouth, ⓙ **although** they may be ⓚ **perceived** at a little different intensities at different sites. ⓛ **Moreover,** the mechanism at work is not ⓜ **place** , but ⓝ **time** . It's not that you taste sweetness at the tip of your tongue, but rather that you register that perception first.

① ⓐ, ⓘ   ② ⓔ, ⓖ   ③ ⓓ, ⓔ, ⓕ
④ ⓔ, ⓕ, ⓘ   ⑤ ⓘ, ⓛ, ⓝ

19. 19)**밑줄 친 ⓐ~ⓘ 중 어법, 혹은 문맥상 어휘의 사용이 어색한 것끼리 짝지어진 것을 고르시오.** 39

No two animals are ⓐ **alike** . Animals from the ⓑ **same** litter will display some of the same features, but will not be exactly the same as each other; therefore, they may not respond in entirely the same way ⓒ **during** a healing session. Environmental factors can also determine how the animal will respond ⓓ **during** the treatment. For instance, a cat in a rescue center will respond very differently than a cat within a domestic home environment. In ⓔ **contrast** , animals that experience healing for physical illness will react differently than those ⓕ **accepting** healing for emotional confusion. With this in mind, every healing session needs to ⓖ **be explored** differently, and each healing treatment should ⓗ **be adjusted** to suit the specific needs of the animal. You will learn as you go; healing is a ⓘ **temporary** learning process.

① ⓒ, ⓖ   ② ⓓ, ⓘ   ③ ⓔ, ⓘ
④ ⓕ, ⓖ   ⑤ ⓒ, ⓔ, ⓖ

20. 20)**밑줄 친 ⓐ~ⓙ 중 어법, 혹은 문맥상 어휘의 사용이 어색한 것끼리 짝지어진 것을 고르시오.** 40

The mind has parts ⓐ **that** are known ⓑ **as** the conscious mind and the subconscious mind. The subconscious mind is very fast to act and doesn't deal with emotions. It deals with memories of your responses to life, your memories and recognition. However, the conscious mind is the one that you have ⓒ **more** control over. You think. You can choose ⓓ **whether** to carry on a thought or to add emotion to it and this is the part of your mind that lets you down ⓔ **frequently** because — ⓕ **separated** by emotions — you make the wrong decisions time and time again. When your judgment is ⓖ **manifested** by emotions, this puts in biases and all kinds of other ⓗ **positivities** that hold you back. Scared of spiders? Scared of the dark? There are reasons for all of these fears, but they originate in the ⓘ **conscious** mind. They only become real fears when the ⓙ **subconscious** mind records your reactions.

① ⓑ, ⓓ, ⓘ   ② ⓑ, ⓕ, ⓘ   ③ ⓒ, ⓕ, ⓗ
④ ⓕ, ⓖ, ⓗ   ⑤ ⓐ, ⓑ, ⓕ, ⓙ

21. 21)밑줄 친 ⓐ~ⓝ 중 **어법, 혹은 문맥상 어휘**의 사용이 어색한 것끼리 짝지어진 것을 고르시오. 41-42

ⓐ **Quirks** are everywhere, defining ⓑ **what** is "normal" and guiding our interpretations of ⓒ **social** life at every turn. As a simple example, there is a norm in Anglo society to say Thank you to strangers who have just done something to help, such as open a door for you, point out that you've just dropped something, or give you directions. There is no law that forces you ⓓ **to say** Thank you. But if people don't say Thank you in these cases it is ⓔ **vague**. People expect that you will say it. You become ⓕ **responsibility** . Failing ⓖ **saying** it will be both ⓗ **surprising** and ⓘ **worthy** of criticism. Not knowing the ⓙ **norms** of another community is the central problem of cross-cultural communication. To continue the Thank you example, even though another ⓚ **culture** may have an expression that appears translatable (many don't), there may be different norms for its usage, for example, such that you should say Thank you only when the cost someone has ⓛ **caused is** ⓜ **considerable**. In such a case it would sound ⓝ **ridiculous** (i.e., unexpected, surprising, and worthy of criticism) if you were to thank someone for something so minor as holding a door open for you.

① ⓑ, ⓔ, ⓚ　　② ⓒ, ⓛ, ⓝ　　③ ⓓ, ⓔ, ⓗ
④ ⓔ, ⓕ, ⓗ　　⑤ ⓐ, ⓔ, ⓕ, ⓖ

22. 22)밑줄 친 ⓐ~ⓘ 중 **어법, 혹은 문맥상 어휘**의 사용이 어색한 것끼리 짝지어진 것을 고르시오. 43-45

Long ago, when the world was young, an old Native American spiritual leader Odawa had a dream on a high mountain. In his dream, Iktomi, the great spirit and searcher of wisdom, ⓐ **appeared** to him in the form of a spider. Iktomi spoke to him in a holy language. Iktomi told Odawa about the cycles of life. He said, "We all begin our lives as babies, move on to childhood, and then to adulthood. Finally, we come to old age, ⓑ **which** we must be taken care of as babies again". Iktomi also told him ⓒ **which** there are good and bad forces in each ⓓ **stage** of life. "If we listen to the good forces, they will guide us in the right direction. But if we listen to the bad forces, they will lead us the wrong way and may harm us", Iktomi said. When Iktomi finished ⓔ **speaking** , he spun a web and gave it to Odawa. He said to Odawa, "The web is a ⓕ **perfect** circle with a hole in the center. Use the web to help your people ⓖ **reach** their goals. Make good use of their ideas, dreams, and visions. If you believe in the great spirit, the web will catch your good ideas and the bad ones will go through the hole". Right after Odawa woke up, he went back to his village. Odawa shared Iktomi's lesson with his people. Today, many Native Americans have dream catchers hanging above their beds. Dream catchers are believed to ⓗ **filter** out bad dreams. The good dreams are captured in the web of life and carried with the people. The bad dreams pass through the hole in the web and ⓘ **are** no longer a part of their lives.

① ⓑ, ⓒ　　② ⓑ, ⓕ　　③ ⓑ, ⓘ
④ ⓒ, ⓔ　　⑤ ⓐ, ⓑ, ⓓ, ⓕ

2024 고1 3월 모의고사

❶ voca ❷ text ❸ [/] ❹ ____ ❺ quiz 1 ❻ quiz 2 ❼ quiz 3 ❽ quiz 4 ❾ quiz 5

1. 1)밑줄 부분 중 어법, 혹은 문맥상 어휘의 쓰임이 어색한 것을 올바르게 고쳐 쓰시오. (5개) [18]

Dear Ms. Jane Watson, I am John Austin, a science teacher at Crestville High School. Recently I was ① **impressing** by the ② **latest** book you wrote about the environment. Also my students read your book and had a class discussion about it. They are big fans of your book, so I'd like to ask you ③ **visiting** our school and give a special lecture. We can ④ **set** the date and time to ⑤ **suiting** your schedule. ⑥ **Have** you at our school would be a fantastic experience for the students. We would be very ⑦ **graceful** if you could come. Best regards, John Austin

기호	어색한 표현		올바른 표현
( )	_____	⇨	_____
( )	_____	⇨	_____
( )	_____	⇨	_____
( )	_____	⇨	_____
( )	_____	⇨	_____

2. 2)밑줄 부분 중 어법, 혹은 문맥상 어휘의 쓰임이 어색한 것을 올바르게 고쳐 쓰시오. (1개) [19]

Marilyn and her three-year-old daughter, Sarah, took a trip to the beach, ① **where** Sarah built her first sandcastle. Moments later, an enormous wave ② **destroyed** Sarah's castle. In response to the ③ **lose** of her sandcastle, tears streamed down Sarah's cheeks and her heart was broken. She ran to Marilyn, saying she would never build a sandcastle again. Marilyn said, "Part of the joy of building a sandcastle is ④ **that** , in the end, we give it as a gift to the ocean". Sarah loved this idea and responded with enthusiasm to the idea of building ⑤ **another** castle — this time, even closer to the water so the ocean would get its gift sooner!

기호	어색한 표현		올바른 표현
( )	_____	⇨	_____

3. 3)밑줄 부분 중 어법, 혹은 문맥상 어휘의 쓰임이 어색한 것을 올바르게 고쳐 쓰시오. (4개) [20]

Magic is ① **that** we all wish for to happen in our life. Do you love the movie Cinderella like me? Well, in real life, you can also create magic. Here's the trick. ② **Write** down all the real-time challenges ③ **that** you face and ④ **deal with**. Just change the challenge statement into ⑤ **negative** statements. Let me give you an example here. If you struggle with getting up early in the morning, then write a positive statement such as "I get up early in the morning at 5:00 am every day". Once you write these statements, get ready to witness magic and ⑥ **confidence** . You will be surprised ⑦ **to** just by writing these statements, there is a shift in the way you think and act. Suddenly you feel ⑧ **less** powerful and positive.

기호	어색한 표현		올바른 표현
( )	_____	⇨	_____
( )	_____	⇨	_____
( )	_____	⇨	_____
( )	_____	⇨	_____

4. 4)밑줄 부분 중 어법, 혹은 문맥상 어휘의 쓰임이 어색한 것을 올바르게 고쳐 쓰시오. (10개) 21

Consider the seemingly simple question How many senses ① **is** there? Around 2,370 years ago, Aristotle wrote that there are five, in both humans and animals — sight, hearing, smell, taste, and touch. ② **So** , according to the philosopher Fiona Macpherson, there are reasons to ③ **expect** it. For a start, Aristotle missed a few in humans: the ④ **deception** of your own body which is different from touch and the sense of balance which has links to both touch and vision. Other animals have senses that are even harder to categorize. Many vertebrates have a different sense system for ⑤ **protecting** odors. Some snakes can detect the body heat of their prey. These examples tell us that "senses ⑥ **can** be clearly divided into a ⑦ **limitless** number of ⑧ **vague** kinds", Macpherson wrote in The Senses. Instead of trying to push animal senses into Aristotelian buckets, we should study them for ⑨ **that** they ⑩ **do** .

기호　　　어색한 표현　　　　　올바른 표현

( )　_____ ⇨ _____
( )　_____ ⇨ _____
( )　_____ ⇨ _____
( )　_____ ⇨ _____
( )　_____ ⇨ _____
( )　_____ ⇨ _____
( )　_____ ⇨ _____
( )　_____ ⇨ _____
( )　_____ ⇨ _____
( )　_____ ⇨ _____

5. 5)밑줄 부분 중 어법, 혹은 문맥상 어휘의 쓰임이 어색한 것을 올바르게 고쳐 쓰시오. (9개) 22

When we think of leaders, we may think of people such as Abraham Lincoln or Martin Luther King, Jr. ① **Whether** you consider the historical importance and far-reaching influence of these individuals, leadership might seem like a ② **novel** and high goal. But like all of us, these people started out as students, workers, and citizens who ③ **are possessed by** ideas about ④ **what** some aspect of daily life could be improved on a larger scale. Through ⑤ **intelligence** and experience, they improved upon their ideas by ⑥ **protecting** them with others, ⑦ **sought** their opinions and feedback and constantly looking for the best way to ⑧ **abandon** goals for a group. Thus we all have the potential to be leaders at school, in our communities, and at work, ⑨ **along with** age or experience.

기호　　　어색한 표현　　　　　올바른 표현

( )　_____ ⇨ _____
( )　_____ ⇨ _____
( )　_____ ⇨ _____
( )　_____ ⇨ _____
( )　_____ ⇨ _____
( )　_____ ⇨ _____
( )　_____ ⇨ _____
( )　_____ ⇨ _____
( )　_____ ⇨ _____

6. ⁶⁾**밑줄 부분 중 어법, 혹은 문맥상 어휘의 쓰임이 어색한 것을 올바르게 고쳐 쓰시오. (1개)** ²³

Crop rotation is the ① **process** ② **in which** farmers change the crops they grow in their fields in a special order. For example, ③ **if** a farmer ④ **has** three fields, he or she may grow carrots in the first field, green beans in the second, and tomatoes in the third. The next year, green beans ⑤ **will** be in the first field, tomatoes in the second field, and carrots ⑥ **will** be in the third. In year three, the crops ⑦ **will** rotate again. By the ⑧ **fourth** year, the crops will go back to their ⑨ **previous** order. Each ⑩ **crop** ⑪ **enriches** the soil for the next crop. This type of farming is ⑫ **sustainable** because the soil stays ⑬ **healthy** .

기호   어색한 표현   올바른 표현

(   ) _____ ⇨ _____

7. ⁷⁾**밑줄 부분 중 어법, 혹은 문맥상 어휘의 쓰임이 어색한 것을 올바르게 고쳐 쓰시오. (2개)** ²⁴

① **Working** around the whole painting, rather ② **than** concentrating on one area at a time, will mean you can stop at any point and the painting can be considered "finished". Artists often find ③ **them** difficult to know when to stop ④ **painting** , and it can be ⑤ **tempting** to keep on adding ⑥ **more** to your work. It is important to take a few steps back from the painting from time to time to ⑦ **assess** your ⑧ **progress**. Putting too much into a painting can ⑨ **spoil** its impact and leave it looking ⑩ **overworked** . If you find yourself ⑪ **struggling** to decide whether you have finished, take a break and come back to it later with fresh eyes. Then you can decide ⑫ **whether** any areas of your painting would ⑬ **benefit** further refinement.

기호   어색한 표현   올바른 표현

(   ) _____ ⇨ _____
(   ) _____ ⇨ _____

8. ⁸⁾**밑줄 부분 중 어법, 혹은 문맥상 어휘의 쓰임이 어색한 것을 올바르게 고쳐 쓰시오. (1개)** ²⁶

Jaroslav Heyrovsky was born in Prague on December 20, 1890, as the ① **fifth** child of Leopold Heyrovsky. In 1901 Jaroslav went to a secondary school ② **called** the Akademicke Gymnasium. Rather ③ **then** Latin and Greek, he showed a strong interest in the ④ **natural** sciences. At Czech University in Prague he studied chemistry, physics, and mathematics. From 1910 to 1914 he continued his studies at University College, London. Throughout the First World War, Jaroslav served in a military hospital. In 1926, Jaroslav became the first Professor of Physical Chemistry at Charles University in Prague. He ⑤ **won** the Nobel Prize in chemistry in 1959.

기호   어색한 표현   올바른 표현

(   ) _____ ⇨ _____

9. 9)밑줄 부분 중 어법, 혹은 문맥상 어휘의 쓰임이 어색한 것을 올바르게 고쳐 쓰시오. (3개) [29]

It would be ① **hard** to overstate how ② **important** meaningful work is to human beings — work that provides a sense of fulfillment and empowerment. Those who have found deeper meaning in their careers find their days much ③ **more** energizing and satisfying, and count their employment as one of their greatest sources of joy and pride. Sonya Lyubomirsky, professor of psychology at the University of California, has ④ **conducted** numerous workplace studies showing that when people are ⑤ **more** fulfilled on the job, they not only produce ⑥ **higher** quality work and a greater output, but also generally earn ⑦ **lower** incomes. Those most ⑧ **satisfied with** their work are also much ⑨ **more** likely to be happier with their lives overall. For her book Happiness at Work, researcher Jessica Pryce-Jones conducted a study of 3,000 workers in seventy-nine countries, finding ⑩ **which** those who took greater satisfaction from their work were 150 percent ⑪ **less** likely to have a happier life overall.

기호	어색한 표현		올바른 표현
( )	_____	⇨	_____
( )	_____	⇨	_____
( )	_____	⇨	_____

10. 10)밑줄 부분 중 어법, 혹은 문맥상 어휘의 쓰임이 어색한 것을 올바르게 고쳐 쓰시오. (11개) [30]

The rate of speed ① **at which** one is traveling will greatly determine the ability to ② **procedure** detail in the environment. In evolutionary terms, human senses are ③ **adopted** to the speed at which humans move through space under their own power ④ **while** walking. Our ability to ⑤ **extinguish** detail in the environment is therefore ideally suited to movement at speeds of perhaps five miles per hour and under. The fastest users of the street, motorists, therefore have a much ⑥ **less** ⑦ **limitless** ability to process details along the street — a motorist simply has ⑧ **few** time or ability to appreciate design details. On the other hand, pedestrian travel, ⑨ **is** much slower, allows for the ⑩ **ignorance** of environmental detail. Joggers and bicyclists fall somewhere in between these ⑪ **solar** opposites; while they travel ⑫ **slower** than pedestrians, their rate of speed is ordinarily much ⑬ **slower** than ⑭ **those** of the typical motorist.

기호	어색한 표현		올바른 표현
( )	_____	⇨	_____
( )	_____	⇨	_____
( )	_____	⇨	_____
( )	_____	⇨	_____
( )	_____	⇨	_____
( )	_____	⇨	_____
( )	_____	⇨	_____
( )	_____	⇨	_____
( )	_____	⇨	_____
( )	_____	⇨	_____
( )	_____	⇨	_____

11. 11)밑줄 부분 중 어법, 혹은 문맥상 어휘의 쓰임이 어색한 것을 올바르게 고쳐 쓰시오. (3개) 31

Every species ① **has** certain ② **climatic** requirements — ③ **that** degree of heat or cold it can endure, for example. When the climate changes, the places that satisfy those requirements change, too. Species are ④ **forced** to follow. All creatures are ⑤ **capable** of some degree of movement. Even creatures that appear ⑥ **mobile** , like trees and barnacles, are ⑦ **capable** of ⑧ **dispersal** at some stage of their life — as a seed, in the case of the tree, or as a larva, in the case of the barnacle. A creature must get from the place it is born — often occupied by its parent — to a place ⑨ **where** it can survive, grow, and reproduce. From fossils, scientists know ⑩ **that** even creatures like trees ⑪ **grew** with surprising speed ⑫ **during** past periods of climate change.

기호	어색한 표현		올바른 표현
( )	_____	⇨	_____
( )	_____	⇨	_____
( )	_____	⇨	_____

12. 12)밑줄 부분 중 어법, 혹은 문맥상 어휘의 쓰임이 어색한 것을 올바르게 고쳐 쓰시오. (10개) 32

No ① **respectable** boss would say, "I make it a point to ② **encourage** my staff ③ **to speak** up, and I maintain a culture that prevents disagreeing viewpoints from ever getting ④ **ignored** ". If anything, most bosses even say that they are ⑤ **pro-assent** . This idea can be found throughout the series of conversations with corporate, university, and nonprofit leaders, published weekly in the business sections of newspapers. In the interviews, the featured leaders ⑥ **asked** about their management techniques, and regularly claim to continually encourage ⑦ **external** protest from ⑧ **less** junior staffers. As Bot Pittman remarked in one of these conversations: "I want us to listen to these ⑨ **assentors** because they may intend to tell you why we can't do something, but if you listen ⑩ **hardly** , what they're really telling you is what you must do to get something ⑪ **doing** ".

기호	어색한 표현		올바른 표현
( )	_____	⇨	_____
( )	_____	⇨	_____
( )	_____	⇨	_____
( )	_____	⇨	_____
( )	_____	⇨	_____
( )	_____	⇨	_____
( )	_____	⇨	_____
( )	_____	⇨	_____
( )	_____	⇨	_____
( )	_____	⇨	_____

13. 13)**밑줄 부분 중 어법, 혹은 문맥상 어휘의 쓰임이 어색한 것을 올바르게 고쳐 쓰시오. (3개)** [33]

One of the most striking characteristics of a sleeping animal or person is ① **that** they do not respond normally to environmental stimuli. If you open the eyelids of a sleeping mammal the eyes will not see normally — they are functionally ② **informed**. Some visual information ③ **apparent** gets in, but it is not normally ④ **processed** as it is shortened or weakened; ⑤ **different** with the other sensing systems. Stimuli ⑥ **are** registered but not processed normally and they fail ⑦ **to wake** the individual. Perceptual ⑧ **disengagement** probably serves the function of protecting sleep, so some authors do not count it as part of the definition of sleep ⑨ **itself** . But as sleep would be impossible ⑩ **without** it, it seems essential to its definition. Nevertheless, many animals (including humans) use the intermediate state of drowsiness to ⑪ **derive** some benefits of sleep ⑫ **without** total perceptual disengagement.

기호	어색한 표현		올바른 표현
( )	_____	⇨	_____
( )	_____	⇨	_____
( )	_____	⇨	_____

14. 14)**밑줄 부분 중 어법, 혹은 문맥상 어휘의 쓰임이 어색한 것을 올바르게 고쳐 쓰시오. (10개)** [34]

A number of research ① **study** have shown how experts in a field often experience difficulties when ② **introduce** newcomers to that field. For example, in a ③ **genuine** training situation, Dr Pamela Hinds found that people expert in using mobile phones were remarkably ④ **more** accurate ⑤ **then** ⑥ **novice** phone users in judging how long it takes people to learn to use the phones. Experts can become ⑦ **sensitive** to how ⑧ **hardly** a task is for the beginner, an effect ⑨ **is referred** to as the 'curse of knowledge'. Dr Hinds was able to show that as people ⑩ **acquired** the skill, they then began to ⑪ **overestimate** the level of difficulty of that skill. Her participants even ⑫ **overestimated** how long it had taken themselves to ⑬ **acquire** that skill in an earlier session. Knowing that experts ⑭ **recognize** how hard ⑮ **it** was for them to learn, we can understand the need to look at the learning process through students' eyes, rather than making assumptions about how students 'should be' learning.

기호	어색한 표현		올바른 표현
( )	_____	⇨	_____
( )	_____	⇨	_____
( )	_____	⇨	_____
( )	_____	⇨	_____
( )	_____	⇨	_____
( )	_____	⇨	_____
( )	_____	⇨	_____
( )	_____	⇨	_____
( )	_____	⇨	_____
( )	_____	⇨	_____

15. 15)**밑줄 부분 중 어법, 혹은 문맥상 어휘의 쓰임이 어색한 것을 올바르게 고쳐 쓰시오. (1개)** 35

A group of psychologists studied individuals with severe ① **mental** illness who experienced weekly group music therapy, including singing familiar songs and composing ② **original** songs. The results showed that the group music therapy improved the quality of participants' life, with those ③ **participating** in a greater number of ④ **sessions** ⑤ **experiencing** the greatest benefits. ⑥ **Focusing** on singing, another group of psychologists reviewed articles on the ⑦ **efficacy** of group singing as a mental health treatment for individuals living with a mental health condition in a community setting. The findings showed that, when people with mental health conditions ⑧ **participated** in a choir, their mental health and wellbeing ⑨ **significant** improved. Group singing provided enjoyment, improved emotional states, developed a sense of belonging and ⑩ **enhanced** self-confidence.

기호   어색한 표현   올바른 표현

(   ) _____ ⇨ _____

16. 16)**밑줄 부분 중 어법, 혹은 문맥상 어휘의 쓰임이 어색한 것을 올바르게 고쳐 쓰시오. (5개)** 36

In many sports, people realized the difficulties and even impossibilities of young children ① **participating** fully in many adult sport environments. They found the road to ② **succession** for young children is ③ **likely** ④ **if** they play on adult fields, courts or arenas with equipment that is too large, too heavy or too fast for them to handle ⑤ **while** trying to ⑥ **complete** in adult-style competition. Common sense has ⑦ **prevalent** : different sports have made ⑧ **adoptions** for children. As examples, baseball has T ball, football has flag football and junior soccer uses a smaller and lighter ball and (sometimes) a smaller field. All have ⑨ **junior** competitive structures ⑩ **where** children play for shorter time periods and often in smaller teams. In a similar way, tennis has ⑪ **adapted** the court areas, balls and rackets to make them more appropriate for children under 10. The ⑫ **adaptations** are ⑬ **progressive** and relate to the age of the child.

기호   어색한 표현   올바른 표현

(   ) _____ ⇨ _____
(   ) _____ ⇨ _____
(   ) _____ ⇨ _____
(   ) _____ ⇨ _____
(   ) _____ ⇨ _____

17. 17)**밑줄 부분 중 어법, 혹은 문맥상 어휘의 쓰임이 어색한 것을 올바르게 고쳐 쓰시오. (6개)** 37

With no horses ① **are available** , the Inca empire ② **failed** at delivering messages on foot. The messengers were ③ **stationed** on the ④ **royal** roads to deliver the Inca king's orders and reports ⑤ **coming** from his lands. ⑥ **Calling** Chasquis, they lived in groups of four to six in huts, ⑦ **placed** from one to two miles apart along the roads. They were all young men and especially good runners who watched the road in both directions. If they ⑧ **were caught** sight of another messenger ⑨ **came** , they hurried out to meet them. The Inca built the huts on high ground, in sight of one ⑩ **another** . When a messenger neared the next hut, he began to call out and repeated the message three or four times to the one who was running out to meet him. The Inca empire could relay messages 1,000 miles (1,610 km) in three or four days ⑪ **over** good conditions.

기호	어색한 표현		올바른 표현
( )	_____	⇨	_____
( )	_____	⇨	_____
( )	_____	⇨	_____
( )	_____	⇨	_____
( )	_____	⇨	_____
( )	_____	⇨	_____

18. 18)**밑줄 부분 중 어법, 혹은 문맥상 어휘의 쓰임이 어색한 것을 올바르게 고쳐 쓰시오. (14개)** 38

The tongue was mapped into ① **integrate** areas ② **which** certain tastes were registered: sweetness at the tip, sourness on the sides, and bitterness at the back of the mouth. Research in the 1980s and 1990s, ③ **thus** , demonstrated that the "tongue map" explanation of how we taste ④ **does** , in fact, totally wrong. As it turns out, the map was a ⑤ **interpretation** and ⑥ **translation** of research ⑦ **conducting** in Germany at the turn of the twentieth century. Today, ⑧ **lead** taste researchers believe ⑨ **what** taste buds are not grouped according to specialty. Sweetness, saltiness, bitterness, and sourness can be tasted everywhere in the mouth, ⑩ **despite** they may be ⑪ **deceived** at a little different intensities at different sites. ⑫ **So,** the mechanism at work is not ⑬ **time** , but ⑭ **place** . It's not that you taste sweetness at the tip of your tongue, but rather that you register that perception first.

기호	어색한 표현		올바른 표현
( )	_____	⇨	_____
( )	_____	⇨	_____
( )	_____	⇨	_____
( )	_____	⇨	_____
( )	_____	⇨	_____
( )	_____	⇨	_____
( )	_____	⇨	_____
( )	_____	⇨	_____
( )	_____	⇨	_____
( )	_____	⇨	_____
( )	_____	⇨	_____
( )	_____	⇨	_____
( )	_____	⇨	_____
( )	_____	⇨	_____

19. 19)**밑줄 부분 중 어법, 혹은 문맥상 어휘의 쓰임이 어색한 것을 올바르게 고쳐 쓰시오. (7개)** 39

No two animals are ① **like** . Animals from the ② **different** litter will display some of the same features, but will not be exactly the same as each other; therefore, they may not respond in entirely the same way ③ **during** a healing session. Environmental factors can also determine how the animal will respond ④ **while** the treatment. For instance, a cat in a rescue center will respond very differently than a cat within a domestic home environment. In ⑤ **addition** , animals that experience healing for physical illness will react differently than those ⑥ **accepted** healing for emotional confusion. With this in mind, every healing session needs to ⑦ **explore** differently, and each healing treatment should ⑧ **adopt** to suit the specific needs of the animal. You will learn as you go; healing is a ⑨ **temporary** learning process.

기호	어색한 표현		올바른 표현
( )	_____	⇨	_____
( )	_____	⇨	_____
( )	_____	⇨	_____
( )	_____	⇨	_____
( )	_____	⇨	_____
( )	_____	⇨	_____
( )	_____	⇨	_____

20. 20)**밑줄 부분 중 어법, 혹은 문맥상 어휘의 쓰임이 어색한 것을 올바르게 고쳐 쓰시오. (3개)** 40

The mind has parts ① **that** are known ② **as** the conscious mind and the subconscious mind. The subconscious mind is very fast to act and doesn't deal with emotions. It deals with memories of your responses to life, your memories and recognition. However, the conscious mind is the one that you have ③ **more** control over. You think. You can choose ④ **if** to carry on a thought or to add emotion to it and this is the part of your mind that lets you down ⑤ **frequently** because — ⑥ **separated** by emotions — you make the wrong decisions time and time again. When your judgment is ⑦ **clouded** by emotions, this puts in biases and all kinds of other ⑧ **negativities** that hold you back. Scared of spiders? Scared of the dark? There are reasons for all of these fears, but they originate in the ⑨ **subconscious** mind. They only become real fears when the ⑩ **subconscious** mind records your reactions.

기호	어색한 표현		올바른 표현
( )	_____	⇨	_____
( )	_____	⇨	_____
( )	_____	⇨	_____

21. 21)**밑줄 부분 중 어법, 혹은 문맥상 어휘의 쓰임이 어색한 것을 올바르게 고쳐 쓰시오. (14개)** 41-42

① **Quirks** are everywhere, defining ② **that** is "normal" and guiding our interpretations of ③ **sociable** life at every turn. As a simple example, there is a norm in Anglo society to say Thank you to strangers who have just done something to help, such as open a door for you, point out that you've just dropped something, or give you directions. There is no law that forces you ④ **say** Thank you. But if people don't say Thank you in these cases it is ⑤ **vague**. People expect that you will say it. You become ⑥ **responsibility** . Failing ⑦ **saying** it will be both ⑧ **surprised** and ⑨ **worth** of criticism. Not knowing the ⑩ **quirks** of another community is the central problem of cross-cultural communication. To continue the Thank you example, even though another ⑪ **cultures** may have an expression that appears translatable (many don't), there may be different norms for its usage, for example, such that you should say Thank you only when the cost someone has ⑫ **caused** ⑬ **considerate**. In such a case it would sound ⑭ **ridiculously** (i.e., unexpected, surprising, and worthy of criticism) if you were to thank someone for something so minor as holding a door open for you.

기호	어색한 표현		올바른 표현
(　　)	_____	⇨	_____
(　　)	_____	⇨	_____
(　　)	_____	⇨	_____
(　　)	_____	⇨	_____
(　　)	_____	⇨	_____
(　　)	_____	⇨	_____
(　　)	_____	⇨	_____
(　　)	_____	⇨	_____
(　　)	_____	⇨	_____
(　　)	_____	⇨	_____
(　　)	_____	⇨	_____
(　　)	_____	⇨	_____
(　　)	_____	⇨	_____
(　　)	_____	⇨	_____

22. 22)밑줄 부분 중 어법, 혹은 문맥상 어휘의 쓰임이 어색한 것을 올바르게 고쳐 쓰시오. (5개) 43-45

Long ago, when the world was young, an old Native American spiritual leader Odawa had a dream on a high mountain. In his dream, Iktomi, the great spirit and searcher of wisdom, ① **was appeared** to him in the form of a spider. Iktomi spoke to him in a holy language. Iktomi told Odawa about the cycles of life. He said, "We all begin our lives as babies, move on to childhood, and then to adulthood. Finally, we come to old age, ② **where** we must be taken care of as babies again". Iktomi also told him ③ **that** there are good and bad forces in each ④ **stage** of life. "If we listen to the good forces, they will guide us in the right direction. But if we listen to the bad forces, they will lead us the wrong way and may harm us", Iktomi said. When Iktomi finished ⑤ **to speak** , he spun a web and gave it to Odawa. He said to Odawa, "The web is a ⑥ **perfect** circle with a hole in the center. Use the web to help your people ⑦ **reaching** their goals. Make good use of their ideas, dreams, and visions. If you believe in the great spirit, the web will catch your good ideas and the bad ones will go through the hole". Right after Odawa woke up, he went back to his village. Odawa shared Iktomi's lesson with his people. Today, many Native Americans have dream catchers hanging above their beds. Dream catchers are believed to ⑧ **be filtered** out bad dreams. The good dreams are captured in the web of life and carried with the people. The bad dreams pass through the hole in the web and ⑨ **being** no longer a part of their lives.

기호	어색한 표현		올바른 표현
(　　)	_____	⇨	_____
(　　)	_____	⇨	_____
(　　)	_____	⇨	_____
(　　)	_____	⇨	_____
(　　)	_____	⇨	_____

2024 고1 3월 모의고사

❶ voca ❷ text ❸ [/] ❹ _____ ❺ quiz 1 ❻ quiz 2 ❼ quiz 3 ❽ quiz 4 ❾ quiz 5

☑ **다음 글을 읽고 물음에 답하시오.** (18.)

Dear Ms. Jane Watson, I am John Austin, a science teacher at Crestville High School. ⓐ Recently I impress the last book you wrote about the environment. Also my students read your book and had a class discussion about them. They are big fans of your book, so I'd like to ask you to visit our school and give a special lecture. We can set the date and time to 들어갈 단어 _____ your schedule. (가) 당신이 우리 학교에 와주신다면 학생들에게 멋진 경험이 될 것 같습니다. We would be very grateful if you could come. Best regards, John Austin

1. 1)힌트를 참고하여 각 빈칸에 알맞은 단어를 쓰시오.

2. 2)밑줄 친 ⓐ에서, 어법 혹은 문맥상 어색한 부분을 찾아 올바르게 고쳐 쓰시오.

   ⓐ   잘못된 표현   바른 표현

   (   ) ⇨ (   )

   (   ) ⇨ (   )

   (   ) ⇨ (   )

3. 3)위 글에 주어진 (가)의 한글과 같은 의미를 가지도록, 각각의 주어진 단어들을 알맞게 배열하시오.

(가) at / the students. / you / our / experience / Having / for / fantastic / a / would / be / school

☑ **다음 글을 읽고 물음에 답하시오.** (19.)

Marilyn and her three-year-old daughter, Sarah, took a trip to the beach, where Sarah built her first sandcastle. Moments later, an 거대한 _____ wave destroyed Sarah's castle. ~에 반응하여 _____ the loss of her sandcastle, tears streamed down Sarah's cheeks and her heart was broken. (가) 그녀는 다시는 모래성을 쌓지 않겠다고 말하며 Marilyn에게 달려갔다. Marilyn said, "Part of the joy of building a sandcastle is that, in the end, we give it as a gift to the ocean". Sarah loved this idea and responded with 열정 _____ to the idea of building another castle — (나) 이번에는 바다와 훨씬 더 가까운 곳에서 바다가 그 선물을 더 빨리 받을 수 있도록

4. 4)힌트를 참고하여 각 빈칸에 알맞은 단어를 쓰시오.

5. 5)위 글에 주어진 (가) ~ (나)의 한글과 같은 의미를 가지도록, 각각의 주어진 단어들을 알맞게 배열하시오.

(가) would / ran / build / a / Marilyn, / She / she / saying / to / again. / sandcastle / never

(나) sooner! / get / even / this time, / the water / so / would / closer / the ocean / its / gift / to

☑ **다음 글을 읽고 물음에 답하시오.** (20.)

(가) <u>마법은 우리 모두 자신의 삶에서 일어나기를 바라는 바이다.</u> Do you love the movie Cinderella like me? Well, in real life, you can also create magic. Here's the trick. (나) <u>여러분이 직면하고 처리하는 모든 실시간의 어려움을 적어라.</u> ⓐ <u>Just change the challenge statement into negative statements. Let me give you an example here. If you struggle in getting up early in the morning, then write a negative statement such as "I get up early in the morning at 5:00 am every day".</u> Once you write these statements, get ready to witness magic and ^{자신감} _____. You will be surprised that just by writing these statements, there is a ^{변화} _____ in the way you think and act. Suddenly you feel more powerful and positive.

6. ⁶⁾힌트를 참고하여 각 <u>빈칸에 알맞은</u> 단어를 쓰시오.

7. ⁷⁾밑줄 친 ⓐ에서, 어법 혹은 문맥상 어색한 부분을 찾아 올바르게 고쳐 쓰시오.

ⓐ	잘못된 표현		바른 표현
(	)	⇨ (	)
(	)	⇨ (	)
(	)	⇨ (	)

8. ⁸⁾위 글에 주어진 (가) ~ (나)의 한글과 같은 의미를 가지도록, 각각의 주어진 단어들을 알맞게 배열하시오.

(가) our / to / wish / life. / happen / we / in / is / for / what / Magic / all

(나) face / you / that / all / Write / down / real-time / the / with. / deal / and / challenges

☑ **다음 글을 읽고 물음에 답하시오.** (21.)

Consider the seemingly simple question. How many senses are there? Around 2,370 years ago, Aristotle wrote that there are five, in both humans and animals — sight, hearing, smell, taste, and touch. However, according to the philosopher Fiona Macpherson, there are reasons to doubt it. For a start, Aristotle missed a few in humans: the perception of your own body which is different from touch and the sense of balance which has links to both touch and vision. Other animals have senses that are even harder to categorize. Many ^{척추동물} _____ have a different sense system for ^{감지하다} _____ ^{냄새} _____. Some snakes can detect the body heat of their prey. These examples tell us that "(가) <u>감각은 제한된 수의 특정한 종류로 명확하게 나누어지지 않을 수 있다</u>" Macpherson wrote in The Senses. (나) <u>동물의 감각을 Aristotle의 양동이로 밀어 넣는 대신, 우리는 그것들을 존재하는 그대로 연구해야 한다.</u>

9. ⁹⁾힌트를 참고하여 각 <u>빈칸에 알맞은</u> 단어를 쓰시오.

10. 10)위 글에 주어진 (가) ~ (나)의 한글과 같은 의미를 가지도록, 각각의 주어진 단어들을 알맞게 배열하시오.

(가) of / divided / number / be / a / kinds, / cannot / specific / clearly / limited / senses / into

(나) buckets, / into / study / are. / of / Aristotelian / they / animal / Instead / them / what / senses / push / for / should / trying / we / to

☑ **다음 글을 읽고 물음에 답하시오.** (22.)

When we think of leaders, we may think of people such as Abraham Lincoln or Martin Luther King, Jr. If you consider the historical importance and ^{광범위한} _____ influence of these individuals, leadership might seem like a noble and high goal. But like all of us, these people started out as students, workers, and citizens who possessed ideas about how some aspect of daily life could be improved on a larger scale. Through ^{근면함} _____ and experience, they improved upon their ideas by sharing them with others, seeking their opinions and feedback and constantly looking for the best way to accomplish goals for a group. Thus we all have the ^{잠재력} _____ to be leaders at school, in our communities, and at work, regardless of age or experience.

11. 11)힌트를 참고하여 각 빈칸에 알맞은 단어를 쓰시오.

☑ **다음 글을 읽고 물음에 답하시오.** (23.)

(가) 윤작은 농부가 자신의 밭에서 재배하는 작물을 특별한 순서로 바꾸는 과정이다. For example, if a farmer has three fields, he or she may grow carrots in the first field, green beans in the second, and tomatoes in the third. The next year, green beans will be in the first field, tomatoes in the second field, and carrots will be in the third. In year three, the crops will ^{들어갈 단어} _____ again. By the fourth year, the crops will go back to their original order. Each crop ^{비옥하게 하다} _____ the soil for the next crop. This type of farming is ^{지속가능한} _____ because the soil stays healthy.

12. 12)힌트를 참고하여 각 빈칸에 알맞은 단어를 쓰시오.

13. 13)위 글에 주어진 (가)의 한글과 같은 의미를 가지도록, 각각의 주어진 단어들을 알맞게 배열하시오.

(가) Crop / a / rotation / they / order. / in / farmers / special / is / the process / their / change / fields / grow / the crops / in / in / which

☑ **다음 글을 읽고 물음에 답하시오.** (24.)

Working around the whole painting, rather than concentrating on one area at a time, will mean you can stop at any point and the painting can be considered "finished". (가) <u>화가인 여러분은 종종 언제 그림을 멈춰야 할지 알기 어렵다는 것을 발견하고,</u> and it can be tempting to keep on adding more to your work. It is important to take a few steps back from the painting from time to time to ^{평가하다} _____ your progress. (나) <u>한 그림에 너무 많은 것을 넣으면 그것의 영향력을 망칠 수 있고 그것이 과하게 작업된 것처럼 보이게 둘 수 있다.</u> If you find yourself struggling to decide whether you have finished, take a break and come back to it later with fresh eyes. Then (다) <u>여러분은 더 정교하게 꾸며서 자신의 그림 어느 부분이 득을 볼지를 결정할 수 있다.</u>

14. ¹⁴⁾힌트를 참고하여 각 <u>빈칸에 알맞은 단어</u>를 쓰시오.

15. ¹⁵⁾위 글에 주어진 (가) ~ (다)의 한글과 같은 의미를 가지도록, 각각의 주어진 단어들을 알맞게 배열하시오.

(가) difficult / find / when / stop / to / painting / Artists / to / it / know / often

(나) much / it / can / too / looking / spoil / and / Putting / overworked. / its / a / leave / painting / impact / into

(다) painting / would / you / can / areas / benefit / of / decide / from / further / refinement. / whether / your / any

☑ **다음 글을 읽고 물음에 답하시오.** (25.)

The above graph shows the ^{정도} _____ to which young people aged 16-25 in six countries had fear about climate change in 2021. The Philippines had the highest percentage of young people who said they were extremely or very worried, at 84 percent, followed by 67 percent in Brazil. More than 60 percent of young people in Portugal said they were extremely worried or very worried. In France, the percentage of young people who were extremely worried was lower than that of young people who were very worried. In the United Kingdom, the percentage of young generation who said that they were very worried was 29 percent. In the United States, the total percentage of extremely worried and very worried youth was the smallest ^{~중에서} _____ the six countries.

16. ¹⁶⁾힌트를 참고하여 각 <u>빈칸에 알맞은 단어</u>를 쓰시오.

☑ 다음 글을 읽고 물음에 답하시오. (26.)

Jaroslav Heyrovsky was born in Prague on December 20, 1890, as the fifth child of Leopold Heyrovsky. In 1901 Jaroslav went to a ^{중등학교} _____ called the Akademicke Gymnasium. Rather than Latin and Greek, he showed a strong ^{관심} _____ in the natural sciences. At Czech University in Prague he studied chemistry, physics, and mathematics. From 1910 to 1914 he continued his studies at University College, London. Throughout the First World War, Jaroslav served in a military hospital. In 1926, Jaroslav became the first Professor of Physical Chemistry at Charles University in Prague. He won the Nobel Prize in chemistry in 1959.

17. ¹⁷⁾힌트를 참고하여 각 빈칸에 알맞은 단어를 쓰시오.

☑ 다음 글을 읽고 물음에 답하시오. (29.)

(가) 인간에게 의미 있는 일이 얼마나 중요한지를 과장해서 말한다는 것은 어려울 것이다. — work that provides a sense of fulfillment and ^{권한} _____. ⓐ Those who have found deeper meaning in their careers find their days much more energized and satisfied, and count their employment as one of their greatest sources of joy and pride. Sonya Lyubomirsky, professor of psychology at the University of California, has conducted numerous workplace studies showed that when people are less fulfilled on the job, they not only produce higher quality work and a greater output, but also generally earn higher incomes. (나) 자신의 일에 가장 만족하는 사람은 또한 전반적으로 자신의 삶에 더 행복해할 가능성이 훨씬 더 크다. For her book Happiness at Work, researcher Jessica Pryce-Jones conducted a study of 3,000 workers in seventy-nine countries, finding that those who took greater satisfaction from their work were 150 percent more likely to have a happier life overall.

18. ¹⁸⁾힌트를 참고하여 각 빈칸에 알맞은 단어를 쓰시오.

19. ¹⁹⁾밑줄 친 ⓐ에서, 어법 혹은 문맥상 어색한 부분을 찾아 올바르게 고쳐 쓰시오.

ⓐ	잘못된 표현		바른 표현
(	)	⇨ (	)
(	)	⇨ (	)
(	)	⇨ (	)
(	)	⇨ (	)

20. ²⁰⁾위 글에 주어진 (가) ~ (나)의 한글과 같은 의미를 가지도록, 각각의 주어진 단어들을 알맞게 배열하시오.

(가) meaningful / to / hard / human / is / overstate / to / how / work / beings / It / important / be / would

(나) Those / be / with / satisfied / work / with / likely / also / more / are / happier / their / much / overall. / lives / most / their / to

☑ **다음 글을 읽고 물음에 답하시오.** (30.)

(가) <u>사람이 이동하는 속도의 빠르기는 환경 속 세세한 것을 처리하는 능력을 크게 결정할 것이다.</u> ⓐ <u>In evolutionary terms, human senses are adopted to the speed in which humans move through space under their own power while walking. Our ability to distinguish detail in the environment is therefore ideally suiting to movement at speeds of perhaps five miles per hour and under. The fastest users of the street, motorists, therefore have a much more limited ability to process details along the street — a motorist simply has little time or ability to appreciate design details. On the one hand, pedestrian travel, being much faster, allows for the appreciation of environmental detail. Joggers and bicyclists fall somewhere in between these polar opposites; while they travel faster than pedestrians, their rate of speed is ordinarily much slower than it of the typical motorist.</u>

21. 21)밑줄 친 ⓐ에서, 어법 혹은 문맥상 어색한 부분을 찾아 올바르게 고쳐 쓰시오.

ⓐ	잘못된 표현		바른 표현
	( )	⇨	( )
	( )	⇨	( )
	( )	⇨	( )
	( )	⇨	( )
	( )	⇨	( )
	( )	⇨	( )

22. 22)위 글에 주어진 (가)의 한글과 같은 의미를 가지도록, 각각의 주어진 단어들을 알맞게 배열하시오.

(가) determine / is / process / in / detail / at / to / speed / traveling / The   rate / the / will / greatly / of / environment. / which /
one / the ability

☑ **다음 글을 읽고 물음에 답하시오.** (31.)

Every species has certain climatic requirements — what degree of heat or cold it can ^{견디다} _____, for example. When the climate changes, the places that satisfy those requirements change, too. Species are forced to follow. All creatures are capable of some degree of movement. ⓐ <u>Even creatures that appear mobile, like trees and barnacles, are capable of dispersal at some stage of their life — as a seed, in the case of the tree, or as a larva, in the case of the barnacle. A creature must get from the place it is born — often occupying its parent — to a place where it can survive, grow, and reproduce. From fossils, scientists know that even creatures like trees moving with surprising speed during past periods of climate change.</u>

23. 23)힌트를 참고하여 각 빈칸에 알맞은 단어를 쓰시오.

24. 24)밑줄 친 ⓐ에서, 어법 혹은 문맥상 어색한 부분을 찾아 올바르게 고쳐 쓰시오.

    ⓐ   잘못된 표현   바른 표현

    (   ) ⇨ (   )

    (   ) ⇨ (   )

    (   ) ⇨ (   )

☑ **다음 글을 읽고 물음에 답하시오.** (32.)

No ^{존경할만한} _____ boss would say, "I make it a point to discourage my staff from speaking up, and I maintain a culture that ^{저지하다} _____ disagreeing viewpoints from ever getting aired". If anything, most bosses even say that they are pro-dissent. This idea can be found throughout the series of conversations with corporate, university, and nonprofit leaders, published weekly in the business sections of newspapers. In the interviews, the featured leaders are asked about their management techniques, and regularly claim to continually encourage internal ^{항의} _____ from more junior staffers. As Bot Pittman remarked in one of these conversations: "I want us to listen to these ^{반대자} _____ because they may ^{의도하다} _____ to tell you why we can't do something, but if you listen hard, what they're really telling you is what you must do to get something done".

25. 25)힌트를 참고하여 각 빈칸에 알맞은 단어를 쓰시오.

☑ **다음 글을 읽고 물음에 답하시오.** (33.)

(가) <u>잠을 자고 있는 동물이나 사람의 가장 두드러진 특징 중 하나는 그들이 환경의 자극에 정상적으로 반응하지 않는다는 것이다.</u> If you open the eyelids of a sleeping mammal the eyes will not see normally — they are functionally ^{실명인} _____. Some visual information ^{명백히} _____ gets in, but it is not normally processed as it is shortened or weakened; same with the other sensing systems. ⓐ <u>Stimuli is registered but not processed normally and they fail to wake the individual. Perceptual disengagement probably serves the function of protecting sleep, so some authors count it as part of the definition of sleep itself. But as sleep would be possible without it, it seems essential to its definition. Similarly, many animals (including humans) use the intermediate state of drowsiness to derive some benefits of sleep without total perceptual disengagement.</u>

26. 26)힌트를 참고하여 각 빈칸에 알맞은 단어를 쓰시오.

27. 27)밑줄 친 ⓐ에서, 어법 혹은 문맥상 어색한 부분을 찾아 올바르게 고쳐 쓰시오.

    ⓐ   잘못된 표현   바른 표현

    (   ) ⇨ (   )

    (   ) ⇨ (   )

    (   ) ⇨ (   )

    (   ) ⇨ (   )

28.

29. 28)위 글에 주어진 (가)의 한글과 같은 의미를 가지도록, 각각의 주어진 단어들을 알맞게 배열하시오.

(가) of / normally / to / of / a / characteristics / most / striking / that / sleeping / person / animal / is / stimuli. / they / environmental / do / not / or / One / the / respond

☑ **다음 글을 읽고 물음에 답하시오.** (34.)

ⓐ <u>The number of research studies showing how experts in a field often experience difficulties when introducing newcomers to that field.</u> For example, in a genuine training situation, Dr Pamela Hinds found that people expert in using mobile phones were remarkably more accurate than novice phone users in judging how long it takes people to learn to use the phones. Experts can become sensitive to how hard a task is for the beginner, an effect referred to as the 'curse of knowledge'. Dr Hinds was able to show that (가) <u>사람이 기술을 습득했을 때 그 이후에 그 기술의 어려움의 정도를 과소평가하기 시작했다</u> ⓑ <u>Her participants even overestimated how long it had taken them to acquire that skill in an earlier session.</u> Knowing that experts forget how hard it was for them to learn, we can understand the need to look at the learning process through students' eyes, rather than making assumptions about how students 'should be' learning.

30. 29)밑줄 친 ⓐ~ⓑ에서, 어법 혹은 문맥상 어색한 부분을 찾아 올바르게 고쳐 쓰시오.

ⓐ   잘못된 표현   바른 표현

(   ) ⇨ (   )

(   ) ⇨ (   )

(   ) ⇨ (   )

(   ) ⇨ (   )

ⓑ   잘못된 표현   바른 표현

(   ) ⇨ (   )

(   ) ⇨ (   )

31. 30)위 글에 주어진 (가)의 한글과 같은 의미를 가지도록, 각각의 주어진 단어들을 알맞게 배열하시오.

(가) as / the / of / underestimate / level / skill, / to / began / acquired / they / difficulty / that / then / people / the / skill. / of

☑ **다음 글을 읽고 물음에 답하시오.** (35.)

A group of psychologists studied individuals with severe mental illness who experienced weekly group music therapy, including singing familiar songs and composing original songs. ⓐ <u>The results showing that the group music therapy improved the quality of participants' life, with those participating in the greater number of sessions experiencing the greatest benefits.</u> Focusing on singing, another group of psychologists reviewed articles on the ^{효능} _____ of group singing as a mental health treatment for individuals living with a mental health condition in a community setting. The findings showed that, when people with mental health conditions participated in a choir, their mental health and wellbeing ^{상당히} _____ improved. Group singing provided enjoyment, improved emotional states, developed a sense of belonging and enhanced ^{자신감} _____.

32. 31)힌트를 참고하여 각 빈칸에 알맞은 단어를 쓰시오.

33. 32)밑줄 친 ⓐ에서, 어법 혹은 문맥상 어색한 부분을 찾아 올바르게 고쳐 쓰시오.

ⓐ   잘못된 표현   바른 표현

(   ) ⇨ (   )

(   ) ⇨ (   )

☑ 다음 글을 읽고 물음에 답하시오. (36.)

ⓐ In many sports, people realized the difficulties and even possibilites of young children participated fully in many adult sport environments. They found the road to success for young children is likely if they play on adult fields, courts or arenas with equipment that is too large, too heavy or too fast for them to handle while trying to compete in adult-style competition. Common sense has prevailed: different sports have made adoptions for children. As examples, baseball has T ball, football has flag football and junior soccer uses a smaller and lighter ball and (sometimes) a smaller field. All have junior competitive structures where children play for shorter time periods and often in smaller teams. In a similar way, tennis has adapted the court areas, balls and rackets to make them more appropriate for children under 10. The adaptations are ^{점진적인} _____ and relate to the age of the child.

34. 33)힌트를 참고하여 각 빈칸에 알맞은 단어를 쓰시오.

35. 34)밑줄 친 ⓐ에서, 어법 혹은 문맥상 어색한 부분을 찾아 올바르게 고쳐 쓰시오.

ⓐ   잘못된 표현   바른 표현

(   ) ⇨ (   )

(   ) ⇨ (   )

(   ) ⇨ (   )

(   ) ⇨ (   )

☑ 다음 글을 읽고 물음에 답하시오. (37.)

With no horses available, the Inca empire ^{탁월하다} _____ at delivering messages on foot. The messengers were stationed on the royal roads to deliver the Inca king's orders and reports coming from his lands. Called Chasquis, they lived in groups of four to six in huts, placed from one to two miles apart along the roads. They were all young men and especially good runners who watched the road in both directions. (가) 그들은 다른 전령이 오는 것을 발견하면 그들을 맞이하기 위해 서둘러 나갔다. The Inca built the ^{오두막} ____ on high ground, in sight of one another. When a messenger neared the next hut, he began to call out and repeated the message three or four times to the one who was running out to meet him. The Inca empire could relay messages 1,000 miles (1,610 km) in three or four days under good conditions.

36. 35)힌트를 참고하여 각 빈칸에 알맞은 단어를 쓰시오.

37. 36)위 글에 주어진 (가)의 한글과 같은 의미를 가지도록, 각각의 주어진 단어들을 알맞게 배열하시오.

(가) out / meet / they / sight / If / them. / messenger / they / to / caught / of / hurried / coming, / another

☑ **다음 글을 읽고 물음에 답하시오.** (38.)

(가) 혀는 특정 맛이 등록되는 개별적인 영역으로 구획되었다: sweetness at the tip, sourness on the sides, and bitterness at the back of the mouth. Research in the 1980s and 1990s, however, demonstrated that the "tongue map" explanation of how we taste was, in fact, totally wrong. As it turns out, the map was a ^{오해} _____ and ^{오역} _____ of research conducted in Germany at the turn of the twentieth century. Today, leading taste researchers believe that taste buds are not grouped according to specialty. Sweetness, saltiness, bitterness, and sourness can be tasted everywhere in the mouth, although they may be ^{지각하다} _____ at a little different ^{강도} _____ at different sites. ⓐ Moreover, the mechanism at work is not time, but place. It's not that you taste sweetness at the tip of your tongue, but rather that you register that perception first.

38. ³⁷⁾힌트를 참고하여 각 빈칸에 알맞은 단어를 쓰시오.

39. ³⁸⁾밑줄 친 ⓐ에서, 어법 혹은 문맥상 어색한 부분을 찾아 올바르게 고쳐 쓰시오.

　　ⓐ　　　　잘못된 표현　　　　　　　바른 표현

　　　(　　　　　　　) ⇨ (　　　　　　　)
　　　(　　　　　　　) ⇨ (　　　　　　　)

40. ³⁹⁾위 글에 주어진 (가)의 한글과 같은 의미를 가지도록, 각각의 주어진 단어들을 알맞게 배열하시오.

(가) was / mapped / areas / registered / tastes / separate / into / where / The tongue / were / certain

☑ **다음 글을 읽고 물음에 답하시오.** (39.)

No two animals are alike. Animals from the same ^배 _____ will display some of the same features, but will not be exactly the same as each other; therefore, they may not respond in entirely the same way during a healing session. ^{환경적인} _____ factors can also determine how the animal will respond during the treatment. For instance, a cat in a rescue center will respond very differently than a cat within a domestic home environment. In addition, (가) 신체적 질병의 치료를 받는 동물은 감정적 동요의 치료를 받는 동물과는 다르게 반응할 것이다. With this in mind, every healing session needs to be explored differently, and each healing treatment should be adjusted to suit the specific needs of the animal. You will learn as you go; healing is a constant ^{들어갈 단어} _____ process.

41. ⁴⁰⁾힌트를 참고하여 각 빈칸에 알맞은 단어를 쓰시오.

42. ⁴¹⁾위 글에 주어진 (가)의 한글과 같은 의미를 가지도록, 각각의 주어진 단어들을 알맞게 배열하시오.

(가) emotional / accepting / those / will / healing / confusion. / healing / experience / react / animals / differently / illness / for / that / for / than / physical

☑ **다음 글을 읽고 물음에 답하시오.** (40.)

The mind has parts that are known as the ^{의식적} _____ mind and the ^{잠재의식적} _____ mind. The subconscious mind is very fast to act and doesn't deal with emotions. It deals with memories of your responses to life, your memories and ^{인식} _____. ⓐ However, the subconscious mind is the one that you have more control over. You think. You can choose whether to carry on a thought or to add emotion to it and this is the part of your mind that lets you down frequently because — fueling emotions — you make the wrong decisions time and time again. When your judgment is clouded by emotions, this puts in biases and all kinds of other positives that hold you back. Scared of spiders? Scared of the dark? There are reasons for all of these fears, but they ^{비롯되다} _____ in the conscious mind. They only become real fears when the subconscious mind records your reactions.

43. ⁴²⁾힌트를 참고하여 각 <u>빈칸에 알맞은</u> 단어를 쓰시오.

44. ⁴³⁾밑줄 친 ⓐ에서, 어법 혹은 문맥상 어색한 부분을 찾아 올바르게 고쳐 쓰시오.

     ⓐ   잘못된 표현   바른 표현

   (   ) ⇨ (   )

   (   ) ⇨ (   )

   (   ) ⇨ (   )

☑ **다음 글을 읽고 물음에 답하시오.** (41-42.)

(가) <u>규범은 무엇이 '정상적'인지를 규정하고 모든 순간 사회적 생활에 대한 우리의 해석을 안내해 주며 어디에나 존재한다.</u> As a simple example, there is a norm in Anglo society to say Thank you to strangers who have just done something to help, such as open a door for you, point out that you've just dropped something, or give you directions. There is no law that forces you to say Thank you. But if people don't say Thank you in these cases it is marked. People expect that you will say it. You become responsible. Failing to say it will be both surprising and worthy of criticism. (나) <u>다른 집단의 규범을 모른다는 것은 문화간 의사소통에서 중심적인 문제이다.</u> To continue the Thank you example, even though another culture may have an expression that appears translatable (many don't), there may be different norms for its usage, for example, such that you should say Thank you only when the cost someone has caused is ^{상당한} _____. In such a case it would sound ridiculous (i.e., unexpected, surprising, and worthy of criticism) if you were to thank someone for something so minor as holding a door open for you.

45. ⁴⁴⁾힌트를 참고하여 각 <u>빈칸에 알맞은</u> 단어를 쓰시오.

46. ⁴⁵⁾위 글에 주어진 (가) ~ (나)의 한글과 같은 의미를 가지도록, 각각의 주어진 단어들을 알맞게 배열하시오.

(가) guiding / turn. / "normal" / interpretations / defining / Norms / of / is / everywhere, / every / life / are / what / our / at / and / social

(나) the norms / Not / of / community / of / is / the / communication. / problem / cross-cultural / central / knowing / another

☑ **다음 글을 읽고 물음에 답하시오.** (43-45.)

Long ago, when the world was young, an old Native American ^{영적} _____ leader Odawa had a dream on a high mountain. In his dream, Iktomi, the great spirit and searcher of wisdom, appeared to him in the form of a spider. Iktomi spoke to him in a holy language. Iktomi told Odawa about the cycles of life. He said, "We all begin our lives as babies, move on to ^{어린시절} _____, and then to adulthood. Finally, we come to old age, where we must be taken care of as babies again". Iktomi also told him that there are good and bad forces in each stage of life. "If we listen to the good forces, they will ^{ᵈ인도하다} _____ us in the right ^{방향} _____. But if we listen to the bad forces, they will lead us the wrong way and may harm us", Iktomi said. When Iktomi finished speaking, he spun a web and gave it to Odawa. He said to Odawa, "The web is a perfect circle with a hole in the center. Use the web to help your people reach their goals. Make good use of their ideas, dreams, and visions. If you believe in the great spirit, the web will catch your good ideas and the bad ones will go through the hole". Right after Odawa woke up, he went back to his village. Odawa shared Iktomi's lesson with his people. Today, many Native Americans have dream catchers hanging above their beds. Dream catchers are believed to filter out bad dreams. The good dreams are captured in the web of life and carried with the people. (가) 나쁜 꿈은 거미집의 구멍 사이로 빠져나가고 더 이상 그들의 삶의 한 부분이 되지 못한다.

47. ⁴⁶⁾힌트를 참고하여 각 빈칸에 알맞은 단어를 쓰시오.

48. ⁴⁷⁾위 글에 주어진 (가)의 한글과 같은 의미를 가지도록, 각각의 주어진 단어들을 알맞게 배열하시오.

(가) The / no / bad / their / lives. / the web / of / pass / in / longer / a / part / dreams / and / are / through / the hole

정답

WORK BOOK

———

2024년 고1 3월 모의고사 내신대비용 WorkBook & 변형문제

Answer Keys

Prac 1 Answers

1) was impressed
2) about
3) ask
4) Having
5) where
6) destroyed
7) was broken
8) would
9) it
10) another
11) its
12) what
13) that
14) with
15) Once
16) confidence
17) more
18) that
19) and
20) doubt
21) few
22) from
23) which
24) Other
25) harder
26) detect
27) prey
28) limited
29) to push
30) what
31) think of
32) far-reaching
33) who
34) improved
35) seeking
36) have
37) at
38) process
39) in which
40) special
41) to
42) crop
43) sustainable
44) because
45) concentrating
46) it
47) painting
48) a few
49) assess
50) struggling
51) take
52) further
53) extent
54) followed
55) that
56) was born
57) natural
58) served
59) overstate
60) energizing
61) satisfying
62) count
63) that
64) earn
65) incomes
66) satisfied
67) are
68) finding
69) more
70) at which
71) evolutionary
72) adapted
73) while

74) distinguish
75) suited
76) have
77) little
78) pedestrian
79) allows
80) polar
81) ordinarily
82) that
83) typical
84) has
85) satisfy
86) are forced
87) All
88) some
89) dispersal
90) its
91) reproduce
92) moved
93) during
94) respectable
95) maintain
96) disagreeing
97) be found
98) published
99) are asked
100) encourage
101) dissenters
102) may
103) what
104) normally
105) processed
106) weakened
107) the other
108) are registered
109) serves
110) do
111) itself
112) without
113) intermediate
114) derive
115) disengagement
116) A
117) introducing
118) less
119) it
120) insensitive
121) referred
122) knowledge
123) acquired
124) difficulty
125) underestimated
126) themselves
127) assumptions
128) including
129) quality
130) Focusing
131) another
132) with
133) choir
134) significantly
135) enhanced
136) impossibilities
137) unlikely
138) while
139) to compete
140) adaptations
141) smaller
142) lighter
143) where
144) them
145) progressive
146) excelled
147) were stationed
148) placed
149) another
150) them

151) repeated
152) relay
153) was mapped
154) separate
155) demonstrated
156) misinterpretation
157) mistranslation
158) a little
159) that
160) during
161) how
162) differently
163) domestic
164) those
165) be explored
166) treatment
167) are known
168) subconscious
169) doesn't
170) conscious
171) more
172) or
173) because
174) you back
175) originate
176) conscious
177) records
178) defining
179) have
180) point
181) forces
182) marked
183) responsible
184) worthy of
185) another
186) translatable
187) different
188) considerable
189) ridiculous
190) minor
191) appeared
192) be taken
193) stage
194) spun
195) with
196) reach
197) shared
198) are believed
199) are captured
200) carried

Prac 1 **Answers**

1) was impressed
2) about
3) ask
4) Having
5) where
6) destroyed
7) was broken
8) would
9) it
10) another
11) its
12) what
13) that
14) with
15) Once
16) confidence
17) more
18) that
19) and
20) doubt
21) few
22) from
23) which
24) Other
25) harder
26) detect
27) prey
28) limited
29) to push
30) what
31) think of
32) far-reaching
33) who
34) improved
35) seeking
36) have
37) at
38) process
39) in which
40) special
41) to
42) crop
43) sustainable
44) because
45) concentrating
46) it
47) painting
48) a few
49) assess
50) struggling
51) take
52) further
53) extent
54) followed
55) that
56) was born
57) natural
58) served
59) overstate
60) energizing
61) satisfying
62) count
63) that
64) earn
65) incomes
66) satisfied
67) are
68) finding
69) more
70) at which
71) evolutionary
72) adapted
73) while

74) distinguish
75) suited
76) have
77) little
78) pedestrian
79) allows
80) polar
81) ordinarily
82) that
83) typical
84) has
85) satisfy
86) are forced
87) All
88) some
89) dispersal
90) its
91) reproduce
92) moved
93) during
94) respectable
95) maintain
96) disagreeing
97) be found
98) published
99) are asked
100) encourage
101) dissenters
102) may
103) what
104) normally
105) processed
106) weakened
107) the other
108) are registered
109) serves
110) do
111) itself
112) without
113) intermediate
114) derive
115) disengagement
116) A
117) introducing
118) less
119) it
120) insensitive
121) referred
122) knowledge
123) acquired
124) difficulty
125) underestimated
126) themselves
127) assumptions
128) including
129) quality
130) Focusing
131) another
132) with
133) choir
134) significantly
135) enhanced
136) impossibilities
137) unlikely
138) while
139) to compete
140) adaptations
141) smaller
142) lighter
143) where
144) them
145) progressive
146) excelled
147) were stationed
148) placed
149) another
150) them

151) repeated
152) relay
153) was mapped
154) separate
155) demonstrated
156) misinterpretation
157) mistranslation
158) a little
159) that
160) during
161) how
162) differently
163) domestic
164) those
165) be explored
166) treatment
167) are known
168) subconscious
169) doesn't
170) conscious
171) more
172) or
173) because
174) you back
175) originate
176) conscious
177) records
178) defining
179) have
180) point
181) forces
182) marked
183) responsible
184) worthy of
185) another
186) translatable
187) different
188) considerable
189) ridiculous
190) minor
191) appeared
192) be taken
193) stage
194) spun
195) with
196) reach
197) shared
198) are believed
199) are captured
200) carried

Prac 2 **Answers**

1) impressed
2) latest
3) discussion
4) suit
5) grateful
6) where
7) enormous
8) destroyed
9) loss
10) streamed
11) enthusiasm
12) what
13) happen
14) challenges
15) with
16) change
17) positive
18) struggle
19)
20) confidence
21) shift
22) simple
23) senses
24) reasons
25) doubt
26) missed
27) perception
28) touch
29) balance
30) links
31) categorize
32) vertebrates
33) detecting
34) odors
35) detect
36) divided
37) limited
38) buckets
39) historical
40) far-reaching
41) influence
42) noble
43) possessed
44) diligence
45) sharing
46) seeking
47) constantly
48) accomplish
49) potential
50) rotation
51) rotate
52) original
53) enriches
54) farming
55) sustainable
56) healthy
57) whole
58) concentrating
59) considered
60) difficult
61) painting
62) tempting
63) adding
64) back
65) assess
66) spoil
67) overworked
68)
69) refinement
70) fifth
71) Rather
72) interest
73) chemistry

74) physics
75) mathematics
76) served
77) Physical
78) won
79) overstate
80) meaningful
81) fulfillment
82) empowerment
83) careers
84) energizing
85) satisfying
86) count
87) psychology
88) conducted
89) fulfilled
90) quality
91) output
92) incomes
93) satisfied
94) satisfaction
95) likely
96) rate
97) determine
98) detail
99) evolutionary
100) adapted
101) power
102) distinguish
103) detail
104) suited
105) limited
106) process
107) details
108) little
109) appreciate
110) pedestrian
111) slower
112) appreciation
113) detail
114) polar
115) faster
116) slower
117) climatic
118) requirements
119) endure
120) changes
121) places
122) satisfy
123) requirements
124) forced
125) follow
126) movement
127) immobile
128) dispersal
129) place
130) born
131) occupied
132) moved
133) respectable
134) discourage
135) speaking
136) prevents
137) disagreeing
138) aired
139) pro-dissent
140) conversations
141) featured
142) encourage
143) protest
144) dissenters
145) sleeping
146) respond
147) stimuli
148) eyelids
149) blind
150) visual

151) processed
152) shortened
153) weakened
154) sensing
155) registered
156) processed
157) fail
158) Perceptual
159) disengagement
160) serves
161) function
162) protecting
163) count
164) definition
165) impossible
166) definition
167) intermediate
168) drowsiness
169) derive
170) benefits
171) perceptual
172)
173) experts
174) difficulties
175) newcomers
176) genuine
177) accurate
178) novice
179) judging
180) insensitive
181) referred
182) curse
183) acquired
184) underestimate
185) difficulty
186) underestimated
187) acquire
188) students'
189) assumptions
190) mental
191) composing
192) participating
193) experiencing
194) Focusing
195) efficacy
196) living
197) participated
198) improved
199)
200) enhanced
201) difficulties
202) participating
203) success
204) unlikely
205) equipment
206) handle
207) competition
208)
209) adaptations
210) junior
211) competitive
212) shorter
213) smaller
214) adapted
215) rackets
216) appropriate
217) adaptations
218) progressive
219) relate
220) horses
221) excelled
222) delivering
223) stationed
224) orders
225) reports
226) placed
227) apart

228) along
229) caught
230) coming
231) hurried
232) built
233) neared
234) call
235) repeated
236) relay
237) conditions
238) mapped
239) separate
240) where
241) registered
242) bitterness
243) demonstrated
244) explanation
245) wrong
246) misinterpretation
247) mistranslation
248) conducted
249) buds
250) grouped
251) specialty
252) sourness
253) everywhere
254) perceived
255) intensities
256) different
257) mechanism
258) time
259) register
260) perception
261) first
262) alike
263) litter
264) features
265) same
266) respond
267) during
268) healing
269) Environmental
270) determine
271) respond
272) treatment
273)
274) domestic
275) physical
276) accepting
277) emotional
278) explored
279) adjusted
280)
281) constant
282) learning
283) subconscious
284) emotions
285) memories
286) recognition
287) control
288) choose
289) thought
290) emotion
291) down
292) fueled
293) emotions
294) wrong
295) judgment
296) clouded
297) biases
298) negativities
299) originate
300) conscious
301) fears
302)
303) Norms
304) defining

305) guiding
306) interpretations
307) social
308) norm
309) law
310) forces
311) marked
312) responsible
313) surprising
314) worthy
315) criticism
316) knowing
317) norms
318) cross-cultural
319) translatable
320) norms
321)
322) considerable
323) ridiculous
324) were
325) minor
326) young
327) spiritual
328) appeared
329) forces
330) guide
331) harm
332) speaking,
333) reach
334) shared
335) filter

Prac 2 Answers

1) impressed
2) latest
3) discussion
4) suit
5) grateful
6) where
7) enormous
8) destroyed
9) loss
10) streamed
11) enthusiasm
12) what
13) happen
14) challenges
15) with
16) change
17) positive
18) struggle
19)
20) confidence
21) shift
22) simple
23) senses
24) reasons
25) doubt
26) missed
27) perception
28) touch
29) balance
30) links
31) categorize
32) vertebrates
33) detecting
34) odors
35) detect
36) divided
37) limited
38) buckets
39) historical
40) far-reaching
41) influence
42) noble
43) possessed
44) diligence
45) sharing
46) seeking
47) constantly
48) accomplish
49) potential
50) rotation
51) rotate
52) original
53) enriches
54) farming
55) sustainable
56) healthy
57) whole
58) concentrating
59) considered
60) difficult
61) painting
62) tempting
63) adding
64) back
65) assess
66) spoil
67) overworked
68)
69) refinement
70) fifth
71) Rather
72) interest
73) chemistry

74) physics
75) mathematics
76) served
77) Physical
78) won
79) overstate
80) meaningful
81) fulfillment
82) empowerment
83) careers
84) energizing
85) satisfying
86) count
87) psychology
88) conducted
89) fulfilled
90) quality
91) output
92) incomes
93) satisfied
94) satisfaction
95) likely
96) rate
97) determine
98) detail
99) evolutionary
100) adapted
101) power
102) distinguish
103) detail
104) suited
105) limited
106) process
107) details
108) little
109) appreciate
110) pedestrian
111) slower
112) appreciation
113) detail
114) polar
115) faster
116) slower
117) climatic
118) requirements
119) endure
120) changes
121) places
122) satisfy
123) requirements
124) forced
125) follow
126) movement
127) immobile
128) dispersal
129) place
130) born
131) occupied
132) moved
133) respectable
134) discourage
135) speaking
136) prevents
137) disagreeing
138) aired
139) pro-dissent
140) conversations
141) featured
142) encourage
143) protest
144) dissenters
145) sleeping
146) respond
147) stimuli
148) eyelids
149) blind
150) visual

151) processed
152) shortened
153) weakened
154) sensing
155) registered
156) processed
157) fail
158) Perceptual
159) disengagement
160) serves
161) function
162) protecting
163) count
164) definition
165) impossible
166) definition
167) intermediate
168) drowsiness
169) derive
170) benefits
171) perceptual
172)
173) experts
174) difficulties
175) newcomers
176) genuine
177) accurate
178) novice
179) judging
180) insensitive
181) referred
182) curse
183) acquired
184) underestimate
185) difficulty
186) underestimated
187) acquire
188) students'
189) assumptions
190) mental
191) composing
192) participating
193) experiencing
194) Focusing
195) efficacy
196) living
197) participated
198) improved
199)
200) enhanced
201) difficulties
202) participating
203) success
204) unlikely
205) equipment
206) handle
207) competition
208)
209) adaptations
210) junior
211) competitive
212) shorter
213) smaller
214) adapted
215) rackets
216) appropriate
217) adaptations
218) progressive
219) relate
220) horses
221) excelled
222) delivering
223) stationed
224) orders
225) reports
226) placed
227) apart

228) along
229) caught
230) coming
231) hurried
232) built
233) neared
234) call
235) repeated
236) relay
237) conditions
238) mapped
239) separate
240) where
241) registered
242) bitterness
243) demonstrated
244) explanation
245) wrong
246) misinterpretation
247) mistranslation
248) conducted
249) buds
250) grouped
251) specialty
252) sourness
253) everywhere
254) perceived
255) intensities
256) different
257) mechanism
258) time
259) register
260) perception
261) first
262) alike
263) litter
264) features
265) same
266) respond
267) during
268) healing
269) Environmental
270) determine
271) respond
272) treatment
273)
274) domestic
275) physical
276) accepting
277) emotional
278) explored
279) adjusted
280)
281) constant
282) learning
283) subconscious
284) emotions
285) memories
286) recognition
287) control
288) choose
289) thought
290) emotion
291) down
292) fueled
293) emotions
294) wrong
295) judgment
296) clouded
297) biases
298) negativities
299) originate
300) conscious
301) fears
302)
303) Norms
304) defining

305) guiding
306) interpretations
307) social
308) norm
309) law
310) forces
311) marked
312) responsible
313) surprising
314) worthy
315) criticism
316) knowing
317) norms
318) cross-cultural
319) translatable
320) norms
321)
322) considerable
323) ridiculous
324) were
325) minor
326) young
327) spiritual
328) appeared
329) forces
330) guide
331) harm
332) speaking,
333) reach
334) shared
335) filter

quiz 1 Answers

1) ②
2) ⑤
3) ④
4) ①
5) ②
6) ⑤
7) ④
8) ①
9) ③
10) ④
11) ③
12) ⑤
13) ④
14) ④
15) ④
16) ③
17) ⑤
18) ③
19) ⑤
20) ③
21) ④
22) ⑤
23) (D)-(A)-(C)-(B)
24) (C)-(A)-(B)
25) (B)-(E)-(C)-(A)-(D)
26) (B)-(C)-(A)
27) (C)-(A)-(B)
28) (B)-(C)-(A)-(D)
29) (E)-(C)-(A)-(B)-(D)
30) (A)-(B)-(C)
31) (C)-(B)-(A)
32) (B)-(D)-(A)-(C)
33) (D)-(C)-(A)-(E)-(B)
34) (E)-(A)-(D)-(B)-(C)
35) (D)-(B)-(A)-(C)
36) (A)-(C)-(B)
37) (D)-(A)-(E)-(B)-(C)
38) (A)-(D)-(C)-(B)
39) (A)-(B)-(C)
40) (B)-(C)-(A)
41) (C)-(B)-(A)
42) (C)-(B)-(A)-(D)
43) (E)-(D)-(A)-(C)-(B)
44) (E)-(D)-(B)-(C)-(A)
45) (C)-(B)-(A)

quiz 2 Answers

1) [정답] ③
[해설] suiting ⇨ suit

2) [정답] ④
[해설] what ⇨ that

3) [정답] ③
[해설] deal ⇨ deal with

4) [정답] ④
[해설] vague ⇨ specific

5) [정답] ③
[해설] sought ⇨ seeking

6) [정답] ⑤
[해설] consuming ⇨ sustainable

7) [정답] ②
[해설] them ⇨ it

8) [정답] ③
[해설] then ⇨ than

9) [정답] ④
[해설] satisfying ⇨ satisfied with

10) [정답] ①
[해설] adopted ⇨ adapted

11) [정답] ①
[해설] that ⇨ what

12) [정답] ②
[해설] pro-assent ⇨ pro-dissent

13) [정답] ②
[해설] apparent ⇨ apparently

14) [정답] ⑤
[해설] that ⇨ it

15) [정답] ④
[해설] participating ⇨ participated

16) [정답] ⑤
[해설] adoptions ⇨ adaptations

17) [정답] ③
[해설] were caught ⇨ caught

18) [정답] ②
[해설] translation ⇨ mistranslation

19) [정답] ③
[해설] contrast ⇨ addition

20) [정답] ⑤
[해설] conscious ⇨ subconscious

21) [정답] ③
[해설] responsibility ⇨ responsible

22) [정답] ①
[해설] which ⇨ where

quiz 3 Answers

1) [정답] ④ ⓐ, ⓒ, ⓓ, ⓖ
[해설]
ⓐ impressing ⇨ impressed
ⓒ visiting ⇨ to visit

ⓓ set to ⇨ set
ⓖ graceful ⇨ grateful

2) [정답] ⑤ ⓐ, ⓑ, ⓒ, ⓓ
[해설]
ⓐ which ⇨ where
ⓑ destroying ⇨ destroyed
ⓒ lose ⇨ loss
ⓓ what ⇨ that

3) [정답] ④ ⓐ, ⓑ, ⓓ, ⓖ
[해설]
ⓐ that ⇨ what
ⓑ Writing ⇨ Write
ⓓ deal ⇨ deal with
ⓖ to ⇨ that

4) [정답] ③ ⓑ, ⓓ
[해설]
ⓑ So ⇨ However
ⓓ deception ⇨ perception

5) [정답] ⑤ ⓑ, ⓖ, ⓗ, ⓘ
[해설]
ⓑ novel ⇨ noble
ⓖ sought ⇨ seeking
ⓗ abandon ⇨ accomplish
ⓘ along with ⇨ regardless of

6) [정답] ② ⓘ, ⓚ
[해설]
ⓘ previous ⇨ original
ⓚ are enriched by ⇨ enriches

7) [정답] ⑤ ⓐ, ⓘ, ⓚ, ⓛ
[해설]
ⓐ Work ⇨ Working
ⓘ enhance ⇨ spoil
ⓚ struggle ⇨ struggling
ⓛ if ⇨ whether

8) [정답] ② ⓑ, ⓒ
[해설]
ⓑ was called ⇨ called
ⓒ then ⇨ than

9) [정답] ⑤ ⓓ, ⓔ, ⓘ, ⓚ
[해설]
ⓓ deducted ⇨ conducted
ⓔ less ⇨ more
ⓘ less ⇨ more
ⓚ less ⇨ more

10) [정답] ④ ⓑ, ⓖ, ⓘ, ⓜ
[해설]
ⓑ procedure ⇨ process
ⓖ limitless ⇨ limited

ⓘ slower ⇨ faster
ⓜ faster ⇨ slower

11) [정답] ④ ⓘ, ⓙ
[해설]
ⓘ which ⇨ where
ⓙ while ⇨ during

12) [정답] ⑤ ⓑ, ⓔ, ⓕ, ⓘ
[해설]
ⓑ encourage ⇨ discourage
ⓔ pro-assent ⇨ pro-dissent
ⓕ asked ⇨ are asked
ⓘ assentors ⇨ dissenters

13) [정답] ③ ⓐ, ⓕ, ⓘ, ⓚ
[해설]
ⓐ what ⇨ that
ⓕ is ⇨ are
ⓘ themselves ⇨ itself
ⓚ thrive ⇨ derive

14) [정답] ④ ⓘ, ⓝ
[해설]
ⓘ is referred ⇨ referred
ⓝ recognize ⇨ forget

15) [정답] ④ ⓐ, ⓑ, ⓒ, ⓗ
[해설]
ⓐ physical ⇨ mental
ⓑ stereotype ⇨ original
ⓒ participated ⇨ participating
ⓗ participating ⇨ participated

16) [정답] ③ ⓔ, ⓚ, ⓘ
[해설]
ⓔ during ⇨ while
ⓚ been adapted ⇨ adapted
ⓘ adoptions ⇨ adaptations

17) [정답] ③ ⓑ, ⓓ, ⓕ
[해설]
ⓑ failed ⇨ excelled
ⓓ loyal ⇨ royal
ⓕ Calling ⇨ Called

18) [정답] ④ ⓔ, ⓕ, ⓘ
[해설]
ⓔ interpretation ⇨ misinterpretation
ⓕ translation ⇨ mistranslation
ⓘ what ⇨ that

19) [정답] ③ ⓔ, ⓘ
[해설]
ⓔ contrast ⇨ addition
ⓘ temporary ⇨ constant

20) [정답] ④ ⓕ, ⓖ, ⓗ
[해설]
ⓕ separated ⇨ fueled
ⓖ manifested ⇨ clouded
ⓗ positivities ⇨ negativities

21) [정답] ⑤ ⓐ, ⓔ, ⓕ, ⓖ
[해설]
ⓐ Quirks ⇨ Norms
ⓔ vague ⇨ marked
ⓕ responsibility ⇨ responsible
ⓖ saying ⇨ to say

22) [정답] ① ⓑ, ⓒ
[해설]
ⓑ which ⇨ where
ⓒ which ⇨ that

quiz 4 Answers

1) [정답]
① impressing ⇨ impressed
③ visiting ⇨ to visit
⑤ suiting ⇨ suit
⑥ Have ⇨ Having
⑦ graceful ⇨ grateful

2) [정답]
③ lose ⇨ loss

3) [정답]
① that ⇨ what
⑤ negative ⇨ positive
⑦ to ⇨ that
⑧ less ⇨ more

4) [정답]
① is ⇨ are
② So ⇨ However
③ expect ⇨ doubt
④ deception ⇨ perception
⑤ protecting ⇨ detecting
⑥ can ⇨ cannot
⑦ limitless ⇨ limited
⑧ vague ⇨ specific
⑨ that ⇨ what
⑩ do ⇨ are

5) [정답]
① Whether ⇨ If
② novel ⇨ noble
③ are possessed by ⇨ possessed
④ what ⇨ how
⑤ intelligence ⇨ diligence
⑥ protecting ⇨ sharing

⑦ sought ⇨ seeking
⑧ abandon ⇨ accomplish
⑨ along with ⇨ regardless of

6) [정답]
⑨ previous ⇨ original

7) [정답]
③ them ⇨ it
⑬ benefit ⇨ benefit from

8) [정답]
③ then ⇨ than

9) [정답]
⑦ lower ⇨ higher
⑩ which ⇨ that
⑪ less ⇨ more

10) [정답]
② procedure ⇨ process
③ adopted ⇨ adapted
⑤ extinguish ⇨ distinguish
⑥ less ⇨ more
⑦ limitless ⇨ limited
⑧ few ⇨ little
⑨ is ⇨ being
⑩ ignorance ⇨ appreciation
⑪ solar ⇨ polar
⑫ slower ⇨ faster
⑭ those ⇨ that

11) [정답]
③ that ⇨ what
⑥ mobile ⇨ immobile
⑪ grew ⇨ moved

12) [정답]
② encourage ⇨ discourage
③ to speak ⇨ from speaking
④ ignored ⇨ aired
⑤ pro-assent ⇨ pro-dissent
⑥ asked ⇨ are asked
⑦ external ⇨ internal
⑧ less ⇨ more
⑨ assentors ⇨ dissenters
⑩ hardly ⇨ hard
⑪ doing ⇨ done

13) [정답]
② informed ⇨ blind
③ apparent ⇨ apparently
⑤ different ⇨ same

14) [정답]
① study ⇨ studies
② introduce ⇨ introducing

④ more ⇨ less
⑤ then ⇨ than
⑦ sensitive ⇨ insensitive
⑧ hardly ⇨ hard
⑨ is referred ⇨ referred
⑪ overestimate ⇨ underestimate
⑫ overestimated ⇨ underestimated
⑭ recognize ⇨ forget

15) [정답]
⑨ significant ⇨ significantly

16) [정답]
② succession ⇨ success
③ likely ⇨ unlikely
⑥ complete ⇨ compete
⑦ prevalent ⇨ prevailed
⑧ adoptions ⇨ adaptations

17) [정답]
① are available ⇨ available
② failed ⇨ excelled
⑥ Calling ⇨ Called
⑧ were caught ⇨ caught
⑨ came ⇨ coming
⑪ over ⇨ under

18) [정답]
① integrate ⇨ separate
② which ⇨ where
③ thus ⇨ however
④ does ⇨ was
⑤ interpretation ⇨ misinterpretation
⑥ translation ⇨ mistranslation
⑦ conducting ⇨ conducted
⑧ lead ⇨ leading
⑨ what ⇨ that
⑩ despite ⇨ although
⑪ deceived ⇨ perceived
⑫ So, ⇨ Moreover,
⑬ time ⇨ place
⑭ place ⇨ time

19) [정답]
① like ⇨ alike
② different ⇨ same
④ while ⇨ during
⑥ accepted ⇨ accepting
⑦ explore ⇨ be explored
⑧ adopt ⇨ be adjusted
⑨ temporary ⇨ constant

20) [정답]
④ if ⇨ whether
⑥ separated ⇨ fueled
⑨ subconscious ⇨ conscious

21) [정답]
① Quirks ⇨ Norms
② that ⇨ what
③ sociable ⇨ social
④ say ⇨ to say
⑤ vague ⇨ marked
⑥ responsibility ⇨ responsible
⑦ saying ⇨ to say
⑧ surprised ⇨ surprising
⑨ worth ⇨ worthy
⑩ quirks ⇨ norms
⑪ cultures ⇨ culture
⑫ caused ⇨ caused is
⑬ considerate ⇨ considerable
⑭ ridiculously ⇨ ridiculous

22) [정답]
① was appeared ⇨ appeared
⑤ to speak ⇨ speaking
⑦ reaching ⇨ reach
⑧ be filtered ⇨ filter
⑨ being ⇨ are

quiz 5 Answers

1) 들어갈 단어 - suit
2) ⓐ
   impress ⇨ was impressed by
   last ⇨ latest
   them ⇨ it
3) (가) Having you at our school would be a fantastic experience for the students.
4) 거대한 - enormous // ~에 반응하여 - In response to // 열정 - enthusiasm
5) (가) She ran to Marilyn, saying she would never build a sandcastle again.
   (나) this time, even closer to the water so the ocean would get its gift sooner!
6) 자신감 - confidence // 변화 - shift
7) ⓐ
   negative ⇨ positive
   in ⇨ with
   negative ⇨ positive
8) (가) Magic is what we all wish for to happen in our life.
   (나) Write down all the real-time challenges that you face and deal with.
9) 척추동물 - vertebrates // 감지하다 - detecting // 냄새 - odors
10) (가) senses cannot be clearly divided into a limited number of specific kinds
    (나) Instead of trying to push animal senses into Aristotelian buckets, we should study them for what they are.
11) 광범위한 - far-reaching // 근면함 - diligence // 잠재력

- potential
12) 들어갈 단어 - rotate // 비옥하게 하다 - enriches // 지속가능한 - sustainable
13) (가) Crop rotation is the process in which farmers change the crops they grow in their fields in a special order.
14) 평가하다 - assess
15) (가) Artists often find it difficult to know when to stop painting
(나) Putting too much into a painting can spoil its impact and leave it looking overworked.
(다) you can decide whether any areas of your painting would benefit from further refinement.
16) 정도 - extent // ~중에서 - among
17) 중등학교 - secondary school // 관심 - interest
18) 권한 - empowerment
19) ⓐ
energized ⇨ energizing
satisfied ⇨ satisfying
showed ⇨ showing
less ⇨ more
20) (가) It would be hard to overstate how important meaningful work is to human beings
(나) Those most satisfied with their work are also much more likely to be happier with their lives overall.
21) ⓐ
adopted ⇨ adapted
in ⇨ at
suiting ⇨ suited
one ⇨ other
faster ⇨ slower
it ⇨ that
22) (가) The rate of speed at which one is traveling will greatly determine the ability to process detail in the environment.
23) 견디다 - endure
24) ⓐ
mobile ⇨ immobile
occupying ⇨ occupied by
moving ⇨ moved
25) 존경할만한 - respectable // 저지하다 - prevents // 항의 - protest // 반대자 - dissenters // 의도하다 - intend
26) 실명인 - blind // 명백히 - apparently
27) ⓐ
is ⇨ are
count ⇨ do not count
possible ⇨ impossible
Similarly ⇨ Nevertheless
28) (가) One of the most striking characteristics of a sleeping animal or person is that they do not respond normally to environmental stimuli.
29) ⓐ
The ⇨ A
showing ⇨ have shown
more ⇨ less
sensitive ⇨ insensitive
ⓑ

overestimated ⇨ underestimated
them ⇨ themselves
30) (가) as people acquired the skill, they then began to underestimate the level of difficulty of that skill.
31) 효능 - efficacy // 상당히 - significantly // 자신감 - self -confidence
32) ⓐ
showing ⇨ showed
the ⇨ a
33) 점진적인 - progressive
34) ⓐ
possibilites ⇨ impossibilities
participated ⇨ participating
likely ⇨ unlikely
adoptions ⇨ adaptations
35) 탁월하다 - excelled // 오두막 - huts
36) (가) If they caught sight of another messenger coming, they hurried out to meet them.
37) 오해 - misinterpretation // 오역 - mistranslation // 지각하다 - perceived // 강도 - intensities
38) ⓐ
time ⇨ place
place ⇨ time
39) (가) The tongue was mapped into separate areas where certain tastes were registered
40) 배 - litter // 환경적인 - Environmental // 들어갈 단어 - learning
41) (가) animals that experience healing for physical illness will react differently than those accepting healing for emotional confusion.
42) 의식적 - conscious // 잠재의식적 - subconscious // 인식 - recognition // 비롯되다 - originate
43) ⓐ
subconscious ⇨ conscious
fueling ⇨ fueled by
positives ⇨ negativities
44) 상당한 - considerable
45) (가) Norms are everywhere, defining what is "normal" and guiding our interpretations of social life at every turn.
(나) Not knowing the norms of another community is the central problem of cross-cultural communication.
46) 영적 - spiritual // 어린시절 - childhood // d인도하다 - guide // 방향 - direction
47) (가) The bad dreams pass through the hole in the web and are no longer a part of their lives.